The Tyranny of Change:
America in the Progressive Era,
1900–1917

The Tyranny of Change:
America in the Progressive Era,
1900–1917

JOHN WHITECLAY CHAMBERS II

Barnard College
Columbia University

Under the General Editorship
of Vincent P. Carosso

St. Martin's Press
New York

To my sons
Bret, Jeff, Adam

Library of Congress Catalog Card Number: 80-50124
Copyright © 1980 by St. Martin's Press, Inc.
All Rights Reserved.
Manufactured in the United States of America.
43210
fedcba
For information, write St. Martin's Press, Inc.,
175 Fifth Avenue, New York, N.Y. 10010
cover design: Pat Vitacco
cloth ISBN: 0-312-82757-1
paper ISBN: 0-312-82758-X

Preface

Modern America was born in the Progressive Era. In the first two decades of the twentieth century, the forces accompanying industrialization sent the familiar nineteenth-century world plummeting towards extinction. A land of family farms and scattered settlements was eclipsed by a modern nation of giant corporations, huge factories and office buildings, sprawling cities, and jostling ethnic groups. "There has never been a time in the world's history," Harvard philosopher Ralph Barton Perry declared in 1916, "in which blind social forces have been so strong." Many Americans felt themselves in the grip of a tyranny of change.

My primary purpose in this volume is to re-examine and explain the developments of the Progressive Era, focusing on the years between 1900 and 1917, the high point of this dramatic period. In this interpretive history, I shall also explore the effect these developments have had on subsequent years. For Americans today are to a significant degree heirs of the legacy of the Progressive Era.

The Progressive Era holds particular significance because it represents America's first full-scale attempt to come to terms with the rapidly emerging multicultural, urban, industrial society. Modernization, a process of change in which social institutions were altered to adapt to mechanization and rising economic productivity, touched virtually every aspect of American life in those years. The transformation to a more cosmopolitan, urban society caused great social and economic shifts.

"The march of events rules and overrules human action," President William McKinley asserted at the turn of the century. But the forces of change can be vulnerable tyrants. While long-range processes such as industrialization shape broad conditions, they do not dictate the adoption of particular policies or determine precise results. People choose among various alternatives and make and remake institutions. My treatment of the Progressive Era combines the sweeping forces of modernization with the actions of particular men and women.

The people who shaped the attitudes and institutions of modern America in its formative years stride the pages of this book. This volume seeks to explain, for example, the role of J. P. Morgan in the formation of supercorporations like United States Steel, Jane Addams in the origin of modern social work, Mary Pickford in early motion pictures, Theodore Roosevelt in the building of the Panama Canal, and Woodrow Wilson in America's entrance into World War I.

Americans sought to master the sweeping forces of change by what I call a "new interventionism." This represented an unprecedented willingness to intrude into the economy, society, and world affairs. The new interventionists believed that intelligently directed effort could control change and manipulate the environment for the improvement of society. This new attitude challenged and modified nineteenth-century beliefs in a self-regulating marketplace, unrestricted individualism, and a foreign policy of isolationism.

The most famous group among these interventionists was the moderate reformers who called themselves progressives. They gave their name to the era and to the particular spirit of the times. The progressive ethos—a mixture of pragmatic, piecemeal reform and an idealistic, quasireligious vision of democracy—inspired millions of middle-class Americans to social activism. It dominated national politics for a decade.

Among historians, the nature of the Progressive Era remains a major source of controversy. My interpretation emphasizes that the developments of this period did not result solely from the action of progressives. Major contributions were made by radicals, conservatives, and important nonprogressive movements, including the corporate reorganization and consolidation movement, the labor movement, the women's movement, and the movements for both cultural homogeneity and ethnic pluralism. This study also stresses the role of private voluntary associations as well as governmental agencies as mechanisms for achieving directed change. It examines the role of reformers and others who worked for change not only in the political and international system but in the private sector: in education, medicine, law, religion, and social and family relationships.

Understanding the nature of the Progressive Era provides significant insight into the nature of reform and social change in America. The power of particular groups fluctuates over time as economic and political situations differ. As a result, periods of reform have appeared cyclically upon the American scene. Examination of the Progressive Era allows us to view an entire phase of the reform cycle and to probe both its origins and accomplishments. As men and women seek to master change, their solutions are not always inevitable or even desirable. Some of the solutions reached in the Progressive Era, such as the juvenile court system, community zoning, and federal regulatory commissions, are being challenged today. Yet others, such as the community chest, chambers of commerce, consumer protection, investigative journalism, urban playgrounds, workmen's compensation, national conservation, the city-manager system, direct election of U.S. Senators and other key federal officials, and women's suffrage, have retained widespread support. Whatever reassessment Americans may make of the legacies of the period, to understand the Progressive Era is to understand the origins of modern America.

John Whiteclay Chambers II
Morningside Heights
New York City
January 14, 1980

Acknowledgments

This work, an interpretive history of the entire Progressive Era, would not have been possible without many earlier essays and specialized studies of the period. My indebtedness in this regard is great. I have drawn upon all of the works listed in the bibliography and many more. I have been especially influenced by the analyses of Samuel P. Hays, Robert H. Wiebe, Louis Galambos, John C. Burnham, and my colleague in the St. Martin's series, Ellis W. Hawley. Substantial insights came from the works of Arthur S. Link, Sidney Fine, Otis L. Graham, Jr., David Thelen, Arthur A. Ekirch, Jr., David Kennedy, Peter Filene, John Buenker, William Chafe, James Patterson, John Garry Clifford, Lewis L. Gould, Thomas K. McCraw, John A. Garraty, John Tipple, Dudley Dillard, and Robert Crunden. An outstanding seminar paper by Duhamel Puig provided valuable information on the development of motion picture censorship.

Many people assisted me in different ways in the preparation of this book. Vincent P. Carosso of New York University and Chilton Williamson, Jr., then an editor at St. Martin's Press, conceived the idea of this series. Bertrand Lummus, senior editor, and Carolyn Eggleston, project editor, at St. Martin's, helped guide the manuscript along. Richard Pious, a scholar of the presidency and a colleague at Barnard College, Columbia University, offered helpful suggestions regarding my treatment of the presidents. Daniel Traister of the New York Public Library helped sharpen my prose. The title was suggested by Sheila Kendall-Franklin. Otis L. Graham, Jr., of the University of California, Santa Barbara, and James R. Kearney of Arizona State University read the manuscript and made many important suggestions. Amy Russo Piro helped prune the text to the publisher's requirements. Annette Kar Baxter, head of the History Department at Barnard College, devoted more time than I could have hoped for to editing the manuscript. She greatly improved it with her valuable comments.

No acknowledgment would be complete without an expression of my great indebtedness to William E. Leuchtenburg and the late Charles Frankel of Columbia University, my mentors, colleagues, and friends. The inspiration they provided through their bold and expansive thought, balanced analyses, and readable scholarship have helped shape my life and work.

To all the individuals mentioned here I owe the strengths of this book. I alone am responsible for its errors and weaknesses.

I dedicate this book to my three sons, Bret, Jeff, and Adam Chambers, who I hope will share my optimism and enthusiasm, and my love of history, as they and America grow another generation older together.

Contents

Editor's Introduction

In less than a generation, the twentieth century will belong entirely to the past. Many of the great personalities and events of the first half of the century already seem remote. To Americans born after World War II and to many others as well, Theodore Roosevelt is little more than a name and a picture in a history book, a bespectacled president with a mustache and a broad and toothy grin. Few people living today remember the young, dynamic Roosevelt—the popular hero of San Juan Hill, the first president to visit a foreign country (Panama) during his term of office and to ride in an automobile. And, indeed, the America of TR's day has all but disappeared.

Since 1901, when Roosevelt assumed the presidency, urbanization and industrialization have wrought profound changes in the United States. At the turn of the century the population was 76 million. Fewer than 40 percent lived in urban areas of 2,500 or more; and although American cities were growing rapidly, only six had a population of a half-million or more, and only three had reached or surpassed a million. In 1900, for the first time, the number of industrial wage earners exceeded the number of farmers and farm laborers, and the value of manufactured goods produced by the nation's workers was more than twice the $4.7 billion attributed to agriculture. The loosely organized, largely agricultural country of less than a half-century earlier was on the way to becoming a tightly integrated, highly industrialized, urban nation. But the road would be far from smooth or straight, and American society would experience unalterable changes over the next eight decades.

By 1970 the nation's population had grown to 205 million, and nearly 74 percent of the people had come to live in cities and their ever-expanding suburbs. Urbanization had changed the face of America, creating vast new metropolitan areas that linked city upon city into huge megalopolises, or "urban conglomerates." Similarly, the continued growth of big business transformed the economic landscape. The United States Steel Corporation, founded in 1901, was the country's first billion-dollar firm; by 1970 over a hundred such corporate leviathans existed. Only a few businesses in 1900 commanded a national market; in the 1970s large corporate enterprises dominated nearly every sector of the nation's economy, and many of these giants exercised increasing might abroad. Industrialism also helped alter the nation's international status. In 1900 the United States, despite its recently acquired overseas possessions, was still a new power of limited influence outside the Western Hemisphere. Following World War II it became one of the two superpowers.

But power, like industrial leadership—the twin developments hailed by many at the turn of the century as signaling the beginning of a new era in the nation—made other observers uneasy. The steady growth of large businesses, the rapidly expanding cities, and increased involvement in international affairs would inevitably create vast changes in American life. Turn-of-the-century commentators and politicians focused on many of the central issues that have faced the American people ever since: how to adapt institutions and policies to the needs of an industrial society; how to protect the environment while promoting material progress; how to provide an equitable and humane judicial system; how to deal with racial and ethnic diversity; how to preserve the nation's security in an increasingly turbulent world and contribute, at the same time, to international peace and stability. The four volumes in this series present America's attempts to respond to such challenges.

Professor Chambers's work, the first volume in the series, covers the opening years of the twentieth century, a time when the American people were seeking to adjust to the vast changes brought about by modern industrialism—the economic, political, social, and cultural dislocations that accompanied the new age of giant enterprise. Neither the American people nor their leaders could agree on specific solutions to the host of problems raised by the rapid economic expansion of the post–Civil War decades. But a great majority of the public, as well as a substantial number of its representatives in government, strongly affirmed the need to moderate the "tyranny of industrial change" that buffeted the country and undermined traditional ways of life. The prevailing mood of America at the turn of the century was one of irritation, observed Mark Sullivan, the perceptive New York City journalist: "The average American in great numbers had the feeling he was being 'put upon' by something he couldn't quite see or get his fingers on; that something was 'riding' him; that some force or other was 'crowding' him." The unseen enemy, Sullivan said, usually turned out to be the business and moneyed interests and their allies and surrogates.

Progressivism, the reform impulse that gave the era its name, represented the dominant American response to the sweeping changes caused by accelerating industrialism, urbanism, and mass immigration. Professor Chambers sees progressivism as the chief source of what he calls a "new interventionism," the willingness to modify the ideal of a self-regulating society and intervene purposefully at home and abroad to improve conditions for Americans. Interventionists included many conservatives and nonprogressive reformers, such as those involved in the movements for women's rights, trade unions, and ethnic pluralism. But the progressives, who combined an evangelical optimism with a belief in the effectiveness of science and business organization, provided a special spirit—the progressive ethos—which dominated the era and helped mobilize millions of people to social activism. Although they differed on the merits of specific programs, progressive leaders like Jane Addams, Louis Brandeis, Robert La Follette, Theodore Roosevelt, and Woodrow Wilson joined together in urging a modification of the classic tenets of unrestricted individualism and the unregulated marketplace, the old laissez faire which allowed blind forces to transform society without regard to social goals and values.

The diverse groups that led the forces of change included men and women from almost every socioeconomic class. They believed that the solution to the problems of the day lay in using modern scientific and

xviii   EDITOR'S INTRODUCTION

business methods to adjust the nation's institutions to the needs of new times and conditions, to move the country into modernity without violating its ideals and heritage. Professor Chambers analyzes the broad sweep of progressive reform by focusing on both the work of voluntary groups—settlement houses, trade and professional associations, and various good-government, consumer, and public health leagues—and the efforts of public officials to expand the power of the state and "use the government," in William Allen White's words of almost a half-century ago, "as an agency of human welfare."

Departing from the disillusionment which has characterized much historical writing about progressivism and other reform movements in recent years, Professor Chambers makes a more positive assessment. Although he recognizes the ambiguous legacy of many of the progressives' specific achievements, he emphasizes their willingness to experiment, their faith in a national destiny to improve the lot of humanity, and their ability to mobilize Americans to work for that goal. By stressing the importance of that effort and ideal, he concludes that the Progressive Era offers a legacy of hope for America as it encounters the challenges of the 1980s.

In his account of change and continuity in the progressive years, Professor Chambers incorporates the findings of a large body of specialized scholarly literature. He deals fully with social and cultural developments as well as with the many significant changes that occurred in the country's political and economic life and in its relationships with the rest of the world. In the following pages, readers will find a balanced, interesting account of the motivations, shortcomings, and accomplishments of twentieth-century America's first major effort at reform.

Vincent P. Carosso

The Tyranny of Change:
America in the Progressive Era,
1900–1917

CHAPTER 1

Prelude to the Twentieth Century

As the rolling peal of bells echoed across the land on New Year's morning in 1900, Americans welcomed the new century with a sense of both awe and anxiety. Within their lifetime, industrialism, urbanism, and massive immigration were transforming a land of isolated agrarian settlements and a few commercial cities into an urban industrial nation and a world power. So great was the change that a person born in the Jacksonian Era who died in the Progressive Era was born in one world and died in another. In the first decade of the twentieth century, the woman who had been the first white child born in Chicago—in 1822, when it consisted of a fur trade fort and five huts—died in what had become a sprawling metropolis.

America prided itself on progress, and there was a great sense of national exhilaration in many of the developments of the final quarter of the nineteenth century. Yet the growth of great cities, the inpouring of millions of immigrants, the sudden rise of giant industries, and the rapid acquisition of an island empire led many people to question whether these innovations did not threaten America's prized tradition and ideals. Many Americans felt themselves caught up in a swirl of uncontrolled change.

THE CRISIS OF THE 1890s

The final decade of the nineteenth century dramatized the dual nature of the emerging urban-industrial society and the hopes and fears of Americans about the course of modernization. The "gay nineties" of popular lore were a time of adventure and excitement. Mustachioed men in derby hats promenaded along tree-lined streets with elegant women in high-buttoned shoes, bustles, and flowing lace dresses. In melodious harmony people crooned the new popular songs like "Daisy" and "The Sidewalks of New York." At the local saloon patrons could still enjoy a free lunch with frosty mugs of beer that cost only a nickel. When the World's Fair opened in Chicago in 1893, people came from all over the country to marvel at the achievements of technology and the evidence of rapid progress demonstrated at "the great white city" erected by the lakefront.

"Life in the States," an English visitor reported in 1900, "is one perpetual whirl of telephones, telegrams, phonographs, electric bells, motors, lifts, and automatic instruments." Enthusiastic admirers of technology, most Americans applauded these inventions. Mammoth new factories delivered thousands of new products: steel girders for skyscrapers and bridges, metal tubing for bicycles, glass for large windows, copper wire for new electrical sources of light and power. Technological improvements enabled people to break through age-old barriers of time and space. At speeds of more than a mile a minute, trains carried travelers across the country in a few days instead of the months it had taken by wagon or coach. Telegraph lines sped words from one coast to another in moments. Mass production provided more goods to consumers at cheaper prices in a national marketplace linked by a network of rails and wires. Henry Adams, a Harvard historian and the descendant of two presidents, mused that "the new American—the child of incalculable coal-power, chemical power, electric power, and radiating energy—must be a sort of God compared with any former creature of nature."

Yet many Americans feared the future, for such rapid modernization seemed to be a mixed blessing. Adams himself worried that the nation's dynamic technology might be out of control, spinning it away from its fundamental beliefs and heritage. The benefits of industrialization came with considerable dislocation, suffering, and jeopardy to American society. The unrestrained growth of industry devoured resources, blackened the skies with smoke, and wore down workers in factories and sweatshops. Intensive ten- and even twelve-hour workdays contributed to one of the highest industrial accident rates in the Western world.

Industrialization also seemed to be dividing the country into hostile classes: the extremely wealthy and the poor. The new industrial rich—plutocrats, many people called them—obtained unprecedented wealth and lived in opulent splendor. In 1900 the steel magnate Andrew Carnegie, shuttling between his baronial mansion on New York's Fifth Avenue and his castle in Scotland, made a tax-free profit of $23 million. At the same time, factories, mines, and railroads employed millions of unskilled or semiskilled workers. Steelworkers worked twelve-hour shifts six days a week and earned an average of $450 a year. Women earned less than men. In garment district sweatshops in New York City, they were paid only $5 for a six-day work week, averaging $260 a year.

The nation seemed to be acquiring a large, unruly proletariat composed largely of recent immigrants from southern and eastern Europe. The growing cities were centers of discontent and seemed to threaten an America which had been dominated by a homogeneous rural or small-town Anglo-Saxon Protestant culture. Those who feared the influx of Catholic and Jewish immigrants into the cities, nativists like the Congregationalist minister Josiah Strong, warned that "the city is the nerve center of our civilization. It is also the storm center. . . . The city has become a serious menace to our civilization."

The 1890s were a time of disastrous events that evoked deep foreboding among Americans. The year 1893, which marked the opening of the World's Fair, also ushered in the worst depression the country had yet experienced. Some 500 banks and 15,000 businesses failed. Hundreds of thousands of people were thrown out of work without savings or relief. For the first time large numbers of tramps roamed the countryside. In one of the first mass protest marches on the nation's capital, a group of jobless men calling themselves "Coxey's Army" marched on Washington, vainly urging federal support. In Chicago railroad management seeking to break a strike of Pullman workers and trainmen obtained assistance from the police and from U.S. cavalrymen. Before the strike was broken, the city echoed with the sound of gunfire and the crackle of flames from burning railroad cars. In the steel town of Homestead, near Pittsburgh, a bitter strike broke into open warfare. When managers at the Carnegie mill dispatched a flotilla of rafts carrying private guards across the Monongahela River from Pittsburgh to land at the town, strikers fired on them with rifles and cannon. Ten persons were killed in the strike, and an anarchist tried to assassinate Henry Clay Frick, the manager of the mill. Industrial violence, crime, disease, and extensive urban poverty challenged American ideals of freedom, democracy, and a relatively classless and harmonious society.

Even in the rural heartland, the Midwest and the South, protest erupted. Populist farmers rose up against the dominance of eastern industrialists, financiers, and railroad tycoons. In 1896 agrarians gained control of the Democratic party in a futile attempt to capture the presidency. Comparing the Populists to the radicals of the French Revolution, a hysterical eastern editor warned that "the Jacobins are in full control. No large political movement in America has ever before spawned such hideous and repulsive vipers."

The crises of the 1890s led large numbers of Americans to wonder whether their belief in a self-regulating society was not contributing to the destruction of that society. Reluctance to intervene in the marketplace seemed to encourage blind social forces. However, the noninterventionist ideal of a free, unregulated marketplace and a limited role for the state had become a major tenet of the national creed in the nineteenth century and was not easily modified. This concept reinforced long-held beliefs in individualism, liberty and opportunity, and suspicion of concentrated power—whether in the state or in the form of private monopoly.

The marketplace ideal, most fully articulated in 1776 in *The Wealth of Nations* by the Scottish economist Adam Smith, coincided with what many Americans already believed: that free individuals pursuing their own self-interest also contributed to the general good of the community. In a famous passage Smith asserted that "the individual intends only his own gain [but is] led by an invisible hand to promote an end which was no part of his intention." Like the colonists who rejected the Crown's grant of a monopoly on tea to the British East India Company, Smith challenged excessive mercantilist regulations as inefficient and oppressive. Neither government nor any individual, he argued, had enough wisdom to direct the complex economic life of a nation. Instead, Smith presumed a natural economic order in which competition among producers would generate the most efficient economic growth and the most adequate goods at the most reasonable prices, to the benefit of society.

Smith's conception of a self-regulating economy was readily adopted by Americans and applied to society as well. It reinforced a belief in individualism which had been encouraged by the opportunities available in America because of a shortage of labor and an abundance of land (exactly the opposite of the situation in Europe). Individualism had also been given divine sanction by evangelical Protestantism's emphasis on individual regeneration and self-worth. Furthermore, when the British government sought to expand its authority, colonial rebels like Patrick Henry, John Adams, and Thomas Jefferson adopted concepts of natural law and certain inalienable natural political rights which belonged to all people and could not be abridged by governments. Individualism and self-regulation had thus helped provide intellectual justification for the American Revolution and the American experiment in a democratic form of government.

The economic growth and industrialization of nineteenth-century America took place in a nation which increasingly emphasized the value of unrestricted individualism, a free and open market economy, and a laissez-faire system of limited government. The admonition of Jeffersonian and Jacksonian democratic agrarians was that the government that governs least governs best. Federalists like Alexander Hamilton and Whigs like Henry Clay who advocated a positive governmental role through active economic promotion found themselves running against a popular trend. Emerson, Thoreau, and the transcendentalists emphasized individualism and restricted government, and so did the classical liberal political economists of Europe and one of the most powerful new concepts of the nineteenth century, Darwinism. As applied to society by sociologists like Herbert Spencer in England and William Graham Sumner in the United States,

Darwin's theory of biological evolution through natural selection explained social change through natural evolutionary laws and the "survival of the fittest." These theorists, who became known as Social Darwinists, defended the automatic functioning of society as being in the best interests of the country's evolutionary progress. They hammered away against proposals for government intervention for either promotion of economic growth or temporary amelioration of hardships as detrimental to natural progress and ultimately futile. In the second half of the nineteenth century, British visitor James Bryce observed that laissez faire had become "the orthodox and accepted doctrine in the sphere both of Federal and of State legislation."

Social Darwinism reinforced ideas already fairly strongly held and justified practices already established. It supported the conservative temper of many Americans at the time and then added seeming scientific justification to the faith in progress that most Americans felt because of the economic abundance, opportunity, and individual advancement in the United States. It justified those who argued for a stable and unmanipulated currency and opposed protective legislation for workers and consumers and government interference in the marketplace. Furthermore, skepticism of government seemed to be reinforced by exposés of widespread political corruption at all levels, from the Tweed Ring in New York to the Grant administration in Washington. Unlike their British counterparts, American economists, clergy, businesspeople, and others tended to assume that principles of individualism, competition, and governmental inefficiency were laws of God and that the social and economic growth and increasingly higher standard of living of the United States were part of a divine plan. Like previous generations, they believed Americans were a chosen people. In a textbook on political economy published in 1870, the economist Francis Bowen asserted that laissez faire meant "'things regulate themselves' . . . which means, of course, that God regulates them by his general laws, which always, in the long run, work to good."

Although in practice laissez faire was accompanied by much governmental promotion—land grants to railroads, protective tariffs, stable currency, and anti-union action to aid industry—the idea of the self-regulating marketplace and society attained the peak of its strength in the nineteenth century, when it was enshrined in both thought and law. But even as it reached its apex, the dramatic changes it encouraged began to undermine popular faith in the marketplace ideal. Without restriction or purposeful social direction, industrialization, urbanization, and immigration seemed to threaten American traditions of individualism, competition, and opportunity and the ideal of a democratic, relatively classless society of independent producers. In the crisis of the 1890s many people began to doubt that industrialization would cure its own ills.

A NEW KIND OF GROWTH

Closing the Frontier

An era of westward growth seemed to come to an end in 1890, when the Census Bureau reported that an unbroken moving line of settlement no longer existed in the United States. The disappearance of America's western frontier, which for three hundred years had served as a symbol of economic expansion and opportunity, was a blow to the nation. Even more than in other frontier societies—western Canada, Argentina, Brazil, and Siberian Russia—the American West and the rugged frontier life had become part of the nation's self-image. In 1893 the historian Frederick Jackson Turner warned that the end of the frontier threatened to curtail American uniqueness, individualism, democracy, and economic growth.

The last frontier had been conquered swiftly. After the Civil War, Americans in great numbers had pushed into the trans-Mississippi West, settling the treeless expanses of the Great Plains, the wooded valleys of the Rockies, and the drier regions of the Southwest. By 1900 the population of the West had quadrupled, reaching 17 million, and the frontier had disappeared.

The federal government had promoted, but not directed, settlement of this region. It granted public land to railroads to help finance construction of transcontinental lines. The first was completed in

1869, and by 1893 four railroads linked the West Coast with the East. Railroads and speculators acquired the best land, but many settlers obtained their farms free from the federal government under the Homestead Act of 1862.

In support of white settlement, the government also intervened to restrict, and often eliminate, the Indians. By 1890, thirty years after the white invasion of the plains began, the buffalo herds and the plains culture had been destroyed, and the decimated tribes were confined to reservations. The triumph of numbers and technology had been assisted by the Indians' inability to overcome centuries of tribal rivalry and unite against the whites.

The tribes had resisted destruction. In 1862 the Santee Sioux in western Minnesota rose against invading whites, killing nearly 800. Cheyennes attacked miners and settlers in Colorado. Whites in turn slaughtered Indians. In the Sand Creek massacre in Colorado, militiamen killed more than 200 men, women, and children in a dawn attack on a Cheyenne village. Pressed by eastern reformers, the government attempted a new "peace policy" of putting the Indians onto large reservations where they would be out of the way of white settlement and missionary agents could Christianize them and teach them farming. Lack of funds and outright starvation on the reservations led to many outbreaks of violence in 1870s and 1880s. In the 1870s twelve military campaigns to return tribes to the reservations cost the lives of 948 soldiers, 460 civilians, and an estimated 4,500 Indians. In 1876 Sioux warriors led by Sitting Bull and Crazy Horse annihilated General George A. Custer's force of 264 men at the Little Big Horn. The Sioux, like the Nez Percé and other tribes, were forced back to the reservations by the army and by the virtual extinction of the buffalo herds on which their society depended. The surrender of Chief Joseph of the Nez Percé in 1877 captured the Indians' despair and resignation:

I am tired of fighting. Our chiefs are killed. . . . The little children are freezing to death. . . . I want to have time to look for my children. . . . My heart is sick and sad. From where the sun now stands I will fight no more forever.

A final outburst came at Wounded Knee, South Dakota, in 1890, when whites, alarmed by the spread of a millenarian movement known as the Ghost Dance, ambushed a Sioux village, killing several hundred men, women, and children in the last tragic massacre of the Indian Wars.

Having defeated their warriors, the federal government tried to assimilate the Indians into American culture. Beginning in the 1870s it sought to destroy the authority of the chiefs and abolished the tradition of dealing with the Indians through treaties as if they were semisovereign domestic nations. Instead, the Indians were brought under federal jurisdiction.

The publication of Helen Hunt Jackson's *A Century of Dishonor* (1881) contributed to the growth of a movement to ameliorate the conditions which were decimating the Indians. The resulting Dawes General Allotment Act of 1887 endeavored to convert them into small yeomen farmers by granting a 160-acre homestead to every Indian who agreed to work it. This attempt to "Americanize" the Indians was a disaster from the start. By 1920 the Indians had lost two-thirds of their land, and the majority were paupers.

In their place, the whites pushed into the West. Prospectors and mining companies moved into California, Nevada, Idaho, Arizona, and the Dakotas in search of gold and silver, copper, iron, and coal. The cattlemen soon followed, bringing steers from Texas to the railheads in Missouri and Kansas in the 1860s and 1870s, and to the grazing lands of the Great Plains in the 1880s. They gave the urbanizing country a string of new frontier heroes and villains: Jesse James, Billy the Kid, Calamity Jane, Annie Oakley, Wild Bill Hickock, and Buffalo Bill Cody, the professional hunter and showman who brought cowboys and Indians to the theaters of the East even as the frontier culture was dying. Last came the farmers: lower-middle-income Americans from nearby farm states or Scandinavian or German immigrants, "sod-busters" who broke open the tough, matted, arid grasslands with new steel plows and brought wheat to the prairies of America.

The rapid settlement of the trans-Mississippi West was a source of great pride but also of anxiety, for it seemed to signal the limits of economic growth as well as the end of the frontier. Some members of the eastern elite, like the young Theodore Roosevelt, feared that the loss of the frontier experience would accelerate the flabbiness and materialism which they saw accompanying the rise of an urban, industrial, heterogeneous society.

The Challenge of Mass Immigration

The new frontier was in the city. Pilgrims to prosperity, 12 million people sailed across the Atlantic to the United States in the last three decades of the nineteenth century. An average of 400,000 immigrants a year came during prosperous times, attracted by the promises of opportunity, relatively inexpensive land, comparatively high wages, and political and religious freedom. Until the 1890s most of these immigrants came from the countries which had supplied immigrants before the Civil War: Britain, Ireland, Germany, and the Scandinavian countries. Beginning in the mid-1880s, however, increasing numbers began to arrive from southern and eastern Europe.

The "new immigrants" came from Italy, Austria-Hungary, Russia, Russian Poland, the Balkans, and Greece. They were pushed from their homelands by economic, religious, and political oppression. As landlords consolidated and mechanized their agricultural holdings, millions of peasants and villagers lost their traditional livelihood. Many fled to neighboring cities. Others set out to find employment in the growing nations of Canada, Argentina, Australia, and the United States. By 1893 they surpassed the "old immigrants" in number and made up the bulk of the new arrivals in the United States each year. They came with high hopes, like Mary Antin, author of *The Promised Land* (1912), who remembered the glowing letters her father, a Jewish teacher and storekeeper, had sent back to Russia from Boston.

> In America, he wrote, it was no disgrace to work at a trade. Workman and capitalists were equal. . . . The cobbler and the teacher had the same title, "Mister." And all the children, boys and girls, Jews and Gentiles, went to school! Education would be ours for the asking, and economic independence also. . . . So at last I was going to America! The boundaries burst. The

winds rushed in from outer space, roaring in my ears, "America! America!"

The immigrants provided the basic work force for America's industrial expansion. Primarily unskilled laborers, less than one in ten had a recognized trade or profession. Few could speak English, and 25 to 50 percent could not read or write any language. The majority were former peasants, a generation or two removed from serfdom.

Typically, a strong, ambitious, but often illiterate young man or woman left an overcrowded peasant village in Italy, Poland, or one of the other agricultural countries, sailed across the Atlantic in steerage class for a few dollars, and arrived in New York or another American port. The young men found themselves confronted by their fellow countrymen—*padrones* in Italian—who sought to hire them out in work gangs to employers in manufacturing, construction, mining, or street or railroad building and repair. It was long, hard work for low wages. Many young immigrant women worked as domestic servants, their hard and lonely life ofter exacerbated by the inability to communicate in English with their employers. If the immigrant did not return home after a few years—as up to 40 percent did during economic cutbacks—he or she would generally try to put away money and bring over other members of the family. This pattern was more typical of the Italians, Greeks, and Slavs than of the Jews from Russia or Russian Poland. Jewish families, persecuted in Czarist pogroms, fled together. Coming from cities and towns, a larger percentage of these immigrants had manual or clerical skills, and they found work in the clothing industry and the expanding stores and shops of the new urban nation.

In the United States the immigrants became urban villagers, clustering in the industrial cities. That made them more visible than previous immigrants and more closely identified with the problems of the big cities. Although the foreign-born never exceeded 15 percent of the American population (compared to 22 percent in Canada and 30 percent in Argentina in the same years), the immigrants and their American-born children represented a significant part of the population in some areas. In 1900 between two-thirds and three-fourths of

the population of Massachusetts, Rhode Island, Wisconsin, and Minnesota had at least one parent born outside the United States. In cities
like Boston, New York, Chicago, and Milwaukee, immigrants and
their children were a majority of the population.

Already fearful of many of the effects of uncontrolled urbanization
and industrialization, many native-born Americans saw the new
immigrants as another threat to traditional society. Prejudice and a
pseudo-scientific racism which assumed levels of races led many people
to view these cultural and religious minorities—predominantly
Catholic and Jewish—as belonging to "inferior Slavic and Mediterranean races." More than one commentator spoke in menacing terms
of "new swarms" of European immigrants "invading America."
Concerned about the declining birthrate among native-born Americans, Brahmins like Henry Cabot Lodge warned of "racial suicide"
and the overwhelming of the native "racial stock" by immigrants and
their large numbers of children. A vigorous new anti-Semitism led
to discriminatory barriers in housing, hotels, clubs, and offices.
Representatives of conservative labor unions like the American
Federation of Labor warned that "pauper labor" undermined wage
rates and the country's standard of living. Many native-born Americans connected immigrants with urban crime, disease, labor violence,
and radicalism, fearing the impact of a new, "unruly and inferior"
urban proletariat.

Nativists who opposed the new immigrants sought to acculturate or
"Americanize" those who were already in the country and to limit the
number of new arrivals. The immigration restriction movement began
in California, where agitation against the "coolie labor" used to build
railroads led Congress to prohibit the immigration of Chinese laborers
in 1882. In the 1890s the American Protective Association and the
Immigration Restriction League joined the American Federation of
Labor, the Daughters of the American Revolution, and other newly
formed nationalistic groups in pressing for a literacy test which would
keep most of the new immigrants out of the country.

Massive immigration did not, however, subvert American culture.
The new immigrants did not force significant changes in the structure
or direction of American family, religious, or political life. Rather,

they and their children usually adopted many of the patterns of the pre-dominant Anglo-Saxon culture. But at the time the nativists feared their impact and linked them with many of the problems of the developing cities.

The Rise of the Metropolis

The cities became the focus of the new America. As the southern plantation and the northern family farm had symbolized the agrarian society of the years before the Civil War, so the industrial city emerged, for better or worse, as the symbol of the transformation of American society. The urban population grew from 20 percent in 1860 to 40 percent in 1900. Rural hamlets became small towns; towns and trading centers grew into medium-sized cities like Minneapolis, Omaha, Cleveland, Pittsburgh, Detroit, and Jersey City. In the urban-industrial heartland of the Northeast–North Central region, an entirely new type of city emerged—the modern industrial metropolis.

The big industrial cities of the North differed in form and function from the old mercantile cities. Previously consisting of a few hundred thousand people clustered in an area of half a dozen square miles, cities like New York, Chicago, Philadelphia, and Boston grew to encompass several million people in areas of up to forty square miles. Technology altered old constraints. Instead of walking to work, people could commute by horsecar and, beginning in the 1890s, electric streetcar. As wealthier residents moved to the periphery in "streetcar suburbs," the poor remained trapped in the urban core. The outward movement segregated large cites into rings and enclaves differentiated by income, ethnicity, and, concomitantly, by rates of crime and disease.

Within the cities, soaring land values encouraged property owners to seek maximum land use. Downtown, where the streetcar lines converged, a central business district developed. Structural steel frameworks and elevators enabled builders to change the skyline of America's cities. Skyscrapers soared above church steeples and the mass of three- to five-story buildings. The downtown area housed the new department stores, banks, professional and office buildings, theaters, restaurants, and hotels which catered to the growing numbers of people who came to the hub of the city to work, shop, and find entertainment.

The city was exciting. Rural life had been dominated by monotony and isolation, but urban dwellers saw new sights and faces almost every day. Entertainment could be found in playgrounds, beaches, parks, dance halls, vaudeville theaters, baseball fields, museums, libraries, ice cream parlors, or the ubiquitous saloons, which served not only as drinking establishments but as political and social clubs for many members of the working classes.

But danger and disease also lurked in the cities. The high price of land contributed to urban congestion, although the housing patterns varied. In Philadelphia and Baltimore, where the tradition of home ownership remained strong, contractors built mile after mile of row houses. In Boston and Newark, they put up four-story buildings with wooden decks. But in New York high rents forced as many as four hundred people to jam themselves into tenements designed for fifty, in which a four-room flat might house fifteen. Dark and foul, the tenements of New York's Lower East Side produced one of the highest mortality rates in the world. Thousands died from typhoid, diphtheria, and tuberculosis. In the notorious Hell's Kitchen on New York's West Side, one reformer, Rev. Walter Rauschenbusch, declared that "one could hear human virtue cracking and crushing all around." Fires destroyed large areas of the cities, including virtually all of Chicago in 1871. Street crime was commonplace.

Startled by the growth of urban poverty and industrial violence and stunned by the angry mobs which roamed the cities during the draft riots of the Civil War and by the great railroad strikes and riots of 1877, several cities and states increased their means of social control. They expanded their police forces and revitalized the militia (now renamed the National Guard) as a defense against mob violence, providing urban militia units with formidable armories patterned after medieval castles with turrets and slotted windows.

Confronted with such threatening developments, reformers began banding together to improve urban conditions. Some sought to save both the souls and bodies of troubled urban dwellers. The Young Men's Christian Association (YMCA) and the Salvation Army set up residential hotels which also served as religious, cultural, and recreational centers. A more secular movement established settlement houses. The first, Hull House in Chicago's immigrant tenement district, was founded by Jane Addams, a young woman from a middle-class Illinois family who rejected the traditional woman's homemaker role to become the founder of modern social work. Many of the immigrant groups formed their own mutual aid societies, and the needy poor also received aid from Catholic churches and Jewish synagogues. Within Protestantism, a number of concerned clergymen, such as Rauschenbusch and Washington Gladden, founded the "Social Gospel movement," which stressed social ethics and ministered to the needs of the urban poor.

When municipal governments had difficulty coping with sanitation, water supply, urban transportation, and public relief, upper- and middle-class citizens often joined in civic reform associations to obtain governmental action. Led by business and professional people, these so-called "good government" groups did much to establish and expand professional public health, fire, and police departments, ensuring proper authority and responsibility in those agencies. In many cases this also meant unseating urban party bosses like William M. Tweed of New York City's Tammany Hall. (The Tweed Ring was broken in 1871.) The "machines" were accused of manipulating the vote of recent immigrants to maintain power, raise taxes, and bilk the city through kickbacks, padded contracts, sales of franchises, and other forms of graft. However, reformers tended to ignore the role played by municipal political machines like Tweed's in providing assistance to the poor and to ethnic groups, and in making the fragmented system of city government work.

Urban reformers of the post–Civil War period often formed permanent organizations which acted as supplemental political vehicles for accomplishing what the constituted governments could not do. They also began to expand the powers of government and modify the policy of laissez faire in areas like public health, where they recognized the need to intervene in the marketplace to exert some control over water supply, garbage and sewage disposal, inspection of milk and meat, and treatment of infectious diseases in order to protect the public welfare.

THE AGE OF INDUSTRIALISM

The Supremacy of Industry

Industrialization transformed America within a single generation. By 1900, surpassing Britain and other industrializing nations, the United States emerged as the manufacturing giant of the world. The change from small shops to the factory system had begun before the Civil War, especially in textiles and iron manufacturing. But in the decades after the war entrepreneurs dramatically expanded production by establishing the factory system and mass production in a growing number of industries. America's factories boosted real gross national product by 120 percent, an average annual gain of 4 percent, between 1870 and 1900. By the turn of the century the value of manufacturing goods exceeded that of agricultural commodities. The United States had become an industrial nation.

This phenomenal boost in manufacturing production came from a triple revolution—in transportation and communication, in production, and in marketing. Railroads and steamship lines created a national and an international market by linking the areas which supplied raw materials and commodities with the industrial regions and the growing urban centers. Drastically reduced transportation costs enabled large, efficient producers to undersell local manufacturers. Steel mills in Pittsburgh could outbid local ironmongers in Philadelphia, New York, and even London. The telegraph provided business with the means of communication and the information required to operate across such distances.

Swiftly developing technology and new sources of power made possible the production revolution which supplied this expanded market. New mining techniques and refining processes provided basic ores. Coal, the major new energy source, replaced the power provided by waterfalls, horses, mules, and oxen. New processes like the Bessemer and open-hearth methods of making steel improved both the product and its production. (By 1900 the United States was producing more steel, and selling it more cheaply, than Britain and Germany combined.)

Inventions created completely new products, especially for urban consumers. Alexander Graham Bell, educator of the deaf and experimenter in acoustics, demonstrated the first magnetoelectric telephone in 1876. The same decade saw the development of the first adding machine with printed totals, as well as the cash register, celluloid, and electric dynamos. In the 1880s, patents were granted for numerous electrical appliances: fans, flatirons, stoves, and sewing machines. An electrical engineer, Thomas Alva Edison, built a research laboratory in Menlo Park, New Jersey, not far from New York City, saying that he intended to turn out " a minor invention every ten days and a big thing every six months or so." A distinctly American concept and a distinct success, Edison's invention factory developed marketable products on a regular basis. The "Wizard of Menlo Park" and his associates produced the phonograph (1873), the incandescent electric light bulb (1879), an improved motion picture projector (1895), and a host of other inventions which helped change the nature of life in America.

A revolution in the structure of American marketing linked the new mass production industries with the emerging mass markets. Before the Civil War, wholesale merchants had managed the distribution of manufactured goods to retailers and consumers. In the postwar era, mass production manufacturers began to circumvent the old system of distribution. In the 1880s and 1890s, Singer Sewing Machine, McCormick (reapers), and the Remingtons (typewriters) pioneered in building national, even international, marketing operations which included traveling salespeople, franchised retail dealers and repair shops, and branch offices to coordinate supplies. When butchers in the East resisted switching from locally slaughtered beef to the products of the Chicago meatpackers, Gustavus Swift bought his own refrigerated warehouses, sales offices, and retail stores. He was able to undersell butchers who had cattle shipped live to the East because, since 60 percent of each animal was inedible, he saved transportation costs by slaughtering in Chicago, where it could be done in volume, and then shipping the meat to market in refrigerated cars. Expansion from production into distribution (and sometimes backward into raw materials) was called vertical integration, and this technique was employed by a number of Swift's imitators, who made Chicago the meatpacking center of the country and Milwaukee and St. Louis the dominant producers of beer for the national market.

Mass production, however, had its own pitfalls. Through extensive use of costly high-speed machinery, manufacturers could turn out millions of units, from steel rails to cigarettes, at a fraction of the average cost per unit for smaller manufacturers. Taking advantage of the cost savings from economies of scale, mass producers expanded their markets by underselling competitors. But when the supply of goods outstripped immediate market demand, as often happened, prices plummeted. American steelmakers increased output from 3 million tons to 30 million tons between 1870 and 1900, and the price of steel rails dropped from $100 to $12 a ton. Consumers benefited from the expanded number of goods and the long-term decline in the overall price index, which dropped 25 percent between 1873 and 1896. But many of the men who ran the high-volume industries complained that mass production had undermined the basis of workable price competition, thereby weakening the foundations of the self-regulating marketplace.

Although many people believed that industrial competition benefited society by maintaining low prices, the managers of railroads and other capital-intensive, high-volume businesses bemoaned the increasingly harsh price wars as "cutthroat" or "ruinous" competition. Adam Smith, they said, had presupposed a market in which small firms freely entered and left. He had assumed that when manufacturers could not sell at a profit because of a temporary oversupply of goods, they would close down until shrinking volume caused prices to increase to a profitable level, at which point they would resume production. But in times of intensive competition for declining markets the new industrial giants would *sell below the costs of production,* rather than shut down, in order to pay some of their enormous overhead expenses, such as interest on indebtedness (the cost of building a steel mill in Pittsburgh, for example, increased from $156,000 during the Civil War to $20 million in 1890).

The intensive price-cutting competition which often drove prices below cost led many entrepreneurs in the mass production industries to seek to ensure profits through other means. Some, like the steel magnate Andrew Carnegie, became increasingly competitive, shaving costs by cutting wages and streamlining procurement, production, and distribution. Some tried to expand their markets through extensive advertising and sales campaigns at home and, especially after the depression of the 1890s, abroad. But many sought to avoid price competition by joining with their rivals to intervene in the marketplace in order to control price fluctuations and ensure profits. Beginning in the railroads and spreading into industry, these interventionists tried a variety of means ranging from cooperation to consolidation. "I like a little competition," explained J. P. Morgan, a Wall Street banker who financed many consolidations, "but I like combination better."

The Origins of Big Business

Combination produced big business and the largest supercorporations the world had ever seen. An organizational revolution transformed American business. Before the Civil War most businesses had been small shops or firms owned by a single proprietor or a few partners. The largest, the New England textile mills, were companies which had been created with $1 million. But in the late nineteenth century new entrepreneurs built a number of behemoth corporations backed up by hundreds of millions of dollars and controlling many plants and thousands of employees. Railroads provided the prototype for large-scale, widespread, hierarchical business organization. But the new form of organization soon spread to mass production industry as industrialists sought to extend their power and control the market for their goods.

Attempts to limit price competition began with pools (or cartels, as they were called in Europe), loose agreements in which a number of rival firms agreed to fix prices and allocate markets. Pools were formed among railroads and in the meatpacking, tobacco, and electrical equipment industries, but they rarely functioned well because they could not be legally enforced. Anglo-American common law did not support combinations in restraint of trade. Instead, business turned to other forms of consolidation: acquisition, merger, and the trust.

John D. Rockefeller organized the first and most famous of the trusts, the Standard Oil Trust, in 1879. The former Cleveland bookkeeper and wholesale merchant had entered the petroleum refining industry at its start and had quickly became the largest refiner of kerosene illuminating oil in America. Chaotic conditions ånd widely fluctuating prices frequently cut profits in the industry, and ruinous price wars were common. Rockefeller's Standard Oil Company of Ohio cut costs through efficiency, but it also used its power to obtain secret rebates from railroads, drive competitors out of business, and influence state legislatures. By the mid-1870s the company had eliminated or absorbed many of its competitors through a process of consolidation known as horizontal integration.

Then in 1879 Standard Oil and its forty leading rivals organized a trust in which the voting stock of the operating companies was turned over to a board of trustees headed by Rockefeller in exchange for trust certificates. The trustees of the new Standard Oil Trust set policy for an organization which controlled 95 percent of America's refined-petroleum output. Profits averaged 19 percent a year for the next decade and a half. When the state of Ohio convicted Standard Oil Company of violating its charter, the trust moved to New Jersey, which in 1889 became the first state to make it legal for a corporation in one state to control a corporation in another. In that year the Standard Oil Company of New Jersey was created as a holding company, a paper corporation with its own board of directors, which held the majority of voting stock in various operating companies and could thus set common pricing and market policies for them.

The Challenge of the Trusts

Although the great majority of American businesses remained highly competitive, the emergence of a significant number of giant industrial monopolies became the focus of substantial public concern in the late nineteenth century. Like industrialization itself, the creation of big business stimulated both pride in American power and achievement and anxiety about the ramifications of this new development. There was also much confusion because many people considered all giant firms monopolies when many were not.

Proponents of consolidation claimed that big business was inevitable, stemming from mass production technology, new sources of power, better organization, and the ability to market goods throughout the United States and the world. They also maintained that big business represented progress, creating more jobs and increasing the standard of living by making more products available at cheaper prices. "To stop co-operation of individuals and aggregation of capital," Samuel Dodd, chief attorney for Standard Oil, declared, "would be to arrest the wheels of progress—to stay the march of civilization."

But many Americans worried about these new concentrations of capital, especially their power. "Relations between rival railroad systems," Louis D. Brandeis, a social reform lawyer, complained, "are like the relations between neighboring kingdoms. The relations of the great trusts to the consumers and to their employees is like that of feudal lords to commoners or dependents." At first, cartoonists portrayed the trusts as grasping octopuses or bulging moneybags with high silk hats looming menacingly over society. Gradually, public sentiment built up against the trusts. Farmers, workers, owners of small businesses, socially concerned ministers, and journalists began to accuse railroad consolidators and industrialists like Rockefeller of being "robber barons" who obtained their enormous wealth and power by predatory means, especially local price cutting and exclusive selling contracts with retailers, which forced competitors out of business. Some critics believed that the benefits of mass production could be achieved by medium-sized firms. Many worried about big business' control over competition and the marketplace, claiming that the trust destroyed opportunities for others to become independent businesspeople.

NEW JOBS FOR OLD

The sweeping forces of industrialization, immigration, and urbanization also transformed the nature of work and the work force. Although millions still labored on farms and in villages, the greatest increase in jobs came in urban areas—in factories, offices, retail shops, and department stores. Increasingly, America became a nation of wage earners. At the time of the Civil War, only slightly more than a million people worked for hourly wages; the majority of white Americans were self-employed on farms or in small shops or other businesses. On the eve of World War I, however, more than 7 million persons worked for someone else for wages, and millions more were salaried employees paid by the week or month. America was becoming a nation of employees.

Factory Labor

The nation's factories drew workers from many sources. Some were skilled artisans displaced by industrialization. Many had been unskilled day laborers. And the sons and daughters of farmers left the land in droves for jobs in the factories. Increasingly, however, the least skilled, heaviest, dirtiest, and most dangerous jobs were done by immigrants.

As people moved from the work routines of the farmer and artisan to factory discipline, the nature of work changed. Mass production and the factory system divided labor into simple, repetitive tasks. Managers used incentives and coercion to adapt rural people to the pace of the machines they operated. Published work rules, bells and whistles, constant supervision, and the piece-rate system, which paid workers on the basis of their output, encouraged productivity. So did fines, suspensions, and firings. Monotonous factory work diminished the sense of self-worth of many workers, who also resented the dependence fostered by the wage system. Many skilled trades and the apprentice–master craftsman system were eliminated or greatly modified. "You can take a boy fresh from the farm," lamented a machinist with thirty years of experience, "and in three days he can manage a machine as well as I can."

Speed of production and lack of safety devices led to one of the highest accident rates in the industrialized world. Steelworkers labored twelve hours a day, six days a week in front of the furnaces. Men and women in the nation's factories put in a work week which averaged sixty hours. Pittsburgh, with its miles of steel mills, seemed to one visitor to be a city "like hell with the lid taken off."

Workers responded to the transformation of work in different ways. Many accepted factory conditions because of the high wages, which generally exceeded those in rural areas of the United States and Europe. Although prices dropped in the last third of the nineteenth century, wages increased as a result of economic growth. Another incentive was the prospect of upward social mobility. Although it was seldom experienced, the "rags-to-riches" myth celebrated in American folklore and the popular novels of Horatio Alger was widely believed. People pointed to Andrew Carnegie, who rose from immigrant factory worker to steel magnate and multimillionaire. Recent studies disclose that although Carnegie was a rare exception, a significant number of people did improve their socioeconomic status somewhat during the period.

Some of those who moved upward were immigrants. Guiseppe Tuoti opened a real estate office in Manhattan in 1885, and his business prospered as Italian immigrants saved their earnings and bought stores and tenements. Within a few years Tuoti had formed a company to develop the town of Woodbridge, New Jersey, as a suburban retreat for Italians and others fleeing Manhattan's slums. Soon he expanded his operations to Staten Island, Brooklyn, and the Bronx. By the time he retired, in 1924, Tuoti had become one of New York's leading realtors, a self-made millionaire. Many other immigrants won a measure of economic success. In America, a Warsaw tailor became a dressmaker; a Pinsk peddler flourished as a storekeeper; a talmudic scholar from Vienna became a leading lawyer.

Small gains in status were much more common. Recent statistical research shows that in some cities one out of five white men, native-born and immigrant, moved from blue- to white-collar occupations in a single decade—the 1880s. Furthermore, many unskilled workers moved into semiskilled positions, and their children often moved on to skilled jobs. A laborer's son might become a factory worker, his grandson a machinist. By sending many members of the family to work and living frugally while putting money in a savings account each week, some families of unskilled and semiskilled workers bought relatively inexpensive houses and became property owners. The realization that improvement was possible may have helped alleviate the massive discontent caused by the trauma of industrialization.

Industrial strife made labor-management relations a series of violent episodes, the fiercest stemming from wage cuts and layoffs. The great railroad strikes of 1877, the Homestead strike of 1892, and the Pullman strike of 1894 all witnessed pitched battles between strikers and police. In 1886 violence flared in Haymarket Square in Chicago during a demonstration in support of the eight-hour day. Someone threw a bomb into the ranks of police, killing half a dozen. Police then fired wildly into the crowd, causing more casualties. Four alleged anarchists were executed for the "massacre."

Some attempts were made to form labor-based political parties. San Francisco and Milwaukee had powerful workers' parties, but on the national level the Greenback Labor party of 1878–1884 and the National Labor party of 1888 were never able to do more than elect a handful of congressmen. Marxian Socialists formed the Socialist Labor party in 1877; less revolutionary, and more influential, socialists established the Socialist Party of America in 1901.

Although most workers remained outside working people's parties and unions, labor's most significant response to the new conditions was to develop national organizations. The earliest national confederations of workers—the National Labor Union (1866–1872) and the Knights of Labor (1878–1893)—organized skilled and unskilled workers and opposed the wage system, seeking alternatives such as consumers' and producers' cooperatives. The most influential unions, however, did not try to eliminate the wage labor market but accepted the corporate industrial wage system and sought to limit competition among skilled craft workers in order to achieve higher wages and better working conditions. The railroad brotherhoods (engineers, conductors, and firemen) and the trade unions, which in 1886 formed the American Federation of Labor (AFL), used their economic power, through strikes and boycotts, to better their conditions.

Following the example of big business, organized labor attempted to protect itself against the more extreme effects of market forces by enrolling all the workers in particular trades—carpenters, teamsters, brewers, railroad workers. American labor was craft conscious rather than class conscious. As leader of the AFL, Samuel Gompers, an English immigrant cigar maker, abandoned radical goals for what he called "unionism pure and simple." Under his direction the AFL grew from 150,000 members in 1886 to 500,000 in 1897, when it represented nearly 60 percent of the union members in America. Labor, like business, challenged and helped modify the free-market system through the organization of interventionist forces.

New Roles for Women

Women became a significant part of the urban industrial work force, just as they had been important to the farm economy, but the new system separated home and work. Single women had worked in the earliest New England textile mills. During the Civil War, they temporarily replaced men in many factories and stores. In the postwar period, they found work as domestic servants in private homes; as workers in commercial laundries, canneries, garment factories, and cigarette and textile mills; and in clerical positions in offices and sales jobs in department stores. The factory system employed women from lower-income families. Most middle-class women did not work for wages in the nineteenth century. A "cult of true womanhood" stressed domesticity and submissiveness as the correct womanly characteristics and emphasized the role of women as wives, mothers, and homemakers.

Beginning in the 1840s, middle-class women like Elizabeth Cady Stanton and Susan B. Anthony founded a women's movement as the start of a major collective search to define and ensure a position for women in society that was not subordinate. They sought not only suffrage but fully equal citizenship and autonomy, or individual self-determination. The expansion of the economy in the post-Civil War era created new jobs for women outside the home and offered employment opportunities for increasing numbers. In 1870, 15 percent of American women worked outside the home; in 1890, 20 percent did. Society was forced to recognize the disparity between the reality of working women and the ideal of the exclusive homemakers. Female academies and women's colleges like Mount Holyoke, Wellesley, Bryn Mawr, Vassar, and Barnard helped prepare women leaders and provided for more assertive intellectuality and greater self-assurance in their occupations. Women found jobs as nurses and schoolteachers, and a handful broke employment barriers to become physicians and professors, primarily at women's colleges but sometimes at predominantly male universities. Alumnae groups, women's clubs, and organizations like the Women's Christian Temperance Union promoted women's activities, provided support networks, and contributed to a new sense of female solidarity.

Most women were not radicals but sought to find a meaningful position for themselves within the prevailing emphasis on the nurturing role of women. Thus, although some women stressed suffrage as a right, the more conservative thought of it as a means of protecting Anglo-Saxon culture from the impact of the immigrant vote. More altruistically, "social feminists" led reform movements to aid immigrants and the poor through settlement house work and public health nursing, and to protect the moral standards of the nation through campaigns against pornography, prostitution, and alcoholism.

More radical feminists stressed autonomy and equality for women. Particularly influential were John Stuart Mill's *Essay on Liberty* (1859) and the ideas of the women's-rights lecturer and activist Frances Wright. In 1872 Victoria Woodhull, a fiery journalist and editor, became the first woman to be nominated for president of the United States, when she was put forward by the People's party, a collection of radical groups. Autonomy was stressed by theorists like the anarchist Emma Goldman and the socialist Charlotte Perkins Gilman, who in *Women and Economics,* published in 1898, provided an economic explanation for the subjugation of women and proposed communal solutions to the problems of child rearing and household labor in order to free women for careers in the work force.

Changes in the nineteenth-century conception of women's place in society frightened many conservatives, who feared that employment outside the home and the drive for women's rights would undermine the family and social stability. In particular, they pointed to the declining birthrate, which had plunged from 52 per 1,000 in 1840 to 33 per 1,000 in 1900, and the divorce rate, which had soared from one in every 21 marriages in 1880 to one in every 12 by 1900.

A New Middle Class

Among the most rapidly growing areas of the economy was the service sector, and the number of white-collar or white-blouse jobs in offices and stores increased dramatically. Clerks and salespeople, typists and secretaries may not have received the same incomes as members of the middle class, but their attire and surroundings made them feel that they were part of it. In addition, large numbers of salaried workers were employed in the expanding areas of education and government. Staff, supervisors, and managers in the new corporations provided part of the new salaried middle class, as did the growing numbers of professionals—lawyers, doctors, engineers, teachers. Increasingly, the new middle class eclipsed the old middle class of artisans, skilled workers, shop owners, and small manufacturers.

Farmers: The Vanishing Yeomen

Although agricultural productivity continued to grow in the late nineteenth century, agriculture's importance declined rapidly compared with that of industry. With increasing mechanization—especially the use of mechanical reapers and threshers—and the expansion of farm acreage from 500 million to 800 million acres between 1870 and 1900, agricultural production grew dramatically. But because of mechanization, this leap in output was accomplished by a smaller number of workers. In 1850, some 60 percent of the population was engaged in agriculture; by 1900, the proportion had dropped to 40 percent. Over the same period, agricultural output fell from 40 percent to 20 percent of gross national product.

Many American farmers found themselves in difficulty in the late nineteenth century. With the vast expansion of agricultural production, the price of commodities generally declined, falling by 50 percent between 1866 and 1900. At the same time, farm mortgages increased as farmers brought new land under production and bought new equipment. Agrarians complained of high interest rates, freight rates, and prices for agricultural machinery, which were kept artificially high by means of the protective tariff. Caught between falling commodity prices and rising costs, many farmers went bankrupt. Farm tenancy increased nationally from 26 percent of all farms in 1880 to 35 percent in 1900. The rise was particularly dramatic in the cotton and wheat states. The yeoman farmer, the symbol and hope of America in the Jeffersonian Era, became an anachronism in a land of large-scale production. An increasingly urban nation looked upon small farmers as a relic of the past, while the farmers became radicalized because of their plight and turned to political action to save themselves and their vision of America.

THE WEAKENED SPRING OF GOVERNMENT

Government was ill prepared to cope with the major forces which were transforming the country. Suspicion of power, a legacy from colonial times, had led Americans to limit central power, fragmenting it through the federal system and the checks and balances on the different branches of government. The Jeffersonian-Jacksonian ideal of a limited state and the policy of laissez faire combined to restrict the functions of the national and state governments. Traditionally, Americans had relied primarily on voluntary private associations rather than public authorities to deal with most of their collective problems. Compared with other nations the United States had, according to a visiting European scholar, M. I. Ostrogorski, only "a weakened spring of government."

Popular Politics

The humorist Mark Twain was fond of saying that it was a good thing Congress had not been present when God said "Let there be light," because otherwise the world would have remained in darkness. Like many others, Twain belittled the politicians in Washington. While the powerful currents of industrialization, urbanization, and immigration were changing the nature of American society, both major parties ignored the new problems from lack of understanding and from timidity. Because Republicans and Democrats were so evenly divided, with control in each house of Congress fluctuating between them, they evaded new issues and avoided bold actions which might have uncertain effects. The result was a politics of dead center in which neither major party sought to disturb the status quo. "The Republican and Democratic parties were like two bottles," the

English observer James Bryce commented. "Each bore a label denoting the kind of liquor it contained, but each was empty."

Paradoxically, at a time when government seemed so superficial, the political participation of Americans reached its highest point in the country's history. In the last third of the century, the turnout of eligible voters reached 80 percent nationally and 95 percent in certain sharply divided states in the Midwest. In those days, in addition to being a ritual affirmation of democracy, politics was a form of popular entertainment, almost a spectator sport. On a hot summer day in 1876, a local paper in a small Indiana town reported that a political rally held during the week was "a spectacle no foreign fiesta could equal."

Sectional and cultural differences also help explain why most people remained intensely loyal to the two major parties despite their ineffectiveness. The divisions which had led to the Civil War continued to shape the polity for generations after the war had ended. The Republican party was based in the North, with a few black voters in the South. The Democratic party was based in the South, with some urban, ethnic-based political machines in the North. In a few midwestern and mid-Atlantic states, the parties were evenly matched. Memories of the Civil War and religious and ethnic values proved more important than class or economic issues in determining how most Americans defined their political loyalties. Seeking to enjoy their own cultural traditions, Irish and German Catholics, Jews, and Lutheran and Episcopalian Protestants, members of "liturgical" churches which emphasized ceremony, ritual, and well-defined dogma, preferred to keep government out of their private lives. They tended to support the Democratic party, which in the North took a more tolerant view of cultural pluralism. In part, these groups reacted against the Republican party's attempts to use the power of the state to regulate ethical behavior and to create a virtuous society, for example, through state and local laws controlling the use of alcoholic beverages and the observance of the Sabbath on Sunday. The GOP appealed especially to evangelical, "pietistic" Protestants, such as Baptists, Methodists, Presbyterians, and Congregationalists, who emphasized personal reformation, inner regeneration, and "right behavior" over ritual and dogma.

The Growth of Government

In its limited fashion the federal government gradually began to expand its functions and to shift from issues related to the Civil War and Reconstruction to policies promoting economic growth and some feeble attempts at regulation. To encourage settlement of the West, Congress provided land for settlers and the railroads. To encourage industrial growth and high wages, it maintained a substantial protective tariff against foreign competition. Both major parties supported tariffs, although most Democrats wanted lower duties, which would benefit agrarian consumers. Reaction against corruption, the spoils system (which rewarded partisans with federal jobs), and the assassination of President James Garfield by a disappointed office seeker led Congress to establish the federal civil service system at a time when the number of civilian federal employees was soaring—it increased from 53,000 in 1871 to 230,000 in 1900.

A wave of protest against combinations in railroading and industry and their dominant influence in the marketplace forced government to take some regulatory action. In 1887 Congress prohibited pooling by the railroads and established the first federal regulatory agency, the Interstate Commerce Commission (ICC), to determine whether freight rates were reasonable. Without rate-fixing authority, however, the ICC was soon reduced to a statistics-gathering bureau by adverse court decisions.

Federal actions against trusts proved ineffective. In 1890, in response to public pressure, Congress passed the Sherman Antitrust Act, which outlawed combinations in restraint of trade and provided for triple damages upon conviction. Perhaps intentionally, the law was too vague to be effective. Congress had acted partly to avoid more radical state action, especially in agrarian regions. The lawmakers did assert federal jurisdiction over interstate commerce and the national marketplace, and they moved to limit the trusts, but they left it to the executive and the judiciary to decide what would be done.

The Supreme Court emasculated the Sherman Act as it applied to business. It took a limited view of the interstate commerce power when it ruled in favor of the sugar trust in the *E. C. Knight* case (1895). The Court, however, proved quite willing to use the antitrust act against labor unions (*In re Debs,* 1895), and upheld injunctions against strikes which obstructed interstate commerce. While upholding formal consolidations like the sugar trust, the Supreme Court invalidated pooling or cartel arrangements among independent companies in the *Addystone Pipe and Steel* case (1899). Nineteenth-century conservatives believed that the judiciary rather than the other popularly elected branches of the federal government should weigh the claims of conflicting groups and determine the proper equilibrium among the rights of individuals, the sanctity of private property, and the welfare of the community. But many Americans expressed discontent about the ineffectiveness of all of the branches of the national government in dealing with the issues of industrialization.

Populism: The Agrarian Revolt

Plagued by declining incomes and mounting debt, many farmers and villagers in the South and West demanded governmental action to ease their plight. "The fruits of the toil of millions," the platform of the newly formed People's party declared in 1892, "are boldly stolen to build up colossal fortunes of a few." The Populists attacked the eastern moneyed interests and the gold standard they supported, and demanded unlimited coinage of silver to boost commodity prices through inflation of the money supply. Despite much confusion and moralistic rhetoric over whether the nation's currency should be backed by gold alone or by silver as well, the basic issue was whether the federal government should actively intervene in the economy and use its power to aid groups like farmers which were hurt by industrialism. The Populists also urged federal ownership of the railroads, government loans on crops and land, an eight-hour day for labor, direct election of U.S. senators, and a federal income tax on the new sources of wealth.

Taking up the Populists' standard, William Jennings Bryan, a Nebraska congressman, won the Democratic party nomination for president in 1896. A powerful orator, Bryan challenged eastern financiers and corporate managers, and the Republican party, in ringing biblical terms: "You shall not press down upon the brow of labor this crown of thorns. You shall not crucify mankind upon a cross of gold." The "great commoner" enlisted millions in his crusade, but he lost to a former Republican congressman and governor of Ohio, William McKinley. It was a crushing defeat for the agrarians. Although it is seldom recognized as such, L. Frank Baum's masterpiece of children's fantasy, *The Wonderful Wizard of Oz* (1900), contained a subtle, symbolic allegory of the populist revolt. It told of the unmasking of a fraudulent wizard by a little girl from Kansas, a farmer, an industrial workman, and a cowardly lion (the pacifist politician William Jennings Bryan?) who followed a yellow (golden?) brick road but were saved by Dorothy's magic *silver* slippers in the Land of Oz (ounce?).

Although few Americans realized it at the time, Bryan's defeat marked the last bid of the nation's farmers for leadership of a national reform movement. It also ended an era of political stalemate and timidity, ushering in a period of a strong Republican majority and bold new political leadership which addressed many contemporary issues.

THE TASTE OF EMPIRE

New Directions

"Barriers of national seclusion are everywhere tumbling like the Great Wall of China," an American historian observed in 1898. By the turn of the century Americans had joined the Europeans and Japanese in the international competition for commerce, colonies, and prestige. Exercising new-found strength, the United States defeated Spain in 1898 and gained not only a major role in the Caribbean and Western Pacific but recognition as a world power as well. Expansionists hailed the end of America's largely self-imposed exclusion from international affairs. "The policy of isolation is dead," *The Washington Post* declared. "A new consciousness seems to have come upon us—the consciousness of strength, and with it a new appetite, a yearning to show our strength. . . . The taste of empire is in the mouth of the people."

This new outward thrust posed a challenge to American traditions. In the past the United States had maintained a realistic, limited foreign policy. Isolated, protected by broad oceans and relatively weak neighbors on either side, and enjoying a large domestic market, Americans paid little attention to events abroad, reacting to those that affected them rather than trying to shape international developments. The United States saw itself serving primarily as a moral example to the world, a beacon of democracy. In the late nineteenth century, however, American policy makers became more willing to enter into foreign adventures.

Expansion was not new to Americans, who had justified their westward conquests as part of a divinely ordained "manifest destiny." But overseas imperialism was different. The acquisition from Spain of an empire of thickly populated islands which the United States intended to administer as colonies, not as potential states of the Union, led many traditionalists to accuse the nation of departing from its unique mission. As the philosopher William James put it in 1898, in the early days of the war with Spain,

> We had supposed ourselves . . . a better nation than the rest, safe at home, and without the old savage ambition, destined to exert great international influence by throwing in our "moral weight." . . . Dreams! Human Nature is everywhere the same; and at the least temptation all the old military passions rise and sweep everything before them.

Fueling America's new expansionism was a growing sense of what the nation could and should accomplish in the role of world power. The idea of mission remained strong, and the descendants of those who had sought to convert the Indians now carried the Bible to "heathens" in Hawaii, Japan, and China. The evangelist Dwight L. Moody echoed the buoyant optimism of many Christian Americans in 1887, when he organized the Student Volunteers for Foreign Missions and called for "the evangelization of the world in this generation." America's traditional sense of itself as the exemplar of free democratic institutions was augmented by Social Darwinism, which, as interpreted by imperialists on both sides of the Atlantic, meant that it was the responsibility of the Anglo-Saxon race ("the white man's burden," Kipling called it) to "civilize" and "uplift" the nonwhite peoples of the world.

Industrial growth gave Americans a new sense of power, but the depressions of the 1870s, the 1880s, and especially the 1890s caused many in industry and government to look for new markets abroad. Exports leaped from $34 million to $1.5 billion during the last three decades of the century. Many prominent Americans saw foreign economic expansion as necessary to great-power status as well as beneficial to national prosperity. "The trade of the world," Senator Albert Beveridge declared, "must and shall be ours." The desire to extend and protect foreign commerce and to be a great power led to the modernization of the U.S. Navy, which by 1900 ranked third among the world's fleets, surpassed only by those of Britain and Germany.

No clearly defined overall foreign policy guided American expansion in the late nineteenth century; rather, decisions were often opportunistic and politically motivated. Nevertheless, despite an erratic course, expansion continued during the three decades after the Civil War. The United States bought Alaska from Russia and established a naval coaling station on Samoa in the South Pacific. It signed trade agreements with countries in Latin America and the Far East. American forces helped wealthy white planters overthrow the native monarchy in Hawaii. Then, in 1895, the Cleveland administration warned Britain to arbitrate the boundary dispute between British Guiana and Venezuela or face the possibility of war with the United States. Active American intervention in international relations involving a major power marked a significant departure from traditional foreign policy, shocked the European nations, and forced the British to back down.

The War with Spain

The Spanish-American War of 1898 continued the United States' rise to global activism. Like a crab scampering sideways across the sand, the country edged hesitantly toward war. After the Cuban Revolution erupted in bloody guerrilla fighting in 1895, Washington tried to persuade Madrid to grant the reforms, the autonomy, and finally the independence necessary to restore stability and commerce on the island. As the conflict dragged on, President McKinley came under increasing pressure for intervention, especially after the U.S.S. *Maine* was sunk in Havana Harbor by an explosion.

In New York the sensationalist Hearst and Pulitzer newspapers, vigorously competing for circulation, helped whip up war hysteria, but sentiment for American action to "free" Cuba was also strong in the agrarian Midwest. When important business interests reluctantly decided that even a potentially unsettling war was preferable to continued disruption of the American political and economic situation, McKinley obtained authority from Congress to use U.S. forces to drive the Spanish out of Cuba and end the war. He also wanted to avoid possible German intervention in the conflict.

Spanish resistance was feeble. American troops quickly seized Cuba and Puerto Rico and defeated a Spanish naval squadron in the Philippine Islands. At the same time, the United States annexed the Hawaiian Islands for their economic and strategic value. America had made the most of what Secretary of State John Hay called a "splendid little war."

An Island Empire

McKinley's decision to demand an island empire—Puerto Rico, Guam, and the Philippines—in the peace treaty with Spain triggered a major debate over the direction of American foreign policy. Both the shapers of foreign policy opinion—government officials, editors, former diplomats, international lawyers, missionaries, and religious and business leaders—and the general public were divided over the issue of annexation.

Expansionists like Theodore Roosevelt and Senators Beveridge and Henry Cabot Lodge supported annexation as the responsibility of a great power. If the United States did not guide, protect, and educate the native peoples toward self-government, they argued, they would be taken over by some other, more aggressive country like Germany or Japan. Advocates of a "large policy" also saw economic benefits for the United States. They viewed the Philippines as the "pickets of the Pacific, standing guard at the entrance to trade with the millions of China." Manila would become an American Hong Kong, an entrepôt to that market. Puerto Rico would provide a site for protecting the trade routes to the Panama Canal.

Anti-imperialists like William James, Andrew Carnegie, and Senator George F. Hoar of Massachusetts viewed the acquisition of colonies in far-flung underdeveloped lands as another dangerous threat posed to American traditions by industrialization. The taking of "vassal states" without the consent of their inhabitants, one senator declared, was "trampling . . . on our own great Charter which recognizes alike the liberty and dignity of individual manhood." Andrew Carnegie offered to write a personal check for $20 million to buy the independence of the Philippines.

Despite their efforts, the anti-imperialists failed to prevent the annexation of an American colonial empire. A few days before the Senate ratified the Treaty of Paris, which ended the Spanish-American War and provided for the annexation of Puerto Rico, Guam, and the Philippines, fighting broke out between American troops and Filipino nationalist forces who wished independence rather than American rule. It took more than two years and 125,000 soldiers to suppress the revolt. The Americans suffered more than 7,000 casualties, and more than 200,000 Philippine civilians died from privation, disease, and brutality during the fierce and ruthless guerrilla war which solidified American power in the Philippines.*

As a Pacific power, the United States began to participate actively in the momentous developments in China. With the decline in the power of the Manchu dynasty, Europeans and Japanese began to carve out spheres of influence in what Western diplomats called "the sick man of Asia." Attempting to enunciate a coherent and defensible American policy toward China, Secretary of State Hay circulated two "Open Door" notes among the great powers in 1899 and 1900. These defined American interest as maintaining the territorial integrity and sovereignty of China and keeping the spheres of influence, or leaseholds, of other powers there open to trade with other nations, such as the United States. The European nations acquiesced in this statement of policy because they feared that a scramble to divide China

---

* Spain went on to spend more money and lose more soldiers in an attempt to regain imperial status by conquering Morocco in North Africa.

might lead to a world war. When Chinese nationalists staged the Boxer Rebellion, the United States added 2,500 troops to a multinational expedition which rescued the foreign legations besieged in Peking. Hay's notes were also designed to reassure Americans that the government did not intend to keep U.S. troops on the Asian mainland, as it had in the Philippines.

The acquisition of an empire and the recognition of great-power status had seemed so easy that many Americans were deceived into believing that intervention in the name of moral idealism could be achieved without significant costs to the nation. But others were concerned about the effects of this new role on American ideals and traditions. As William Graham Sumner argued in an 1899 article entitled "The Conquest of the United States by Spain," it might do much harm:

> We cannot govern dependencies consistently with our political system, and . . . if we try it, the state which our fathers founded will suffer a reaction which will transform it into another empire just after the fashion of all the old ones. That is what imperialism means.

THE CHALLENGE OF CHANGE

"My country in 1900," Henry Adams wrote, "is something totally different from my own country in 1860. I am wholly a stranger in it. Neither I, nor anyone else, understands it." Americans considered change to be part of the progress ordained for their nation, and many applauded the industrial growth which by the turn of the century had made the United States one of the most powerful nations on earth. But the developments of the end of the nineteenth century—the closing of the frontier, industrialization and the emergence of the trusts, massive new immigration, the rise of giant metropolises, and the conquest of a far-flung island empire—were so new and rapid that many people were not sure they represented progress. Indeed, Harvard art historian Charles Eliot Norton concluded that it was a "degenerate and unlovely age."

Cracks in the Victorian Order

The old order of thought was also disintegrating under changing social conditions and a new ferment in the intellectual world. America and the Western world were beginning the transition from an age of confidence to an age of doubt. The United States had been born in the Enlightenment and had grown to maturity in the Victorian period with its emphasis on an orderly, Newtonian universe of natural laws, fixed moral principles, the dignity of humanity, the omnipotence of God, and the benevolence of nature. Nature and experience had justified the optimism of Americans, who saw evidence of progress in the growth of their country's wealth and power. But this comfortable Victorian concept of life and the universe began to fall apart under the impact of industrialization and the blows of Darwinism.

One of the most influential concepts of the nineteenth century, Darwinism caused an intellectual revolution not only in biology but also in people's attitudes about the place of humankind in nature. In what he called "the struggle for existence," the English naturalist Charles Darwin concluded that the organisms that were best equipped to get food and shelter would inherit whatever favorable variations occurred in their genetic makeup. Gradually, through a long process of "natural selection," higher, more developed species would evolve. The English sociologist Herbert Spencer applied Darwin's theories of evolution and "survival of the fittest" to society as well. His work was popularized in the United States by the sociologist William Graham Sumner and the philosopher John Fiske.

Evolution banished the absolute and knowable Newtonian universe and substituted one that was in constant flux, whose beginning and end were unknown. The process of natural selection relegated God and individual human beings to virtually passive roles. It also took away the moral authority of institutions and, by subjecting them to the law of evolution, required that they justify themselves. Evolution provided a scientific foundation for the march toward a better civilization, but since the process operated relentlessly through natural selection there was little room for people as active agents. Thus, the price of scientific determinism was submission and conformity. Americans could accept evolution because the notion of change and growth was part of their experience, but they could not accept determinism, which implied that individuals had little or no control over their destiny.

The New Social Criticism

In the late nineteenth century many writers, social scientists, and other intellectuals began to attack the assumptions of the Victorian order and such prevailing concepts as Social Darwinism, unrestricted individualism, the unregulated marketplace, and laissez faire. Investigative journalists like Henry Demarest Lloyd in *Wealth against Commonwealth* (1894), an attack on Standard Oil, and Jacob Riis in *How the Other Half Lives* (1890), a study of poverty in New York City, stressed the brutality of contemporary life. The most important manifestoes awakening middle-class readers to the need for reform were Henry George's *Progress and Poverty* (1879) and Edward Bellamy's *Looking Backward* (1888). Although their solutions to the problems of industrialization differed—George suggested a single tax on rising land values and Bellamy advocated nationalization of industry—both vividly portrayed the shocking contrast between vast wealth and extensive poverty in the emerging industrial society.

Probing and protesting much of the change that industrialism brought to American life, novelists challenged the genteel Victorian literary tradition. Mark Twain, in such later works as *The Man That Corrupted Hadleyburg* and *The Mysterious Stranger,* and William Dean Howells, in *A Hazard of New Fortunes* and *Traveler from Altruria,* had criticized the irresponsibility of acquisitive capitalism and industrialism and the disintegration of traditional standards of morality. But the gentle criticism of "realists" like Howells was supplemented in the 1890s with a harsher new literature, "naturalism," which documented and confronted the dilemmas and problems of urban industrial society. Stephen Crane dealt with subjects that were previously taboo to most American writers as he portrayed prostitution in *Maggie, A Girl of the Streets* (1893). Never before had American writers been so sharply estranged from contemporary society.

Deterministic violence permeated the works of Frank Norris, beginning with *McTeague* (1890) and *The Octopus* (1901), the first volume in his trilogy about the struggle between wheat growers and the Southern Pacific Railroad. It fascinated Jack London, whose *The Call of the Wild* (1903) told of a great dog who escaped from civilization to lead a wolf pack in Alaska. In *Sister Carrie* (1900), Theodore Dreiser's first major work, men and women were portrayed as poor creatures driven by violent desires that they neither create nor control in circumstances beyond their ability to change. As one of Dreiser's characters in *The Genius* concluded exhaustedly, "life was nothing save dark forces moving aimlessly." Despite their pessimistic determinism, Dreiser and the other naturalist critics hoped, like their model, the French social critic Emile Zola, that people would be so repelled by the inhumanity they portrayed that they would somehow repudiate it and create a better world.

But even while the naturalists pursued their mood of doubt, another group of writers represented tradition instead of change. These "traditionalists" shared Victorian convictions that there were standards and that style was important. Henry James, sensitive and subtle, disdained the materialism of a pecuniary civilization in books like *The American* (1877). He stressed the need to preserve moral integrity and artistic values. Edith Wharton focused on ethical values ranged against social or material values in her portraits of the changes in upper-class New York society. Like James, she was unhappy but not outraged at contemporary life in America.

Origins of Interventionism

Americans believed too strongly in the idea of progress and in their destiny as a chosen people to wish to bring the process of change and modernization to a halt. But the society was in such turmoil that Americans began an extensive struggle to gain some kind of control over the process. Few mechanisms existed for directing such widespread change. National institutions like the federal government and the major political parties were hampered by timidity and traditional checks on the power of the central government. Traditionally, Americans had not relied primarily upon government but upon individuals and institutions in the private sector and the market system to determine the direction of society and the allocation of resources. But the developments accompanying industrialization—especially the shock of the depression of the 1890s—caused many people to fear undirected social change. In an increasingly complex, interrelated society, people began to turn to collective action. "We live in an atmosphere of organization," the leader of the organized charity movement in Baltimore wrote in the 1890s. "Men are learning the disadvantages of isolated action.

"We have to act," the philosopher John Dewey asserted, "in order to keep secure amid the moving flux of circumstances." Although they initially represented a minority in the late nineteenth century, some scholars began to revolt against abstract and formalistic determinist thought and advocated collective action, including expanded governmental power, to improve social conditions. They began to challenge laissez faire and the idea of a self-regulating society. Beginning in the 1880s the sociologist Lester Frank Ward assailed the concept of inevitability in evolution as mindless and wasteful. Intervention could improve matters through purposeful manipulation.

The most active advocates of increased governmental action in the marketplace were a group of rebellious young economists who challenged Adam Smith and classical political economy. They did not think the self-interest of individuals necessarily coincided with the best interests of society. "Private self-interest," Henry Carter Adams declared in 1887, "is too powerful, or too ignorant, or too immoral to promote the common good without compulsion." Although they did not think government should intervene everywhere, the interventionist economists did believe, as Richard T. Ely declared in 1885, "that the conflict of labor and capital has brought to the front a vast number of social problems whose solution is impossible without the united efforts of church, state, and science." From his position at Johns Hopkins and, later, the University of Wisconsin, Ely urged a program of social reform and full publicity (along with personal responsibility on the part of the directors) about the corporations in order to raise the level of competition to a higher moral plane. Simon Patten at the University of Pennsylvania urged the need for national planning to help Americans adjust to the new industrial environment. But the neoclassical economist John Bates Clark argued that competition was the "social guarantor of progress," and he proposed to regulate and enforce competition by prohibiting unfair practices which had led to monopoly.

New-school economists and other social critics began to lay the groundwork for interventionism to curtail the harshness of the marketplace. The dramatic changes of the late nineteenth century and the proposals of the interventionists created a brittle tension between modernizers and traditionalists and between those who followed different paths to modernization. Most of the problems of industrialization were clear by the end of the century: growing poverty, increasing class distinctions, maldistribution of wealth and opportunity, increased crime rates, violence, pollution of the environment, and corruption of American values. Ex-President Rutherford B. Hayes complained in his diary in 1890 about "the wrongs and evils of the money-piling tendency of our country," which were "giving all power to the rich and bringing in pauperism and its attendant crimes and wretchedness like a flood." In 1900 Americans looked into the new century with a mixture of hope and fear.

CHAPTER 2

The Corporate Revolution

On a snowy evening as the new century opened, two men in tuxedos paced in front of a crackling fire in the library of a brownstone mansion in New York City. Shadows of dancing flames flickered on stained-glass windows and Renaissance masterpieces. Amidst a collection of art treasures from the past, two modern titans helped shape the economic structure of the future as they put together the largest manufacturing company the world had ever seen, the United States Steel Corporation.

Sparring with each other verbally, the two men stood in striking contrast: the vigorous young contender and the deliberate old warrior. Combining captivating warmth, optimism, and driving ambition, 38-year-old Charles Schwab, the son of a stable-keeper on Andrew Carnegie's estate, had scrambled up to become the manager of Carnegie's mills. His host, J. P. Morgan, had inherited his father's banking company and, through his own skill and awesome personal authority, expanded it into the most powerful investment banking house in the United States. At 64, "Old Jupiter," a gruff and towering figure with piercing eyes and a walrus mustache, was one of the world's leading bankers.

In his meeting with Morgan on that winter evening, Schwab thrust forward his proposal: consolidation of most of the major steel companies, with the giant Carnegie firm as the centerpiece. The combination could prevent a potentially destructive price war and might well stabilize both American and international markets. Cautiously, Morgan probed and tested Schwab's assertions. As dawn streamed through the stained-glass windows, the banker finally acquiesced. All that remained was the asking price for Carnegie's holdings. Without a word, Schwab handed Morgan a piece of paper with the figure $492,000,000 on it. Silently, Morgan scrutinized it, then tersely gave his answer: "I accept."

Within a year Morgan's banking syndicate created the United States Steel Corporation, a giant industrial combine which controlled iron and steel works, shipping and railroad lines, and ore and coal properties. The company owned 156 major factories and several hundred smaller plants in a dozen states. It employed 168,000 workers and was capitalized at $1.4 billion. When it was created in 1901, U.S. Steel controlled 60 percent of American steel production. With an annual gross income which soon exceeded that of the U.S. Treasury, the new industrial behemoth was bigger and more powerful than many nations.

The creation of U.S. Steel—the world's first billion-dollar corporation—symbolized one aspect of a virtual corporate revolution. Before the turn of the century there were only a few supercorporations. Yet in only a half-dozen years, from 1897 to 1903, a sudden wave of reorganizations and consolidations created vast new empires in industry, railroads, and finance. This dramatic private intervention in the marketplace through the consolidation of economic power led to an oligopolistic pattern in which a small number of giant firms dominated the most important industries. Economic growth produced structural change, which led to new behavior, new attitudes, and new tensions as it reshaped traditional American society.

THE GREAT MERGER MOVEMENT

The combination movement resulted largely from the belief of financiers and corporate managers that some kind of consolidation and intervention was necessary to curb price competition and reduce the in-

stability created by an unregulated marketplace. Using successful consolidations like Standard Oil as a model, corporate reorganizers
created a revolution in the structure of American industry as the new
century began. The Great Merger Movement saw more than 3,000
substantial manufacturing companies—many, like Carnegie Steel,
already huge firms—combined through mergers or holding companies
into a few hundred supercorporations. Like U.S. Steel, each
dominated a particular industry: General Electric, the National Bis-
cuit Company (Nabisco), American Can Company, Eastman Kodak,
U.S. Rubber (later Uniroyal), the American Telephone and Telegraph Company, and many others. By 1904 the 300 largest industrial
corporations owned $20 billion in assets, or more than 40 percent of
the industrial wealth of the United States.

At the same time, Morgan and railroad entrepreneurs like Edward
H. Harriman of the Union Pacific, James J. Hill of the Great
Northern, the Vanderbilts of the New York Central, and the wealthy
Philadelphians who controlled the Pennsylvania Railroad transformed
the nation's rail system. During the depression of the 1890s at least
one quarter of the trackage in the country went into the hands of
bankruptcy receivers. In 1897, as economic recovery began, the half-
dozen reorganizers pumped new funds into the carriers and consolidated the railroad network from hundreds of independent and often
competing lines into a few large, noncompetitive rail systems, each of
which exercised virtual monopoly control in a particular region. In a
reference to the trusts which applied to these new rail consolidations
as well, James J. Hill wrote in 1901 that they "came into being as the
result of an effort to obviate ruinous competition."

A favorable economic and legal climate spurred the consolidation
movement. Although many businesses went bankrupt in the depression of 1893–1896, trusts like Standard Oil, American Sugar, and
American Tobacco kept making profits by limiting the decline of
prices in their industries. When prosperity and investor confidence
returned, reorganizers tried to emulate their achievement by consoli-
dating other industries. With the endorsement of respected financiers
like Morgan, a market developed for the stocks of the industrial corporations (the securities market had previously been limited primarily
to railroad and government issues). Consolidators sold stock in the

new supercorporations to banks, trust funds, insurance companies, and wealthy investors. By the late 1890s the legal framework seemed to ensure the legitimacy of the giant corporation. States like New Jersey and Delaware had authorized the corporate holding company device, and despite passage of the Sherman Antitrust Act, the Supreme Court had agreed with attorneys for the American Sugar Company and upheld the legality of that monopoly in the *E. C. Knight* case. "What looks like a stone wall to a layman," one critic declared, "is a triumphal arch to the corporation lawyer."

The creation of big business and the supercorporations also led to an internal revolution in management and the rise of substantial corporate bureaucracies. Having formed these large-scale, multiplant companies, the organizers and managers had to provide administrative structures and procedures so that they would function effectively. Information had to flow upward and directives downward. Managers, many of them more accustomed to competing than cooperating, had to adopt new roles, values, and modes of action. Some corporations, like Du Pont, General Electric, and International Harvester, worked out effective new administrative structures rapidly. Others, like U.S. Steel and Westinghouse, did so more slowly. But all developed structures which were similar in their basic design. Production, distribution, and purchasing facilities were placed in new functional departments, and staff agencies were constructed to deal with engineering, accounting, traffic, legal, and research and development matters. In a major departure from the old trade associations or cartels, the integrated corporations developed a new institution—the central coordinating agency. This body, headed by an executive committee often composed of the president and the heads of the major departments, provided overall corporate direction.

The bureaucratic environment of these vast enterprises produced a new kind of corporate leadership. Managerially minded men succeeded the dynamic, individualistic capitalist entrepreneurs. The bureaucrat replaced the robber baron at the helm of American industry. The shift of leadership from men like Carnegie and Vanderbilt to lesser-known figures like Theodore Vail of AT&T, Elbert Gary of U.S. Steel, and George Perkins of International Harvester represented the transition from creating new industries and giant firms to maintaining and expanding them. Capitalists like Carnegie and Vanderbilt had been rugged competitors with a zest for combat. The new managers were the servants of the corporation, salaried employees rather than owners, and they were more cautious and less willing to take extreme risks. They wanted to control, not exploit, ruthless price competition, and they were willing to intervene in the marketplace and to maintain a live-and-let-live philosophy. The new corporate managers were less flamboyant than their individualistic predecessors, but they were no less successful in accomplishing their aims. The aggressive competition of the open marketplace began to be brought under some control.

The attempts of the new interventionists to modify the operation of the marketplace were more successful in certain areas than in others. Control of price competition proved most effective in capital-intensive, technologically advanced industries like steel and petroleum, which obtained genuine economies of scale, and in those which built up consumer loyalty through extensive advertising of brand names. In these industries, prices were often "administered" rather than set entirely by market forces. A dominant firm became the "price leader," setting a profitable price with the rest of the industry following suit. With regard to steel, for example, the price of steel rails, which had fluctuated between $85 and $16 a ton during the era of fierce competition between 1880 and 1901, sold consistently for $28 a ton in the fifteen years after the formation of U.S. Steel. In oil, farm machinery, and a number of other industries, price leadership reduced the dangers of unrestricted price competition in mass production industries.

But in many areas the marketplace proved unconquerable. When attempted monopolies like American Bicycle, U.S. Leather, and National Salt raised prices too high, aggressive new competitors swarmed in, won over customers, and drove the debt-ridden giants into receivership. Much of American industry thus remained highly competitive. Small and medium-sized firms, operating locally or regionally, battled each other vigorously in textiles, clothing, leather goods, furniture, lumber, and printing. At the retail level, price competition remained a major characteristic of small business, as contrasted to the administered prices of big business. To protect their own interests—but not administer prices—small businesses formed their own trade associations and joined local chambers of commerce, the latter uniting nationally in 1912 to form the U.S. Chamber of Commerce.

Even big business did not eliminate competition entirely. Indeed, during the Progressive Era many of the supercorporations lost some of their dominance of the market to newer, more aggressive competitors. U.S. Steel, for instance, proved slower than its rivals to convert to new technology and shift to the growing market for lighter, alloy steel products. Its share of the market dropped from 62 percent in 1901 to 40 percent in 1920. Similarly, Standard Oil, which had refined 90 percent of the nation's petroleum at its peak in 1899, lost its monopolistic position to new companies like Texaco, Gulf, and Union, which rushed in to develop the oil fields discovered in Texas and California. The new companies also led in exploiting the use of petroleum as gasoline and fuel oil for heating homes and running ships and automobiles. By 1907 Standard's share of the market had eroded to 84 percent, and it was 80 percent in 1911 (the year the Supreme Court ordered its division into several lesser companies, among them Standard Oil of New Jersey, Ohio, and California). By 1920 their combined share had dropped to 50 percent of the market.

Oligopoly, in which a handful of large firms dominated the market, characterized American industry, not monopoly. But the giants did mute price competition, replacing it with less destructive competition in such areas as sales promotion, advertising, cost reduction, and quality of goods and services. The fact that some competition remained reassured many Americans that the market system continued to operate. On the other hand, many also became fearful of the concentration of power in yet another area—finance.

The Wall Street Connection

From the financial centers of the East, investment bankers emerged as powerful agents of industrial development and consolidation. With access to capital from investors in the United States and Europe, they underwrote the expansion and reorganization of American railroads and industry. Acting as middlemen between investors and the corporations, they promoted and financed consolidations through massive issuances of stock. The underwriters received a handsome profit (the Morgan syndicate earned perhaps $60 million for organizing U.S. Steel), but they also saw themselves as financial statesmen, directing the flow of capital and credit to avoid ruinous competition and encourage orderly and sustained economic growth.

The most prestigious investment banking houses located in New York, Boston, and Philadelphia did not number more than a dozen firms. The majority, such as J. P. Morgan; Kidder, Peabody; and Lee Higginson, were run by a handful of old-line Anglo-Saxon Protestants, who usually came from successful merchant or banking families. There were also a few German Jewish firms like J. & W. Seligman, Lehman Brothers, and Kuhn, Loeb. The Jewish bankers represented rags-to-riches stories which could have been written by Horatio Alger.

The Seligmans personified that success story. Joseph Seligman arrived in steerage class from Bavaria in 1837, at the age of 17. He immediately set out on foot as a peddler. Soon he and his three brothers were tramping through the rural areas of the Northeast and the South with their backs bent under packs filled with bolts of cloth, lace, ribbons, pins and needles, and dozens of other items for farm families. Putting their profits together, they bought peddlers' wagons and then a chain of small dry-goods stores.

When gold was discovered in California, two of the brothers took $20,000 worth of merchandise by boat to Panama, then by mule across the isthmus, and then, again by ship, to San Francisco. In that inflationary boom town their goods soared in value. The gold they received in payment was shipped back East and then to Europe to buy more supplies for the Seligman stores. In their move from dry-goods merchants to buyers and sellers of gold bullion, the Seligmans found a considerable difference. Undershirts could bring profits only while the store was open to sell them, but money stayed active around the clock. "Money," Joseph wrote to his brothers, "earns money even while you sleep."

During the Civil War, J. & W. Seligman & Co. received the main contract to supply uniforms to the Union Army. Accepting risky government bonds in payment, the company, with Lincoln's support, became not only a major government contractor but also one of the primary marketers of Union bonds in the United States and Europe.

After the war it turned to marketing the stocks and bonds of railroads as well as states, municipalities, and the federal government. President Grant offered Seligman the post of secretary of the treasury, but the New York banker turned it down. In 1879 the man who had risen from immigrant foot peddler to millionaire merchant-banker and financial adviser to presidents died, leaving a fortune estimated at more than $30 million.

Beginning in the 1890s a number of bankers began to expand into new areas of investment. In addition to railroad and government securities, they began to finance the reorganization of the giant new companies in mining, refining, and manufacturing. They also began to demand a share in management in return for assisting the corporations in meeting their capital and credit needs. Morgan representatives, for example, went onto the boards of directors (often as chairmen) of companies like U.S. Steel, General Electric, and International Harvester. At the same time, Morgan and other investment bankers established "interlocking directorates" with institutions which were the sources of funds—commercial banks, trust companies, and the rapidly growing life insurance companies, which accumulated millions of dollars from the premiums of policyholders. Investment bankers sought to limit the unpredictability of the money market by ensuring coordination of further economic development.

The Reaction to Consolidation

"If the carboniferous age returned and the earth repeopled itself with dinosaurs," one economist observed, "the change would scarcely seem greater than that made in the business world by these monster corporations." The sudden emergence of huge concentrations of economic power in industry and finance within a few years startled most Americans. Many feared that such combinations, if allowed to continue, would take on all the worst attributes of monopoly: prevention of competition, inefficiency, arrogance, destruction of the marketplace, and corruption of the political system.

The greatest fear was that the financiers had created a "money trust" which monopolized the credit resources of the country. When agrarian Democrats gained control of the House of Representatives, the Pujo Committee launched an investigation of this alleged "trust." The committee found a significant concentration of control over investment funds in the House of Morgan and the Rockefellers, whose profits from Standard Oil provided an enormous source of funds which were channeled through National City Bank and other New York financial institutions into controlling interests in other companies. In 1913 the Pujo Committee report concluded that four allied financial institutions in New York City, representing primarily Morgan and the Rockefellers, held 341 interlocking directorships in 112 major banks, railroads, public utilities, and insurance companies, whose aggregate resources totaled $22 billion, an amount equal to half the gross national product of the United States at the time.

Although the Pujo Committee did not prove that a monopolistic "money trust" existed (there remained substantial competition in banking), it did demonstrate the high degree of concentration that had taken place in the last two decades. It also enshrined the "directing power" of New York investment bankers as part of American folklore and thus helped generate support for some form of public, decentralized body in the banking system, a sentiment which contributed to the creation of the Federal Reserve System.

The Progressive Era was the time when Americans most fully debated what was called "the trust issue." Traditionally suspicious of centralized power, many Americans—particularly people in small and medium-sized businesses, workers, farmers, consumers, reformers, and radicals—assailed the trusts as "great engines of oppression." They feared that the giant corporations were closing out opportunities for people to become independent, whether as artisans, mechanics, or owners of small businesses. Life within the corporate structure was very different from life in a small business, warned Hazen Pingree, governor of Michigan and a former businessman:

> They [the employees] become a part of a vast industrial army. Their personal identity is lost. . . . There is no real advance for them. They may perhaps become larger cogs or larger wheels in the great complicated machine, but they can never look forward to a life of business freedom.

Critics also feared that the giant corporations were destroying the market system. They blamed administered prices for the inflation which began with the return of prosperity in 1897 and continued for the next two decades. The muckraker Henry Demarest Lloyd listed some of the evils of the trusts in 1910:

> Blowing up competitors, as the oil monopoly has done;
> shutting up works and throwing men out of employment, as the sugar monopoly has done;
> selling the machinery of rivals for junk, as the nail monopoly has done;
> paying big bonuses to others not to run, as the steel monopoly has done;
> restricting production, as the coal monopoly has done; and
> buying up and suppressing new patents, as the telephone monopoly has done.

Defending big business against this onslaught, corporate leaders and many clergymen, writers, economists, and political leaders argued that the giant firms were an inevitable and beneficial result of industrialization. Consolidation was also occurring in Europe, and American defenders of the supercorporation asserted that such a structure was necessary to compete effectively against European cartels in the international market. Furthermore, supporters of big business claimed that through mass production, efficiencies of scale, and the elimination of middlemen and local monopolies, the giant corporations could provide more products at lower prices. Although some industrialists, such as Rockefeller, were reluctant to accept limitations on their power, some other corporate managers, such as George Perkins, the Morgan partner who headed International Harvester, accepted the notion that the mammoth corporations, funded as they were through the sale of stock to the public, were in fact quasi-public enterprises and not strictly private property. Perkins warned recalcitrant industrialists in 1911 that they would have to accept some kind of federal regulation and reform. "If we continue to fight against it much longer," he cautioned, "the incoming tide may sweep the question along either to Government ownership or socialism."

From different perspectives and interests, Americans in the Progressive Era generally clustered into five schools of thought regarding big business. Many continued to believe in *laissez faire* and argued either that big business was inevitable and beneficial or, like William Graham Sumner, that the marketplace which had temporarily produced monopoly would restore competition by inviting new competitors if necessary. Others, such as economist John Bates Clark, believed that some governmental intervention was needed to restore the marketplace. Jeffersonian agrarians like Bryan urged the use of *antitrust* suits and the taxing power to reduce those corporations which exceeded a specified size. They also argued that patents and the protective tariff, which encouraged trusts, should be modified or eliminated. Some corporate managers and heads of industrial trade associations envisioned a new kind of *self-regulation* or *associationalism,* in which business would cooperate through private groups like trade associations to reduce the problems of destructive price competition, waste, unemployment, and violence in labor relations.

Others, including Perkins, Theodore Roosevelt, and economists Richard Ely and Simon Patten, believed *governmental regulation* was required to ensure that the giant firms did not operate to the disadvantage of the public interest. Roosevelt eventually recommended federal charters and supervision of capitalization as well as wage and price policy. Still others argued for *government ownership.* A substantial number, including Ely, recommended it for natural monopolies like railroads, streetcar lines, and utilities like gas, water, electricity, and even the telegraph and telephone. A minority, mainly socialists and radical agrarians, urged that the government take over the giant manufacturing firms in steel production, petroleum refining, and other essential industries.

Much confusion existed in the early years of the twentieth century over what was happening in industry and what to do about "the trusts." Part, the uncertainty came from the difficulty of differentiating large-scale businesses from consolidations of many firms into trusts. People were also confused about the shape of the corporate economy which was emerging, about whether it was characterized by monopoly or oligopoly and whether that made a significant difference. The fact that some competition continued, though in a different manner, led many people to believe that the marketplace remained despite the trusts. Furthermore, many feared that the complete breakup of big business would create chaos and jeopardize economic growth and the new material goods that were being produced in the developing mass consumption society.

THE MASS PRODUCTION/MASS CONSUMPTION ECONOMY

The organizational revolution which produced the supercorporations took place in an economy which was booming with the mass production of industrial and consumer goods. Mounting industrial output boosted real gross national product an average of 6 percent annually between 1897 and 1914. National income increased by nearly one-third. This economic growth was accompanied by the first sustained period of inflation since the Civil War. The cost of living went up 39 percent between 1897 and 1914, an average annual inflation rate of 3 percent. Although there was no sustained depression, the recessions of 1907 and 1914 were sharp despite their brevity. Nevertheless, the era was viewed by many as one of great economic growth in productivity and in the standard of living.

Economic growth came partly from a crackling new power source. Electricity was hailed by George Westinghouse, the developer of long-distance systems of transmitting alternating electrical current, as a modern Aladdin's genie which would relieve men and women of the burden of heavy toil in factory and home. It offered an efficient, convenient, and uniform source of energy, and it was cheaper than the steam-powered belts and pulleys which it replaced. In the first twenty years of the century, more than one-third of America's manufacturing plants converted to electrical power for their machines; Westinghouse's genie also began to turn the motors in the first mass-marketed electric fans, vacuum cleaners, and washing machines.

Production of consumer goods for the mass market, a process which had begun in the late nineteenth century, dramatically expanded in the early years of the new century. The birth of the mass consumption society was made possible by staggering leaps in productivity, which enabled manufacturers to reduce the prices of goods to a level within the purchasing power of millions of consumers. The most significant single increase in productivity came from the introduction of the moving assembly line. This American invention had been used in the nineteenth century for watches, sewing machines, typewriters, and bicycles, but in 1913 a lanky farm boy–mechanic turned auto maker,

Henry Ford, brought it to maturity by using it to make automobiles consisting of several thousand parts. America became the master of mass production and mass consumption, and Ford emerged as the presiding genius of the new flow technology, which Europeans reverently labeled "Fordismus." Interchangeable standardized parts and precise new automatic machines made the new technology possible. Putting these together in a moving assembly line, Ford converted the construction of automobiles from a jerky, unpredictable process to a smoothly flowing stream. To do this, he decided to make all cars alike. "The way to make automobiles," he explained, "is to make one automobile like another automobile . . . just as one pin is like another pin when it comes from a pin factory." In 1913, at his plant in Highland Park outside of Detroit, Michigan, he subdivided the work of assembling the chassis of a Model T Ford and put the components on a moving line. Slicing assembly time from 12½ to 1½ hours, Ford cranked out 500,000 Model Ts a year and eventually chopped the base price from $950 to $290.

Ford proved tremendously successful at expanding the market. By cutting costs, he brought his cars down to what he called "the buying power." He sold 15 million of his "tin Lizzies" or "flivvers" before he changed to the Model A Ford in 1927. At the same time, he also expanded his market and amazed the nation by establishing "the five-dollar day" for his workers, a pay scale that was nearly double the average daily earnings of industrial workers. The pay hike not only increased workers' purchasing power but also reduced absenteeism and turnover on the assembly line and helped forestall unionization. A self-made millionaire who boosted wages and provided people with a new form of travel, Ford became a folk hero. In addition, his success convinced many other industrialists of the efficacy of mass production techniques, and they began a changeover which accelerated during World War I and the 1920s. The assembly line, like the supercorporation, became a symbol of the mass production/mass consumption economy and the new industrial America.

To absorb greatly increased production, American business needed to stimulate demand for consumer goods. Advertising was the key. During the Progressive Era ad agencies developed slogans and jingles, made greater use of syndicated display advertisements, and began to use psychological appeals to create mass consumer demand. Instead of merely advertising the curative or other functional aspects of products, the agencies began to associate happiness, attractiveness, and status with products ranging from soap to automobiles. As the psychologist Walter Dill Scott wrote in 1911, "Goods offered as means of gaining social prestige make their appeals to one of the most profound human instincts."

Mass production meant major changes in retailing to handle the new flood of consumer goods. Some manufacturers, like the automakers, established local dealers who marketed, financed, and serviced their products. The oil companies erected service stations. Department stores which had first been established at the time of the Civil War grew into giant emporia: Macy's, Lord & Taylor, Wanamaker's, and Marshall Field. Mail order houses like Montgomery Ward, founded in 1872, and Sears Roebuck, established in 1895, revolutionized rural retailing. Chain stores like Woolworth's "5-and-10-cent" store, which opened in Utica, New York, in 1879, and J. C. Penney, which was founded in 1902, spread rapidly.

The materialism encouraged by the mass production/mass consumption economy proved almost as controversial as the giant corporations themselves. Like them, consumerism was both praised and pilloried. Some thought abundance of consumer goods might replace abundance of arable land as a frontier of economic growth. Many saw this growth as a sign not only of increased well-being but also of improved morality. "Material prosperity," asserted a Massachusetts bishop in 1901, "is helping to make the national character sweeter, more joyous, more unselfish, more Christlike."

Critics found much of the gospel of mass production and consumption appalling. Blanching at the excesses of advertising as it sought to stimulate mass demand, Walter Lippmann warned how powerless the public was against such advertising:

> . . . the eastern sky ablaze with chewing gum, the northern with toothbrushes and underwear, the western with whiskey, and the southern with petticoats, the whole heavens brilliant with monstrously flirtatious women.

More radical critics like the economist Thorstein Veblen feared that the emphasis on consumption of material goods would divert discontented industrial workers from attacking the economic system and lead them to accept the wage system and seek satisfaction in immediate symbols of status and achievement.

CHANGES IN WORK AND THE WORK FORCE

In the early years of the century, new immigrants from southern and eastern Europe filled the bottom ranks of heavy industry and construction and helped produce significant changes in the nature of the work force and, consequently, of society itself. Although the foreign-born accounted for only 20 percent of the working population, they made up more than 60 percent of the wage workers in heavy industry. Much transition occurred in these years. Until the 1890s, most of the anthracite miners in Pennsylvania had been English-speaking men from Britain, Ireland, and Wales. By 1919, however, over 90 percent were Slavs, Italians, or Greeks. The steel mills of Pittsburgh and the textile factories of Lawrence, Massachusetts, presented a similar picture.

Increasing numbers of rural Americans also trekked to industrial jobs in the cities. One of the most significant population shifts in these years was the beginning of the mass migration of southern blacks into northern cities. When World War I caused a labor shortage, more than 330,000 blacks fled the poverty and discrimination of the South. "I should have been here 20 years ago," a black carpenter wrote home to Hattiesburg, Mississippi, from Chicago in 1917. "I just begin to feel like a man." The black exodus had an important impact on race relations in the North. Small, scattered settlements of blacks were consolidated into large ghettos, such as Harlem in New York and the south side of Chicago. Immigrants, blacks, and Hispanic workers (in the Southwest) composed the bottom level of the industrial work force. Thus, race and ethnicity increasingly became the basis for social class and stratification, to a degree that was unique among major industrial societies.

Millions of women joined the work force at the turn of the century. One woman out of five had worked outside the home in 1890, but by 1910 one out of four did so. Before the 1920s most women who obtained gainful employment were working only temporarily, a stage between living with their parents and marrying. The ideal woman's role remained that of wife and mother, taking care of the home and family, not working outside it. But a minority of women—predominantly black or foreign-born—were forced by economic necessity to perform both roles. As late as 1870, 50 percent of all working women (again primarily the black and foreign-born) had toiled as domestic servants and washerwomen, but as often as could most young women workers turned to jobs offering greater status and personal freedom. By 1920, only 16 percent of working women were paid household workers.

Blacks, who became the primary servant group in the North, worked as day servants and returned to their own homes at night. White women, especially immigrants, were able to gain more freedom in factories which did work formerly done in the home—laundries, garment factories, canneries, and textile mills. The hours were often long and the wages scanty. "I didn't live," one woman factory hand told a New York State investigating commission, "I merely existed." Native-born women who went to work often found clerical positions in the new department stores or in the growing number of offices created by the bureaucratization of business. A small but growing number of middle-class women pursued careers as nurses, teachers, or physicians.

Many children spent their days working in mines and mills instead of in school. During the last decade of the nineteenth century, the percentage of boys and girls between the ages of 10 and 15 who worked for wages increased dramatically, especially in the South, where a threefold rise in the number of employed children led to widespread protest. Opposition to the use of child labor helped cut that percentage in half in the second decade of the twentieth century through prohibitive legislation.

The Costs of Industrialism

America paid a high price for industrial supremacy. At the turn of the century, industrial accidents killed 35,000 workers each year and maimed 500,000 others. Only when scores of workers perished in a single disaster did the American public rise in indignation. The Triangle fire in New York City in 1911 was such a tragedy. The blaze broke out in the Triangle Shirtwaist Company factory in the top of a ten-story loft building just as some 500 young Jewish and Italian immigrant women were preparing to leave work on a Saturday afternoon. Swirling flames quickly turned the shop into a raging furnace. In panic and confusion, workers pressed against one another, pushing toward the exits. But the fire doors had been locked from the outside for fear that the women would steal pieces of fabric. When firemen entered the factory rooms, they found the women's charred bodies piled up behind the locked doors. Other fleeing workers jammed themselves into two freight elevators, but women who were still trapped on the top floors jumped into the elevator shafts to escape, and their bodies jammed the mechanism and halted the elevators' descent. Dozens of women leaped from the roof of the building to their deaths on the streets below, many holding hands and jumping in groups. By the time firemen brought the blaze under control, 146 young women were dead. Investigation placed the blame on the owners, the insurance company, and the city's building and fire departments, although no one was convicted on criminal charges.

The public outrage that resulted from the Triangle fire and a series of mining disasters led to the passage of a number of laws designed to increase factory safety standards and improve working conditions, especially of women and children. Together with workers' organizations and some employers' groups, reformers pressed state legislatures to enact mine and factory safety laws, new inspection requirements, and workmen's compensation legislation which placed a larger share of the cost of accidents in the hands of employers. Nevertheless, America's industrial accident rate remained among the highest in the world.

Industrial violence was another cost of the harsh and rapid pace of industrialization. Wage cuts and layoffs frequently triggered massive resistance by workers. Violence often stemmed from workers' attempts to organize unions and management's attempts to destroy them. In the first decade of the new century, twice as many strikes erupted as in the last decade of the nineteenth century. Many were bitter, several brutal, but the bloodiest was in the mining region of Ludlow, Colorado.

Few places exceeded the dismal exploitation of the feudalistic mining camps of southeastern Colorado. In the soft-coal fields of the foothills of the Rockies, some 30,000 Italians, Slavs, Greeks, and Mexicans scratched a living out of the earth in isolated canyon communities. Three corporations, one of them owned by the Rockefellers, controlled the lives of these people, not only employing them but owning the land on which their shacks were built—as well as the schools, churches, saloons, and the company store where food, clothing, and supplies were sold at marked-up prices. The corporations censored movies, magazines, and books, proscribing the works of Marx and Darwin and Omar Khayyám's *Rubáiyát*. "We wish to protect our people from erroneous ideas," an official explained. Wages were lower than elsewhere, the disease rate high, and the death rate in the mines twice the national average. But the company maintained control through force and terrorism, employing spies and dominating the civil government and the police. Protestors found themselves ejected from their jobs, their homes, and the community. In short, the corporate tyranny deprived the workers and their families of their fundamental rights as citizens.

In a snowstorm in late September of 1913, some 9,000 workers and their families went on strike for an eight-hour day and recognition of their union. They moved out of company housing and into tent colonies in the canyons. The companies imported strikebreakers and constructed an armored machine gun vehicle called the "Death Special" to protect them and terrorize the strikers. Fighting broke out between the two sides and several persons were killed. Then, in an act of senseless violence, the militia, sent in by the governor, attacked the largest tent colony near Ludlow, firing into it and then burning it to the ground. Twenty-one residents of the tent community were killed in the melee, including three women and eleven children. In retaliation for what was called the Ludlow Massacre, the miners lashed out against the companies and the militia. Thirty persons died before President Wilson sent in the U.S. Cavalry and brought the open warfare to a halt. Despite much public castigation, the companies won the struggle, for after fifteen months the miners voted to go back to work with some improved conditions and a company union the only fruits of their long struggle.

The civil war in the Colorado minefields was extreme but not unique in this period. Violence among strikers, police, militia, and strikebreakers erupted in a number of places. The old mill towns of

Lawrence, Massachusetts, and Paterson, New Jersey, became battlefields as employers sought to crush strikes. Labor radicals retaliated
against anti-union violence in Idaho by assassinating the governor of
that state, Frank Steunenburg, in 1905. In 1911, radicals blew up the
anti-union *Los Angeles Times,* killing twenty persons.

In the wake of this violence Congress appointed a Commission on
Industrial Relations, a relatively new device, an ad hoc national committee of private citizens and officials, to investigate, hold hearings, and
try to discover the underlying causes of the strife and make policy
recommendations to the federal government. The commission concluded that industrial violence stemmed primarily from industrial
oppression and lack of adequate worker representation. Workers
needed mechanisms to protect themselves, the commission's director of
research concluded, or they would be "driven by necessity and
oppression to the extreme of revolt."

Scientific Management

Industry realized the difficulties that worker resistance posed to its
labor policies, which were designed to obtain maximum productivity
from employees while keeping labor costs to a minimum. "Scientific
management" was the system it devised to improve the performance of
the work force.

The enormous increase in productivity in the early years of the new
century came with hardly any boost in the percentage of the labor force
engaged in manufacturing. The gains in productivity came primarily
from mechanization, as illustrated by the introduction of the assembly
line. But corporate managers sought to bolster production even further
by making the most efficient use of workers as well as machines. The
process they employed to try to remold human activities so as to
eliminate wasted motions was called Taylorism. The founder of modern
scientific management, Frederick W. Taylor, preached a gospel of efficiency in order to produce more goods more cheaply and effectively. His
efficiency ethic subordinated individuals to the goal of expanded
production, which Taylor hoped would lead to a higher standard of
living. "In the past," he wrote in 1911, "the man has been first; in the
future the system must be first."

An eccentric genius, Taylor applied this maxim even to his own daily life. For instance, he designed and wore slip-on shoes with elastic sides to save the time needed to put on the high-button shoes popular in that era. As a consultant to industry, he broke down every operation in a factory into its simplest tasks. Then, using a stopwatch, he timed each operation and ascertained the most economical way of performing it. Taylor hoped that industrial cost saving would result in shorter working hours and higher wages, and that the savings would be passed on to consumers in the form of lower prices. In practice, however, Taylorism often meant work speedups and the elimination of jobs in industries adopting Taylor's methods. As a result, Taylorism was vigorously resisted by labor unions.

When Workers Organize

Labor made rapid strides toward organization at the turn of the century. Union membership leapt from less than 500,000 in 1897 to more than 2 million by 1904. The greatest growth came in the American Federation of Labor (AFL). Like the trusts, the AFL survived the depression of the 1890s virtually intact, demonstrating a greater degree of stability than any previous American labor organization. With the return of prosperity, AFL membership soared. The growing economy created a tighter labor market, giving workers more leverage. In addition, inflation spurred workers to seek wage boosts to compensate for rising prices. Labor also benefited from widespread public criticism of deplorable working conditions. In the first decade and a half of the new century, the AFL grew from 55 unions, representing 60 percent of organized labor, in 1900 to more than a hundred unions, with 80 percent of union members, in 1914.

The growth of big labor increased the reputation and stature of Samuel Gompers, the moderate leader of the AFL. Following the model of the trusts, Gompers sought to combine and intervene to eliminate or greatly reduce competition, in this case in the labor market. Much earlier he had renounced his youthful belief in socialism and accepted capitalism and the wage system. Now he accepted the trusts: "We welcome their organization. . . . When they assume a right for themselves, they cannot deny that same right to us. They are organizing; organization is the order of the day."

Organized labor, like organized business, was a protest against the destructive forces of the free marketplace. Unlike the socialists, who advocated complete removal of competition from the labor market through the elimination of capitalism, Gompers did not aim at completely eradicating the labor market; instead, he tried to limit competition in certain ways. Workers protested that labor was not a commodity, like grain or potatoes, whose price was to be determined by supply and demand. Such a view, they claimed, was repugnant to human dignity, a position validated by Congress in a section of the Clayton Antitrust Act of 1914 which upheld the right of workers to organize and declared flatly that "labor is not a commodity." To obtain higher wages, shorter hours, and better working conditions, the skilled craft unions of the AFL—carpenters, machinists, and others— used their economic power to withhold their labor, engaging in strikes or boycotts when necessary. In order to increase their leverage, the unions tried to include all the members of a particular craft. The growth of organized labor, like that of organized business, helped modify the free-market system in the pursuit of other goals.

Gompers not only rejected the socialists' call for revolution but also argued against the creation of an independent labor party. Distrustful of government, which in the nineteenth century had usually acted against labor, Gompers emphasized "voluntarism," collective action by workers in the private sector. The conservative leaders of the AFL craft unions generally opposed minimum wage legislation (they thought it would be translated into maximum wages) and government-run social security programs (they preferred their own pension programs). Gompers and the others sought to make gains through their economic strength in the marketplace. "Economic need and economic betterment," Gompers declared, "could best be served by mobilizing and controlling economic power." Nevertheless, the AFL increased its political activity, shifting in 1906 from purely lobbying tactics to electioneering for its friends and against its enemies.

In this era of organization the AFL unions prospered, with growing membership rolls and swelling treasuries. They became large, stable, hierarchical, and business-oriented institutions. Union staffs moved out of rented rooms and into permanent headquarters. Union officers consolidated their power and began to serve for longer terms, sometimes for life (Gompers remained president of the AFL until his death in 1924). The collective-bargaining agreement signed as a contract between union officials and management not only bound the employer to a specific schedule of wages and working conditions but restricted employees as well, requiring adherence by workers to minutely delineated formal work rules. It made the union a kind of mediating force in industrialization. By holding their members to the provisions of the contract, craft unions, in return for recognition as the bargaining agent for the workers and improved wages and conditions, helped accommodate the skilled workers to the new corporate industrial system.

Ironically, just as the labor movement obtained dramatic success on the basis of stable trade unions and collective-bargaining agreements, it was undermined by a drastic change in the nature of industrial conditions. The spread of mass production and scientific management increased management's opposition to collective bargaining and impeded the union strategy of controlling the labor market. For the greatest growth in the mass production industries was not in the skilled trades of the AFL but among the unskilled or semiskilled machine tenders, the operatives on the assembly lines, who increasingly were immigrants from southern or eastern Europe. To a great extent the AFL was barred from the heart of the new mass production industries by its own trade union conservatism, its male chauvinism, and its Anglo-Saxon racism (AFL leaders considered women, blacks, and new immigrant workers transient and inferior), as well as the hostility of the judiciary and anti-union businesspeople.

Only in a few industries, such as coal and clothing, were AFL unions able to organize new workers successfully, and there they did it on an industry rather than a craft basis. In the hard-coal fields of Pennsylvania, the United Mine Workers under the leadership of John Mitchell built a union which numbered more than 100,000 members at the turn of the century. Through a major strike, and governmental support in 1902, the UMW obtained a substantial wage increase. Even more dramatic, however, was the mobilization of the garment workers in New York, which caught the city and the country by surprise. Their action was the first industry-wide strike of immigrant workers in the nation's largest city. In several hundred small dress factories and sweatshops in Lower Manhattan, thousands of young Italian and Russian Jewish women toiled at sewing machines for 56 hours a week, Monday through Saturday, for wages as low as $6.00 a week. Worse still, some employers charged them for mistakes or deducted fees for "rental" of the machines and use of electricity. In 1909, thousands walked off their jobs in a strike called "the Uprising of the 20,000." Employers brought in unemployed blacks to break the effort, but several hundred joined the strikers. "It's a good thing, this strike is," one young black woman wrote in her diary. "It makes you feel like a real grown-up person."

Demonstrating unusual solidarity, the women workers marched in picket lines during the long winter months. They gained widespread public sympathy and support. Early in 1910 the International Ladies' Garment Workers' Union (ILGWU), aided by mediator Louis D. Brandeis, won a pay hike, a reduced work week, a preferential union shop, and arbitration machinery composed of representatives of labor, management, and the public. ILGWU membership soared from only 400 to 65,000 as the victory demonstrated the potential power of female and ethnic workers and of collective action.

The Challenge of the Left

Radical labor groups challenged the AFL's policy of exclusive trade unionism and accommodation with management. They advocated industry-wide organization of workers and urged the overthrow, or at least major overhaul, of the capitalist system so as to distribute the benefits of mass production more equitably. The socialists urged the nationalization of all major industries, utilities, banks, and railroads. The more militant minority which made up the Socialist Labor party, founded by the theoretician Daniel DeLeon in 1877, demanded separate socialist unions and worker seizure of power. The majority of American socialists took a more moderate position. They tried to convert the AFL unions to socialism and, at the same time, work toward political power through the Socialist Party of America, which they founded in 1901.

Despite their factionalism, American socialists won significant strength in labor and politics. At their peak in 1912 they accounted for nearly one-third of the delegates to the AFL national convention, representing unions with more than 300,000 members. In that year the Socialist party candidate for president garnered 900,000 votes, 6 percent of the total vote. The Socialists elected 2 members of Congress, 56 mayors (in cities like Milwaukee, Schenectady, and Berkeley), 33 state legislators (in 17 states), and nearly 1,000 city councilmen and aldermen. Like the European socialist parties, the Socialist Party of America grew dramatically in the years before World War I, fed by popular dissatisfaction with the status quo.

Eugene V. Debs, a former railroad worker from Indiana, was the missionary of American socialism. He ran for president five times on the party ticket. A magnetic orator, the kind-hearted Hoosier became an American folk hero, preaching in his broad midwestern accent the need for the workers to block the capitalists. As a young man he had been deeply stirred by the writings of Bellamy and George, but not until he found himself in prison for his activities in the Pullman strike of 1894 did he read Marx. Then, as he recalled, "my eyes opened—and in the gleam of every bayonet and the flash of every rifle the class struggle revealed itself."

The most aggressive force in the class struggle and industrial warfare was the tough, defiant IWW, the Industrial Workers of the World, whose members were called "wobblies." Sprouting up in 1905 among exploited miners, lumberjacks, and migrant field hands of the West, the IWW's membership never exceeded 100,000, but its radicalism and its successful participation in several important eastern strikes, such as those in Lawrence and Paterson, frightened many Americans. IWW leaders believed in syndicalism, a position then in vogue in the French, Italian, and Scandinavian labor movements, which emphasized the takeover and operation of industries by autonomous worker unions or syndicates. The organizers and martyrs of the IWW—especially William "Big Bill" Haywood, the six-foot-tall hard-rock miner and symbolic proletarian leader of the Wobblies—became part of the legend of the American left.

Employers Counterattack

Seeing the growth of radicalism and organized labor as major challenges to the economic system, the marketplace ideal, and their own position, many employers joined forces to launch substantial counteroffensives. The most aggressive of these came not from the trusts but from small and medium-sized businesses. Branding the AFL as "un-American, illegal, and indecent," the National Association of Manufacturers (NAM) argued that "labor trusts" were "contrary to law and the rights of man." It helped drive unions out of a number of midwestern cities.

After the spurt of unionization at the turn of the century, labor's organizing drive lagged for almost a decade. Comparatively few American workers belonged to unions. A tradition of rugged individualism, a belief in opportunity, and a desire for self-improvement, and ultimately self-employment, led many Americans to dislike the idea of joining class-conscious unions. Unlike European workers, American industrial workers did not have to band together to obtain the vote; suffrage came before industrialization. Moreover, many believed in their freedom to work when and where they wanted. The ethnic and racial diversity of the American work force also hampered unionization. So did the hiring policies of employers, who put together ethnic groups which traditionally were suspicious of each other: Russians and Poles, Greeks and Turks, Irish and English, blacks and whites. In addition, they harassed union organizers, required prospective workers to sign agreements not to join unions (so-called "yellow-dog contracts"), and hired spies and private guards to identify and oust unionists. During strikes, employers obtained police, National Guard, and sometimes U.S. Army assistance in protecting company property and allowing strikebreakers to enter plants. The conservative attitude of the judiciary also hampered the labor movement. Courts issued injunctions against strikes, boycotts, and picketing on the ground that these actions deprived the employer of property without due process of law.

During the second decade of the twentieth century, as reform sentiment grew, the labor movement resumed its progress, so that by 1917 more than 3 million men and women, or 11 percent of the work force, held union cards. The federal government began to provide some support for more moderate unions in the AFL and the railroad brotherhoods. However, radical labor organizations like the few socialist unions and the IWW were suppressed by government authorities during World War I. As the Progressive Era ended, organized labor, though a significant new force, exerted relatively little influence on most industrial workers or on the labor market as a whole. The limited number of workers in the skilled trades had been the primary beneficiaries of union activities. Not until the Great Depression, the New Deal, the founding of the Congress of Industrial Organizations (CIO), and the spread of unionization through the mass production industries in the 1930s and 1940s did organized labor achieve substantial control over the industrial labor market.

A GOLDEN AGE FOR AGRICULTURE

Mass production led to fundamental changes in agriculture. The number of new farms increased much less rapidly than it had in the late nineteenth century, and declined after World War I. For nearly twenty-five years after the recovery began in 1897, American farmers enjoyed substantial prosperity. Increased use of chemical fertilizers and new farm machinery helped farmers grow more cotton, tobacco, wheat, corn, and citrus fruits with fewer workers. Agricultural production increased by nearly one-third between 1897 and 1917. With massive immigration and longer life expectancy due to better sanitation and health care, the American population grew faster than the farmers' output of cereal grains. The result was higher commodity prices and larger incomes for the cash-crop farmers.

As America became a nation of city dwellers, it not only expanded its food consumption but also began to change the commodities it consumed. Americans continued to buy large quantities of beef, pork, bread, and milk. But, in response to changes in fashion, modern urbanites wanted more vitamins and less fattening foods. They consumed increasing amounts of protein in the form of dairy and poultry products. Less strenuous work and better-heated homes and offices also led to fewer requests for starchy, energy-producing foods and more calls for lighter fruits and vegetables. Improvements in irrigation opened up land for extensive citrus groves in California and Florida, and refrigerated cars enabled fresh oranges and grapefruit to be transported to the cities of the North. The tastes and life styles of urban residents also led to increased consumption of coffee and sugar. The urban-industrial tempo also led to a growth in alcohol consumption and a dramatic increase in cigarette smoking.

World War I triggered a rapid expansion of farm production. With agriculture dislocated in the warring European nations, high prices and government exhortations encouraged farmers to go into debt to bring more land under cultivation and buy tractors to increase production. Responding to slogans like "Food will win the war," American farmers supplied the needs of the United States and much of western Europe during the conflict. But after the armistice, production far exceeded demand, and American agriculture plunged into a slump from which it did not fully recover until World War II.

Increased costs and lower prices due to overproduction eventually cut down the number of farmers at the same time that employment in urban areas was growing. With national income rising, people spent a lower proportion of their paychecks on food, and agriculture played a declining part in the nation's economy. Agriculture's response to industrialism and mass production meant some product shifts and increased production by fewer farmers. The prosperous years of the Progressive Era proved to be an aberration. The problem of overproduction returned after World War I to plague the farmers and lead ultimately to government aid and intervention to modify the impact of the market system by restricting output and dumping surpluses abroad.

SUPPLIER TO THE WORLD

Throughout much of its history the United States had been a farmer in the world markets. Midwesterners shipped wheat and corn to European cities. Growers in Virginia and the Carolinas supplied tobacco. Southern planters sent millions of bales of cotton to the textile mills of England and the continent. But early in the twentieth century the United States also became manufacturer and banker to the world. It exported capital and credit and a variety of manufactured goods ranging from sewing machines to locomotives. By the end of World War I, America had become the leading economic power in the international marketplace.

In the first two decades of the new century, American foreign trade expanded faster than at any time since the Civil War. As exports and imports doubled by 1914 and spurted again during the war years, manufactured goods became America's leading overseas shipments. Longshoremen swung giant loads of crates aboard ships bound for Europe, Canada, Mexico, and sometimes the Far East. Like an enormous factory, the United States took in supplies for its machines and additional foodstuffs for its workers. Freighters unloaded copper, rubber, tin, manganese, nickel, and zinc for the metal factories, hides for shoes and leather goods, and sugar and coffee for American appetites.

Corporations and wealthy individuals transformed America's foreign investment pattern. Traditionally a debtor nation, the United States had obtained significant European capital for its development. Now, however, Americans began to invest large sums overseas in the construction of foreign railroads and industrial facilities. They also helped underwrite the expenses of the Boer War and the Russo-Japanese War. Between 1897 and 1914, American investment abroad multiplied fivefold, from $700 million to $3.5 billion. During World War I, Americans brought billions of dollars' worth of Allied war bonds. Consequently, the United States was transformed from a debtor to a creditor nation. In a major shift in international cash flow, New York replaced London as the financial center of the world.

Multinational U.S. enterprises emerged in the early years of the twentieth century. Following the depression of the 1890s, several of the new supercorporations expanded overseas. In a number of the mass production industries, production outran immediate domestic demand. "Dependent solely upon local business," John D. Rockefeller explained in 1899, "we should have failed long ago. We were forced to extend our markets and to seek for export trade."

As they probed for new markets, the supercorporations established sales outlets and then manufacturing plants abroad. The first great multinational corporation, Singer Sewing Machine, set up sales offices in half a dozen countries. American Tobacco built a cigarette-rolling mill in China; Ford erected auto plants in Britain and France. Industrial and consumer goods companies such as these concentrated primarily in high-income countries like Europe and Canada, but the extractive industries engaged in mining and transportation operations in underdeveloped nations. For instance, American Smelting and Refining, the Guggenheim company, owned mines, smelters, railroads, and port facilities in Mexico and Chile. Unlike the farmers, who could not affect world markets, the giant corporations could and did seek to limit international competition. American Tobacco Company signed agreements with British competitors to divide and share world markets rather than engage in destructive price competition. Similarly, many other American supercorporations split overseas markets with European cartels.

American foreign-policy makers encouraged the expansion of American business, believing that active foreign trade and investment would stimulate a prosperous, expanding domestic economy, which in turn would contribute to national power and prestige. "America has only just begun to assume that commanding position in the international business world which we believe will more and more be hers," President Theodore Roosevelt asserted in 1901.

THE CORPORATE ECONOMY

Trusts, multinational corporations, Wall Street, labor unions—these became the symbols of the organizational revolution which accompanied the mass production/mass consumption economy. New men of power—financiers, corporate managers, and, to a much lesser extent, the heads of trade associations and the leaders of labor unions—built and managed new mechanisms aimed at alleviating the rigors of the marketplace. Economic growth led to new forms of organization and new types of behavior. Americans took pride in the nation's industrial progress but worried about the challenges these developments posed to its ideals.

Industrialization posed similar problems in other countries. Although the nations of western Europe experienced the mechanization of industry, the rise of mass production, the growth of large-scale enterprise, the migration of the labor force from the farms to the cities, and the growth of unions, each nation responded somewhat differently because of its peculiar characteristics. In Germany, the legal system and the banks encouraged the formation of cartels among large and medium-sized firms to reduce the otherwise ruinous price competition in the coal, steel, potash, electrical, and chemical industries. In France, where the development of mass production lagged, small-scale, family-owned enterprises which emphasized quality rather than quantity continued to characterize the economy, although there were some rather weak trade associations. Britain had a legal system most like that of the United States. Since cartels were illegal there, outright consolidation was more common, and amalgamation led to oligopoly.

In Europe, the rapid rise of nationally organized industrial labor in the second half of the nineteenth century coincided with worker agitation for the vote and the prevalence of a class-conscious socialist philosophy. Militant unions organized millions of skilled and unskilled industrial workers. This set of circumstances helped politicize the European labor movements and led to socialist-oriented labor parties, which gained significant influence in Britain and Germany in the first decade of the twentieth century.

By the end of the first decade of the new century, several trends of industrialism had emerged in the United States, western Europe, and Japan. Accelerated economic growth and the development of mass production industries led to the creation of large new centers of economic power, encouraged massive shifts in population and the work force, and challenged old relationships, traditions, and ideals. The future remained uncertain. It was not known what impact these forces would have on society. Nor was it clear what would be the effect on the economy of the growth of organizations like trusts, trade associations, and labor unions, which sought to limit some aspects of the operation of the marketplace. The changes accompanying industrialization were affecting virtually every institution in society. The scope and pace of change and the pressure for collective intervention posed a major challenge to the American faith in a self-regulating society.

CHAPTER 3

An Age of Adjustment

"Never in the history of the world was society in so terrific flux as it is right now," the novelist Jack London wrote in 1907. As he explained:

> The swift changes in our industrial system are causing equally swift changes in our religious, political, and social structures. An unseen and fearful revolution is taking place in the fiber and structure of society. One can only dimly feel these things, but they are in the air, now, today.

The Progressive Era was a time of general awakening of social thought, a new spirit which saw Americans thinking about their society in new ways, re-examining institutions, attitudes, and the culture itself. The pace of economic and demographic change put great strains on a society whose institutions were created for a land of agrarian settlements. Urbanization and industrialization pushed people toward more collective action. In larger groups they could better control the forces that affected their lives. The discipline of industrial life proved constraining for a people which prided itself on individuality and freedom. Yet mass production offered a higher material standard of living for Americans and reinforced their sense of abundance. From European thinkers—Ibsen, Bergson, Nietzsche, and others—came a new emphasis on the liberation of the individual and the importance of self-realization and fulfillment. Amid the new century's challenges to agrarian America and the Victorian order of the nineteenth century, Americans struggled to understand the changes that were occurring around them.

"There isn't a human relation, whether of parent and child, husband and wife, worker and employer, that doesn't move in a strange situation," Walter Lippmann observed. "There are no precedents to guide us, no wisdom that wasn't made for a simpler age. We have changed our environment more quickly than we know how to change ourselves." In the Progressive Era Americans tried actively to adjust their institutions to the conditions of a new age.

A GROWING NATION

America experienced a virtual population explosion. The population leaped from 76 million to 106 million in the first two decades of the new century. The greatest part of this expansion came from a natural rate of increase due to better living conditions resulting from higher income, more adequate food and shelter, and improvements in health care. The result was longer life expectancy. Medical science made great strides toward eliminating traditional causes of premature death. Following the acceptance of the germ theory of disease, bacterial enemies came under attack through improvements in antiseptic procedures, personal hygiene, and public sanitation. Physicians and public health workers helped curb the infant mortality rate, reduced the number of deaths from tuberculosis, typhoid fever, pneumonia, and diphtheria, and practically eliminated smallpox and malaria. Consequently, life expectancy among white males, for example, grew almost 20 percent, from 46 to 55 years, between 1900 and 1920. Thus, despite a declining birthrate, the number of native-born Americans increased.

With life expectancy increasing and the birthrate falling, older people became a larger proportion of the population. The percentage of people over 65 nearly doubled, rising from 3 to 5 percent between 1870 and 1920. Old age became a social problem in the Progressive Era. Like other "social problems" which had previously been private in nature, the plight of the elderly came to be seen as a concern of the entire community and one which called for community action. The short but severe panic and recession of 1907–1908 dramatized the devastating economic problems of older people in an industrial society. The pace of factory work and the lack of security in the wage system forced older people out of the job market. Many retired in poverty. Although most European nations had compulsory old-age insurance programs, the United States did not. In 1909 the first public commission on aging, which studied the situation of the elderly in Massachusetts, found that 25 percent of those over 65 were on some form of dole. For a long while, however, attempts to deal with this problem were frustrated. The first state pension plan, adopted by Arizona in 1915, was declared unconstitutional. Not until 1935 was the federal social security system established.

Immigrants and Nativists

The most visible increase in the American population came from immigrants to the United States. Fifteen million entered between 1900 and 1915, as many as had arrived in the preceding forty years. They accounted for nearly a third of the nation's population growth. More than 70 percent were "new immigrants" from southern and eastern Europe. Typically, several young men from a village would set out together for America and find work in the same mill, factory, or mine. They would live in a boardinghouse or with friends or relatives who had preceded them. Many intended to live in America only long enough to save money and return home to buy land or redeem the family mortgage, but many remained in the United States.

Nativists saw the immigrants clustering in ethnic "ghettos" and warned of the "Balkanization" of the United States. The immigrants themselves drew much succor from the churches, schools, foreign-language newspapers, and social and cultural associations they created to sustain them in the different and often threatening American urban environment. Nevertheless, recent research indicates that contemporaries exaggerated the homogeneity of the so-called ghettos, which were actually composed of people from many different villages and provinces who had little in common. Immigrant neighborhoods contained a variety of nationalities. Only rarely did a single ethnic group dominate an area of several city blocks, and even then many immigrants soon moved out of such areas. The Lower East Side of Manhattan was known as the Jewish ghetto in 1892, when three out of four of New York's Jews lived there, but twenty-five years later the district contained less than one out of four of the city's Jews. Thousands had moved uptown or to the Bronx, Queens, Brooklyn, or Staten Island. Like those who had arrived before them, the new immigrants were a mobile people.

The immigration of Catholics and Jews from southern and eastern Europe in numbers reaching more than a million a year frightened many Americans, especially those who were already suspicious of the challenges to traditional American culture and values presented by the growth of industry and cities. The immigrants bore the brunt of the anti-urban bias of rural Americans. They were also objects of disdain to Social Darwinists, who argued that Mediterranean and Slavic peoples were genetically less fit than Anglo-Saxons. Nativists feared the diminution of American traditions, ideals, and standards of living.

The question of whether the United States should have a homogeneous or heterogeneous culture became a major national issue in the Progressive Era. Many believed that society should resemble a "melting pot" (indeed, the term was first used in a play written at that time), in which all immigrants were blended into a new cultural type: the American. But a few intellectuals, including philosophers Horace Kallen and John Dewey, and settlement house workers such as Jane Addams, and some representatives of the immigrants themselves, put forward an alternative—cultural pluralism—in which each cultural group would make its own contribution to the range, variety, and richness of what Kallen called "the orchestra of mankind."

Massive immigration challenged the faith of native-born Americans in the wisdom of the open marketplace as it applied to the flow of immigrant labor into the United States. Many began to question the tradition of open immigration. Under pressure from the Immigration Restriction League, the Daughters of the American Revolution, the American Federation of Labor, and other groups, Congress established the Dillingham Commission to investigate the impact of the new immigration. Its report confirmed some of the nativists' worst fears: that the new immigrants were largely unskilled, illiterate, and transient males from southern and eastern Europe, and that the areas in which they lived had high crime and disease rates. (The commission correlated these social indexes with ethnic characteristics rather than with economic conditions.)

Although they were opposed by industry, which still desired a large pool of unskilled labor, nativists sought to limit the flow of immigrants and preserve the traditional ethnic mixture of the American population. In response to their pressure Congress passed a literacy test requirement in 1913 and 1915, but it was successfully vetoed by Presidents Taft and Wilson. Not until 1917, as a result of the intense nationalism of World War I, did Congress finally succeed in overriding a presidential veto and enacting a literacy test, thereby modifying the traditional policy of open immigration. Immigration restriction was placed on a new and more permanent basis in the 1920s.

An "Americanization" movement to acculturate the immigrants became powerful during the Progressive Era. Part of it was educational, as settlement houses, the YMCA, night school civics classes, and some large corporations taught the English language and American forms of dress, behavior, and ideals. In its most coercive form, the Americanization movement became an effort to get immigrants to change their culture—their religion, language, behavior, patterns of thought and action. During World War I the movement for "one-hundred percent Americanism," led by such groups as the National Americanization Committee and local vigilante bodies, became a national crusade involving schools, churches, patriotic societies, and civic organizations. Violence and harassment were used to force people of German birth or descent to give up their language, foreign-language newspapers, clubs and associations, and parochial schools. Intervention for "Americanism" produced tensions in American society which were exacerbated in the 1920s.

Submerged Minorities

Like the new immigrants, America's blacks suffered from the virulent racism of the time. In the South, the drive to eliminate blacks from political and social life gained strength at the turn of the century.

Within twenty years whites disfranchised blacks through poll taxes and literacy tests and segregated them through Jim Crow laws. To keep the blacks subservient, white judges meted out long sentences on chain gangs for trivial offenses. Lynch mobs hanged or burned more than 1,100 blacks during the first dozen years of the twentieth century. The doctrine of white surpremacy also prevailed in the North. Whites in Springfield, Illinois, sought to drive blacks out of town in 1908, destroying their homes and stores and burning three of them to death.

Confronted with such intense racism and repression, America's blacks struggled to survive and to improve their situation. They listened to the opposing arguments of two black leaders. Booker T. Washington, a former slave educated at Hampton Institute and the founder of Tuskegee Institute, succeeded Frederick Douglass as the main spokesman for black Americans between 1895 and his death in 1915. Washington recommended that blacks acquiesce temporarily in the loss of their political liberties and concentrate on becoming economically productive and self-sufficient. He urged them to become efficient farmers, tradespeople, teachers, and businesspeople. His message to white southerners summarized his appeal. "In all things that are purely social," he declared, "we can be as separate as the fingers, yet one as the hand in all things essential to mutual progress." Tuskegeeism, with its conciliatory spirit and emphasis on gradual improvement, pleased white Americans and enabled Washington to become the conduit for the funds of northern white philanthropists and the patronage of Republican presidents.

Opposition came from W. E. B. DuBois, a Harvard-educated black professor who advocated immediate direct action to obtain civil rights and economic equality for blacks. He joined other northern black intellectuals in 1905 to form the Niagara Movement "to refuse to allow the impression to remain that the Negro-American assents to inferiority, is submissive under oppression, and apologetic before insults." Five years later DuBois joined a number of white reformers—including Oswald Garrison Villard, grandson of a leading abolitionist, Jane Addams, and John Dewey—to form the National Association for the Advancement of Colored People (NAACP), whose purpose was to work for the recognition of blacks' constitutional rights. Despite these efforts, however, the status of American blacks, like that of other nonwhites grew worse during the Progressive Era.

By the turn of the century Mexican-Americans in the Southwest were being forced into virtual peasantry. Giant commercial farms destroyed the old rancho system and drove the Chicano farmers from their land. The dislocation of native-born Hispanic Americans was aggravated by heavy immigration of Mexicans after the upheavals of the Mexican Revolution, which began in 1910. Chicanos provided much of the labor for American produce growers. In the cities, *barrios* (ghettos), or colonies of Mexican immigrants, developed. Whites tried to impose Anglo-conformity on the Chicanos, but at the same time they feared the influx of new workers and their preindustrial culture. Collective labor action by Mexican-Americans began with strikes by California beet workers in 1903 and Arizona copper miners in 1915.

Anti-Chinese sentiment on the West Coast had led Congress in 1882 to prohibit additional immigration of Chinese laborers. From that time until 1943, when Chinese people were again allowed to immigrate, the Chinese-American population declined as tens of thousands returned to Kwangtung. They were succeeded by Japanese workers, most of whom were literate and came with families. Beginning in the 1870s they settled in Hawaii to work in the sugar cane fields. Many moved on to the West Coast, where they worked as seasonal field hands, saved their money, leased land, and grew vegetables for market. Some 130,000 arrived in the United States in the 1900s, but rising anti-Japanese sentiment led to segregation by the San Francisco School Board and the prohibition of Japanese-Americans from buying land in California. A "Gentlemen's Agreement" between the United States and the Imperial Japanese government in 1907–1908 led the school board to rescind the order and the Japanese government to bar its citizens from coming to the United States.

CLASS AND STATUS IN AMERICAN SOCIETY

As the plight of the nation's submerged minorities indicates, American society remained significantly stratified. Nonwhites found themselves relegated to the lowest socioeconomic level. The religion and ethnicity of new immigrants also affected their status. Catholics and Jews from southern and eastern Europe were forced into low-paid menial employment.

Reformers exposed the conditions in which minorities were forced to live and the extent of poverty and suffering in the new urban–industrial America. The sociologist Robert Hunter, in his path-breaking study *Poverty* (1904), presented statistical evidence to support his contention that six million people, or one-fifth of the population of the industrial states, lived in abject poverty. One out of every ten persons who died in New York City did not have enough money for a funeral and was buried in Potter's Field. Investigators like Hunter challenged the traditional view that poverty stemmed from immorality. Instead, they concluded that it resulted from the failure of the economic system to meet the needs of all Americans. Plagued by unemployment, the poor were inadequately fed, clad, and sheltered. "My people do not live in America, they live underneath America," declared a Ruthenian priest in Yonkers, New York. "America does not begin till a man is a workingman, till he is earning two dollars a day. A laborer cannot afford to be an American."

The poor lived and died in misery. They skimped on food, substituting condensed or evaporated milk for fresh milk, leaf lard or beef suet for butter. Their children suffered from rickets. In general, health, like income, differed along class and racial lines. The life expectancy of a black man was ten years less than that of a white man, a result of inadequate health care and a greater incidence of malnutrition and disease. By vividly exposing the miseries of the poor, especially the immigrants in the cities, investigative journalists and other reformers helped convince hundreds of thousands of middle- and upper-class Americans that the causes of mass poverty were beyond the individual's control and the poor were the responsibility of society.

Above the poor and the lower-paid workers in the American social structure was a broad and heterogeneous middle class. Outside of the South, with its large numbers of poor white residents, the middle class included most native white Americans. Its members were descended from families who had come from western and central Europe. They included the old middle class of artisans, skilled workers, and self-employed shopkeepers, small businesspeople, farmers, and small manufacturers, as well as members of the professions—teachers, lawyers, and doctors. But these were joined by a growing new middle class—white collar employees who worked in the proliferating urban shops and offices. They lived in homes which ranged from the row houses of the cities to the more spacious single-family houses of the suburbs and country towns, or on prosperous farms.

At the apex of the socioeconomic hierarchy were the upper-class elite. Powerful and prestigious, they included old wealthy families who had inherited money earned in commerce and land speculation—the Cabots and Lodges of Boston, the Browns of Providence, the Roosevelts and Astors of New York, the Drexels and Biddles of Philadelphia—and the new industrial rich and their allies, the financiers, corporation lawyers, and managers—the Rockefellers, Vanderbilts, Carnegies, Dukes, Guggenheims, Seligmans, Lehmans, Morgans, Schwabs, Fricks, and Fords. They were, on the whole, Protestants, along with a few Catholics and Jews, from Britain, Germany, Holland, or France. They lived in mansions in the cities or suburbs and had summer palaces in Newport or Bar Harbor. They belonged to exclusive clubs and sent their children to eastern preparatory schools and then to the colleges of the Ivy League or the Seven Sisters.

The wealth of the super-rich was enormous. The figures of Professor Willard King showed at the time that the rich, less than 2 percent of the population, owned 60 percent of the total wealth of the country. In contrast, the poor and very poor, 65 percent of the population, owned not more than 5 percent of the wealth. The middle class, 33 percent of the nation, owned 35 percent of the wealth. In 1910 it was estimated that the seventy richest Americans each had a fortune of at least $35 million and together owned one-sixteenth of the nation's wealth. Many millionaires spent their money lavishly. The more sensationalist newspapers exposed the excesses of what Thorstein Veblen labeled "conspicuous consumption," the ivory and ebony bedsteads inlaid with gold, the $15,000 diamond-studded dog collars, and the parties at which the guests smoked cigarettes wrapped in $100 bills.

Despite the discrepancies in wealth and stratification, America remained a society in flux. Carnegie and Schwab, self-made millionaires, demonstrated the most extreme and rarest kind of success. But whites, both immigrant and native-born, often achieved significant upward occupational mobility or saw the possibility of it. Amedeo Obici built a pushcart operation into the Planter Peanut Company, and when A. P. Giannini discovered that California banks were refusing credit to Italian immigrants, he created the Bank of America chain in that state and made it one of the largest private banking systems in the world. Among Italians and East European Jews who remained in Manhattan between 1905 and 1915, 32 percent moved from blue-collar to white-collar occupations. In addition, there was a large transient population, primarily poor, who moved from one city to another looking for work. A number of studies suggest the existence of a highly fluid society in white America. Modern industrialism may have increased the distance between the rich and the poor by creating a class of enormously wealthy families, but it also tremendously expanded the middle class through the creation of a wide range of new occupations.

THE FAMILY AND THE STATUS OF WOMEN

Developments of the Progressive Era accelerated changes in the family and in the status of women. Industrialization and urban growth continued to create new economic opportunities for women. At the same time, new ideas from Bergson, Ibsen, Nietzsche, and others emphasized individualism and self-realization and encouraged the growing belief that a person should be able to control his or her own destiny to a large degree. By the early twentieth century it had become clear that the family was changing significantly: social and intellectual forces were reducing its size, modifying its functions, and individualizing and democratizing its structure.

Under such pressures the stability of the family declined. In a society as heterogeneous as America, wide variations existed among class, ethnic–religious, and racial groups in terms of the relations between husband and wife, the status of women, and the socialization of children. The new trends toward smaller families and more liberal divorce laws, along with expanded rights for women, first appeared in the upper- and middle-class white Anglo-Saxon Protestant culture. Lower-income and ethnic groups retained the patriarchal family. Nevertheless, desertion was a common means of ending oppressive marriages, and by the 1920s the divorce rate among the working class equaled that of the middle class.

The trend toward smaller families became prominent among the middle class early in the century. Compulsory education and child labor laws postponed children's economic contribution to the family and lengthened their period of dependence. Consequently, youngsters became economic liabilities rather than assets. Since fewer died at birth or in infancy, it became unnecessary to have large numbers of children to ensure that some would survive. Among higher socioeconomic groups in urban areas, families of half a dozen or more gave way to a norm of two or three children.

To educate middle- and lower-income women in family planning, a nurse, Margaret Sanger, organized the modern movement for birth control, a term she originated. Concerned with women's health and autonomy, Sanger declared that they "are determined to decide for themselves whether they shall become mothers, under what conditions, and when." But the law classified birth control information as pornography and prohibited even physicians from providing advice about contraception. Authorities sent Sanger to jail for opening the first birth control clinic in 1916, in the slums of Brooklyn. It took her twenty years to achieve legalization of birth control.

An Age of Adolescence

During the early years of the new century, the modern concept of adolescence was developed. Industrialization displaced many young people from the jobs they would have held on the farm or in the shop in an agrarian society. The decline in the birthrate and the wide spacing of children, together with the fact that adults lived longer, meant that families in which all children were teenagers became common. Consequently, between 1890 and 1920 a host of urban reformers, educators, youth workers, and psychologists reclassified young people as adolescents. Young people were seen as less in need of advice than of adult manipulation of their environment to improve their personal growth and development. In a time of rapid social change, many people viewed children as instruments of modernization, more malleable than adults. At the very least, child rearing and the socialization of adolescents should equip boys and girls with the security, flexibility, knowledge, and skills to make choices and develop intellectually and emotionally in a changing social order.

To help prepare young people for the strains of modern life, parents, educators, and youth workers formed child study associations, nursery schools, and kindergartens for young children and a number of other institutions for adolescents to provide them with organized peer-group activities emphasizing healthy competition and social interaction. From boys' clubs sponsored by city churches and settlement houses to the playground movement, YMCA programs, 4-H clubs for farm youth, and the more authoritarian and disciplined Boy Scouts of America, these agencies attempted to prepare young people for membership in social and economic groups.

The proliferation of organizations for young people was not without opposition. Many Catholics saw such organizations as attempts to convert their children to Protestantism, and many fundamentalist Protestants, especially in the rural South, viewed them as secularizing agencies which distracted young people from issues of sin and salvation.

The increasing link between romantic love and courtship rapidly transformed sexual customs and moral values in the new century. Despite much resistance by their elders, many young people challenged longstanding restraints and taboos of the Victorian Era. Young women began to make extensive use of cosmetics, which a decade earlier would have been considered sinful. They piled their hair above their necks, threw away their wasp-waisted, bone-and-steel corsets, and hiked their skirts above their ankles. Advertising and the new motion pictures emphasized glamour and sexiness.

The former separation of boys and girls during adolescence receded like the surf at low tide, and coeducation became widespread. The chaperon went the way of the horse and buggy as young couples set out without supervision for a drive in an automobile, a visit to the movies, or to a dance hall to jerk and sway to new, more sensual dances like the tango and the fox trot and the ragtime rhythm of the bunny hug, grizzly bear, and turkey trot. By 1915 critics had coined the term "flapper" to characterize the "New Woman" who sought personal enjoyment, fulfillment, and romantic love. To many young people, it was a thrilling time. The past was overthrown, and Victorianism came to mean "flabby and futile, prudish and trite, grandmotherly and sentimental."

Changing Relationships

Within the family, reform began to redefine relationships between husband and wife. The growing emphasis on individualistic and democratic values and the new economic opportunities for women undermined patriarchal authority. Slowly a new, alternative ideal was created, one which emphasized more equal relationships and shared decision making. By 1909 the word "obey" had been dropped from civil marriage vows, and many churches had also eliminated it. But the new ideal faced much resistance, and the continued subjugation of women in the family set many feminists on the road to political activism. Although most women continued to marry and become homemakers and mothers, a different possibility began to be discussed actively. Scores of magazines and novels portrayed the "New Woman," as young, educated, unmarried, and in revolt against what she considered the smothering Victorian image of womanhood.

Changing views also affected marriage and the divorce rate. A significant minority came to see marriage as based on romantic love and individual interests, and thus as resting on mutual agreement and contract rather than sacrament. A mounting number of marriages ended when affection and respect disappeared. During the early years of the century, the divorce rate soared from one in every 21 marriages in 1880 to one in every 12 by 1900 and one in every 9 by 1916. People spoke of a divorce crisis and a threat to the foundations of social order. Traditionalists, led by many clergymen, tried to tighten legislation so as to restrict the spread of divorce. But feminists, social scientists, liberal clergymen, and other modernists urged the easing of divorce laws not only to allow people to escape from tyrannical marriages but also to permit greater freedom and equality in wedlock and thus help strengthen the institution of marriage. The movement to restrict divorce by statute had failed by the end of the Progressive Era. As in other modernizing countries, divorce laws were liberalized in the

United States, an indication of greater public toleration and acceptance of divorce and of the complex transformation of moral values and sexual customs which would become more widespread in the 1920s.

The Women's Movement

"I have an important piece of news to give you," the president-elect of the General Federation of Women's Clubs in 1904 told the organization, which had over half a million members. "Dante is dead. He has been dead for several centuries, and I think it is time we dropped the study of his *Inferno* and turned our attention to our own." In the Progressive Era women joined together in record numbers to improve their situation in a changing society and give support to each other. Two broad and somewhat conflicting goals characterized the movement. One was to provide special protection for female workers against economic exploitation. Accepting part of the Victorian image of women, many activists fought for and obtained a number of state laws prohibiting long hours, low wages, and dangerous working conditions for women. Another goal was equal access to all the rights and opportunities of modern life and the achievement of individual autonomy for women. Radical feminists like Charlotte Perkins Gilman, a prolific writer who developed one of the first systematic analyses of the feminist position in the United States, called for communal and professionally staffed kitchens, cleaning services, and nurseries, which could give women the freedom to earn a living on an equal basis with men. A few radical feminists, such as the anarchist Emma Goldman, rejected marriage as an institution and advocated monogamous unions in which both partners preserved their freedom to have sexual relations with whomever they chose.

A number of educated upper-middle-class women formed organizations to benefit women and society. The leaders of these national and sometimes international organizations belied traditional attitudes toward women as they displayed the skills and judgment necessary to run large-scale organizations. Female support networks proved very valuable to women activists like Jane Addams, the founder of the settlement house movement; Lillian Wald, the originator of the visiting-nurse system; and Florence Kelley, the organizer of the National Consumers' League. The league, like the National Child Labor Committee and the Women's Trade Union League, in which working women joined forces with socialites, sought through private organization and collective action such as consumer boycotts and political lobbying to eliminate sweatshop wages and conditions.

In the second decade of the twentieth century, the drive for female suffrage became the primary focus of the women's movement, pushing broader social and economic aims into the background. By 1914 the suffrage movement consumed the energy of hundreds of thousands of women and their male allies. Bidding for male support, many suffragists de-emphasized more radical feminist goals. Instead, they accepted elements of the Victorian image of womanhood and asserted that female voters could help male reformers reduce political corruption.

A more favorable political climate gave hope to the suffragists. A former journalist, Carrie Chapman Catt, headed the more conservative National American Woman Suffrage Association (NAWSA) in putting pressure on Congress for a federal amendment. A militant Quaker, Alice Paul, led the more extreme members of the Woman's party in the first major picketing of the White House. When they were imprisoned, the women pickets went on a hunger strike to continue their protest. The suffragists finally won presidential support after the United States entered World War I. After the Armistice, Congress passed the Nineteenth Amendment, which was ratified in time for the 1920 election. "Now at last we can begin," feminist labor lawyer Crystal Eastman declared. "What we must do is to create conditions of outward freedom in which a free woman's soul can be born and grow."

MODERNISM AND INSTITUTIONS: SCHOOLS, HOSPITALS, CHURCHES

Progressive Education

Schools, like the home, could be instruments of both conservation and change. The transformation of education in the Progressive Era put the school in the forefront of change, but it met with much resentment from traditionalists. Educators responded to new conditions by deemphasizing the classical tradition and reshaping the educational system to prepare increasing numbers of people for a continually changing urban industrial society. To provide mass education, the number of public high schools doubled and the number of students there quadrupled. The percentage of high school graduates among 17-year-olds tripled between 1900 and 1920, reaching 16 percent.

Progressive education revolutionized teaching. Its leading advocate, the Columbia University philosopher John Dewey, stressed the child's own experience and the need to "learn by doing" rather than by rote memorization. Despite much resistance, the schools developed broader and more flexible curricula, less formality in the classrooms, the classification of students by intelligence and achievement tests, and the addition of gymnasiums, laboratories, manual arts shops, and rooms for art and music. Progressive education aimed at relevant education which would awaken children to human values and capabilities and instill good moral habits which would serve both them and a changing society.

Colleges and universities expanded their campuses and doubled their enrollment to 600,000 students. The universities, which had begun to emerge in the late nineteenth century, graduated thousands of technicians, managers, and professionals. Educators sought to inculcate the traditions and values of a liberal democratic culture. Many university presidents and professors saw the institution's role as including useful social research to help meet the challenges of change. But the alumni and the public seemed more concerned with the football and fraternity craze which swept the campuses and became immortalized in the high jinks of the fabled Dink Stover of Yale.

Physical and Mental Health Care

The re-examination of institutions which occurred during the Progressive Era led to major changes in the system of health care. Part of the improvement came from developments in medical knowledge and new techniques for diagnosis and treatment: the use of X-rays, improved anesthetics, and the ability to provide blood transfusions. But part came from specific social actions to enhance medical knowledge and service. John D. Rockefeller, for example, established the Rockefeller Institute for Medical Research in New York City in 1901; six years later, serum was discovered for treating spinal meningitis. Andrew Carnegie established the Carnegie Foundation for the Advancement of Teaching in 1910, and one of its first activities was the study and exposure of abuses in medical education. A report by the Flexner Commission recommended significant reforms, especially the need to link medical education with the new universities and hospitals.

At the turn of the century, the mental health movement was inaugurated by Adolf Meyer and others, who discovered that serious mental disorders might yield to chemical and other treatments. In 1909 a movement for additional and improved mental hospitals was founded, and in the same year the European psychiatrists Sigmund Freud and Carl Jung gave guest lectures at Clark University in Massachusetts and helped expand the use of psychoanalysis in the United States.

The modern general hospital emerged in the Progressive Era. In the past, hospitals had been stigmatized as houses of infection and contagion and places where the poor went to die. Those who could afford it received medical treatment, including surgery, in their homes or in the doctor's office. But the use of antisepsis, the availability of costly new medical equipment and therapies, and a wide variety of medical specialists made the hospital a more effective institution for the protection of life and the treatment of injury and disease. In the fifty years between 1875 and 1925, hospitals proliferated in the United States, with their numbers increasing from 150 to 7,000.

Social and economic changes helped transform the hospital. Under the financial pressures of the depression of the 1890s, the old free-treatment philanthropic institutions gave way to business-oriented establishments which began to charge for health care. To encourage paying customers to use their facilities, they offered different classes of service within the hospital for the first time. By the end of the Progressive Era, the hospital had emerged as a center for advanced medical practice and a primary instrument in health care for all classes.

Despite the development of patient payment as the basis for hospital care, the United States differed from most other industrial nations by not adopting a program of national health insurance to spread the increasing costs of medical care. Nevertheless, by 1920 the hospital had moved from a peripheral role to a new position as a major, accepted part of the community.

Modernism and Organized Religion

Organized religion was beset by the secular tendencies of modern life and the challenge of science and rational thought to nonrationalistic systems of belief. The tension between accommodation to change and reassertion of old traditions triggered intensive debate during the Progressive Era.

Modernists who emphasized liberalism and social action existed in each major faith. They won control of most Protestant denominations through the Social Gospel movement, which attacked problems of poverty, vice, corruption, and exploitation of workers. Among Catholics and Jews, modernism and social activism existed but met more resistance.

Traditionalists mustered significant support. Within the Roman Catholic Church, Pope Pius X condemned modernism for substituting subjective criteria for the authority of the church in matters of faith and morals. Lacking central authority, Protestant denominations included both modernists and fundamentalists. Theologically conservative churchmen opposed departure from belief in the literal truth of Scripture. Revivalist preachers like Dwight L. Moody and William A. "Billy" Sunday emphasized another alternative, evangelism, which urged individual regeneration.

The Jewish community was sharply split. The relatively few Jews who had arrived in America before 1880, primarily from Germany, had accommodated to the New World culture and established a Reform Judaism which rejected many old customs and beliefs. But the Jewish immigrants who arrived from eastern Europe in the late nineteenth and early twentieth centuries maintained the Orthodox rituals, customs, and beliefs. Conservative Judaism was created as a cultural compromise between the two divisions in the Jewish community. Attempting to reconcile tradition with change, Jewish history with American reality, Conservative Judaism gained strength in the Progressive Era. In Judaism, as in the other faiths, the tension between modernism and traditionalism remained a continuing source of controversy and division into the 1920s, when, at least within Protestantism, it beame a major national political issue.

THE CHALLENGE OF THE CITY

The cities became the focus of the new America. In the second decade of the century, the United States passed a milestone like the closing of the frontier a generation earlier; it became a nation of cities. The 1920 census showed that for the first time a majority (51 percent) of the population lived in urban areas. These were years of growth for the cities. America developed more large urban areas than any other country. New York, Chicago, Pittsburgh, Detroit, and Cleveland doubled in size during this period. Smaller cities like Los Angeles, Seattle, Atlanta, and Birmingham were transformed. Boom towns skyrocketed with the opening of new oil fields in the Southwest; Dallas, Houston, Tulsa, and Oklahoma City were among them. "The city has become the central feature of modern civilization," the municipal reformer and social scientist Frederic C. Howe wrote in 1906. "Man has entered on an urban age."

The modern metropolis raised the specter of a new and dangerous America. Many people agreed with James Bryce when he said in 1912 that "a great city is a great evil." Many thought the metropolises, with their congestion, hectic pace, lack of adequate air and space, and their crime, violence, and pollution, would destroy not only their residents but American civilization as well. "This life of great cities," Henry George warned in 1898, "is not the natural life of man. He must under such conditions deteriorate, physically, mentally, morally."

Despite such gloomy predictions, the Progressive Era was permeated with a spirit of hope and optimism that people working together could improve the environment and in turn create a better society. The problems of the cities, Frederic Howe argued, were not ethical or personal but economic, and they could be solved through planning and the assertion of public intervention and direction. As Howe wrote in 1912,

> The American city is inconvenient, dirty, lacking in charm and beauty because the individual land owner has been permitted to plan it, to build, to do as he willed with his land. There has been no community control, no sense of the public as opposed to private rights.

In the Progressive Era urban reformers began to challenge the nineteenth-century tradition of an unrestricted marketplace and unrestrained individualism.

Some attempts at planning the urban environment were initiated in the private sector. The 1893 World's Fair in Chicago presented the artificial but stunning "great white city" as a demonstration of the results of an entirely planned environment. It launched the City Beautiful movement, which resulted in the development in several cities of master plans, civic centers, tree-lined boulevards, public fountains and parks, underground electrical and telephone lines, and increased use of ornamentation. Influenced in part by the development of the garden city, a planned community, in England, several companies created carefully laid out housing projects, the most famous being Forest Hills Gardens in New York City. A middle-class community of Tudor-style homes, spacious lawns, and a shopping center, this model of large-scale comprehensive planning was sponsored by the Russell Sage Foundation.

More influential in the Progressive Era was the expansion of governmental influence on urban growth. The response of the first generation of urban planners to the increasing problem of congestion was deconcentration through garden cities and zoning. Businesspeople concerned with protecting their investment, especially in the downtown area, joined with reformers like Lillian Wald, Florence Kelley, and Lawrence Veiller to argue the need for governmental intervention for humanitarian reasons. Together, they obtained the first major zoning law in American history. The New York City law of 1916 exerted public control over the use, height, and area of urban land and construction. With deference to existing private investments, the zoning law aroused interest throughout the nation, and more than a thousand American cities adopted similar ordinances within the next decade. Like much of the legislation of the Progressive Era, zoning was primarily negative in its effects. It did not give government the power to encourage or provide adequate housing, nor did it provide a workable basis for coordinating housing and planning. But New York's zoning act did mark a major transition toward governmental intervention in the marketplace and the recognition that cities would continue to be a major aspect of America.

A NEW MASS CULTURE

The growth of cities also contributed to the transformation of American culture. The Progressive Era witnessed the rise of a new mass culture midway between local or regional folk cultures and the more sophisticated culture of the elite. The new, more standardized culture was based on the concentrated mass markets of the cities and technological developments which provided new forms of mass communication and entertainment. The telephone, mass circulation newspapers and magazines, and motion pictures helped break down localism and encourage a more national and cosmopolitan outlook. Like other forces of industrialism, they helped weave a previously scattered people into a more integrated national society. But they also challenged old values and ideals and led some groups to seek to ensure that mass entertainment served the public welfare.

The telephone helped bring news of the outside world into the home. It also enabled business to expand. The telephone network grew rapidly. At the turn of the century only one person in a hundred had a telephone, but a dozen years later almost one in ten had one of the bulky instruments and there were more than 10 million phones in service. "What startles and frightens backward Europeans," said a visiting English author, "is the efficiency and fearful universality of the telephone."

The staid and simple newspapers of the nineteenth century vanished in the face of sensational new mass circulation dailies which provided not only information but entertainment and advertising. New high-speed rotary presses, linotype machines, and the photoengraving process enabled publishers to create exciting mass-appeal newspapers. Some, like *The New York Times,* won praise as sources of news. But others, like William Randolph Hearst's *New York Journal* and Joseph Pulitzer's *New York World,* deteriorated into "yellow journalism" through sensationalism and even fabrication to cultivate and satisfy the public taste for excitement and controversy. The value of the press in raising public issues and exposing corruption was hailed, but many condemned the more incendiary journals for inflaming public opinion and unsettling foreign affairs. Specifically, critics blamed the press for contributing to American intervention in the Spanish-American War and exacerbating tense relations between the United States and Japan into a war scare in 1907.

Newspapers were a private enterprise with a public function, informing the citizenry. But the free marketplace of ideas was eroded when publishers sought to limit the operation of the economic market by expanding their holdings and reducing competition. By the end of the Progressive Era, a half-dozen newspaper chains controlled more than eighty dailies with a circulation of nearly 10 million. Like industry, the press had intervened in the marketplace and become big business.

Organized Leisure

In preindustrial societies leisure enjoyment for the masses had been provided through religious holidays and festivals. But in an increasingly industrial society with growing amounts of leisure (the work week dropped from 66 hours in 1850 to 56 hours in 1900 and 41 hours by 1920), new forms of organized entertainment were required for the urban masses. Much arose spontaneously; in addition, municipal governments built parks, playgrounds, and zoos, and joined private groups in developing libraries and museums. Entrepreneurs like P. T. Barnum had demonstrated the popularity of circuses. Also, in the late nineteenth century the availability of rail transportation permitted the development of seashore resorts like Atlantic City and amusement parks like Coney Island for the enjoyment of the urban residents.

Most dramatic, however, was the rise of urban spectator sports in the late nineteenth and early twentieth centuries. Professional baseball became a major American institution. "Baseball and football matches," an English visitor observed in 1905, "excite an interest greater than any other public events except the Presidential election." Crowds flocked to the ball fields and baseball became a lucrative industry. A "World Series" was begun in 1903.

Popular music also became a major entertainment industry. Mass production made pianos available to thousands of middle-class families. Beginning in the 1890s New York's "Tin Pan Alley" publishing houses began turning out thousands of simple, but catchy, sentimental songs to be sung around the piano. Some became all-time favorites: "Take Me Out to the Ball Game," "Daisy," and "The Sidewalks of New York." By 1900, however, a powerful new challenger, the phonograph, had almost ruined the piano and sheet music business. Originally developed as a business recording machine, the phonograph was marketed in the Progressive Era for home entertainment. Millions bought the new phonograph records and danced to new, more suggestive lyrics such as the 1906 hit "You Can Go as Far as You Like with Me in My Merry Oldsmobile."

Flickering Images on the Silent Screen

The greatest impact on entertainment and mass culture was that of the movies, the first of the modern mass entertainment media. Emerging in the 1890s, motion pictures established their dominance within two decades. They had come to America through Thomas Alva Edison's kinetoscope, a peephole viewing machine. The film used to produce the movies had been invented by George Eastman. Enterprising operators, including a number of immigrant fur workers and salesmen, used Edison's kinetoscope and later his large-screen motion picture projectors. They put them in amusement parks, penny arcades, and vacant stores, which were converted into "nickelodeon" theaters in working-class districts in the major cities. By 1910 national attendance at movie theaters had reached 500,000 on Sundays; the movies had become a major attraction.

From the beginning, American movie makers geared their product to mass audiences and to a fantasy of escape from the tedium and harshness of urban industrial life. An early advertising jingle enticed potential customers thus:

If you're tired of life, go to the picture show.
You'll forget your unpaid bills, rheumatism and other ills,
If you'll stow away your pills, and go to the picture show.

Producers soon discovered that, of the many one- and two-reel films they showed, subjects like *Taking a Bath* and *Who's in the Bedroom?* drew more audiences than *Otters at Play* or *Sleigh Riding in Central Park.* Sex and risqué skits were introduced almost from the beginning.

In the early years of the century, Edison and the immigrant entrepreneurs began to create longer narrative films. In 1903 Edison cameraman Edwin S. Porter combined plot and characterization in *The Great Train Robbery,* the first motion picture in the modern sense. By 1913, after the industry had moved from New York and New Jersey to Hollywood, California, producers began to create so-called feature films, which ran for more than an hour and were designed to appeal to the huge middle-class market. Based on classic works and popular books and plays, these films featured stars like comedians Harold Lloyd and Charlie Chaplin, western heroes like Tom Mix and William S. Hart, swashbuckling Douglas Fairbanks, the glamorous Gloria Swanson, and the ingénue Mary Pickford, billed as "America's sweetheart." In 1915 director D. W. Griffith set the style of the modern movie epic in his highly biased Civil War saga, *The Birth of a Nation.* Griffith included many of the techniques of modern film making: the close-up, the long shot, cross-cutting, and shadow and profile lighting.

As producers expanded from the tenement trade, they enticed the middle class with more sophisticated films and more attractive movie theaters. The nickelodeons were replaced by ornate palaces rivaling opera houses in grandeur. The Strand, which opened on Times Square in 1914, had thickly carpeted lounges, crystal chandeliers, original oil paintings, comfortable seats, an orchestra and organ, and a corps of uniformed ushers. The program included a comedy, a newsreel, a travelog, and the feature film.

By the end of World War I, the motion picture industry had become big business. Hollywood had a payroll of $20 million a year and dominated both the American and world markets. In the 1920s the former nickelodeon managers, self-made men who had risen from the immigrant communities of New York and Chicago—men like

Adolph Zukor, William Fox, Carl Laemmle, Samuel Goldwyn, and Louis Mayer—consolidated their holdings. They established giant companies—Paramount, Metro-Goldwyn-Mayer (MGM), Columbia, Radio-Keith-Orpheum (RKO), and Warner Brothers—which owned studios, distribution exchanges, and theater chains.

Americans quickly recognized the movies as a powerful new medium capable of influencing masses of people and manipulating thought and behavior. Traditional custodians of culture—educators, editors, clergy, publishers, critics—were divided in their assessment. Some hailed film as "authentic democratic art, straight from the hearts of the humble classes." Many, however, criticized the movies for sensationalism and creating dangerous emotions among the masses. *Good Housekeeping* in 1910 called films "a primary school for criminals . . . teaching obscenity, crime, murder, and debauchery for a nickel." Early critics of the movies often compared the storefront ghetto nickelodeons with saloons. Both attracted many of the same patrons and served as social and entertainment centers for the working classes. Middle-class conservatives and reformers condemned both as unseemly, germ-ridden places which jeopardized the health and morals of the people who went there.

Civic leaders, both reformers and conservatives, were particularly concerned about the influence the movies had on young people. They were incensed by the vivid detail with which crime was portrayed in such films as *The Badger Game* (1905), in which a confidence man swindles the elderly. *The School Children's Strike* (1906), in which rebellious youngsters take revenge against the strict discipline of the principal by burning down the schoolhouse, also proved too provocative for the critics.

Intervention to curb the direct influence of the movies in the Progressive Era took the form of attempts to limit the youthful audience through age restrictions for certain films, zoning requirements to keep theaters, like saloons, confined to specific areas, and censorship and outright suppression. Censorship—a form of cultural intervention—came through local government agencies or private voluntary review boards set up by citizens' groups, sometimes with the cooperation of the industry itself.

Typically, a coalition of community leaders—settlement house and youth workers, members of women's clubs, and civic and business leaders who were concerned with young people and moral standards—either formed their own review board or prodded the city into establishing censorship commissions. In Chicago, New York, and other cities, these censors banned parts or all of hundreds of movies. They excluded scenes which depicted criminals as heroes, ridiculed public authorities, or degraded women. Out came shots showing a ballerina smoking a cigarette or a policeman standing in his underwear. By 1922 the demands for stricter censorship had grown so strong that the studio heads formed their own national review board headed by Will Hays, who had been postmaster general during the Harding administration.

The custodians of culture hoped that the movies would convey middle-class values to lower-income groups. The producers' aim, however, was not to bring high culture to the masses but to entertain them. In the process the movies helped teach new city dwellers the routines of urban industrial life, in addition to which they also poked fun at them, making them more bearable through humor. Culturally, motion pictures assisted in bringing to the mass audience a sophistication in speech, dress, manners, and social attitudes which was unknown to the preceding generation.

Through the movies and other forms of mass entertainment and communication, information was conveyed to millions of people quickly and directly. These new tools helped develop a new mass culture which in many ways supplemented or replaced the old folk culture and more personal transmission of culture. Mass communication, like mass production and mass consumption, helped set the style of modern life.

MODERNISM IN THOUGHT AND ART

"Nothing is done in this country as it was done twenty years ago," Woodrow Wilson declared in 1913. "We are in the presence of a new organization of society. . . . We have changed our economic conditions, absolutely, from top to bottom; and, with our economic society, the organization of our life." Despite the doubts of many critics, such as Walter Lippmann, about the nation's ability to adjust to the new conditions, in the Progressive Era Americans remade many of their institutions, redirected much of their behavior, and began to recast their ways of looking at the world.

While the entrepreneurs of the communication and entertainment industries worked to build a new mass culture based largely on the ethic of consumption and the pleasure principle, traditionalists resisted such a change and modernizers shattered old ways of thought and contributed to the fragmentation of American culture. A sharp tension separated those who wanted to cling to tradition from those who emphasized the need for broad and rapid modernization. In the reform period of the Progressive Era, traditionalists—those in rural areas as well as urban dwellers who continued to assert the primacy of nineteenth-century standards of culture and morality—were on the defensive. Modernizers had the force of change behind them. But many of the social–cultural tensions of these years remained unresolved and in the 1920s were exacerbated into a national conflict over the direction of American society.

The Revolt Against Formalism

The comfortable Victorian cosmos of middle-class mores and the tenets of scientific progress could not sustain the assaults of industrial change and the scientific discoveries of the nineteenth century. On both sides of the Atlantic artists, novelists, dramatists, social scientists, and philosophers revolted against the abstract, formalistic logic of the Victorian Era. Abandoning the quest for a single "truth," they moved toward a more pluralistic acceptance of the possibility that there were many different apprehensions of truth. The emphasis on relativism and change placed the focus on the process of becoming rather than on the end itself.

Pragmatism was the most original American contribution to this relativism. Nicely suited to American optimism during a time of flux in which old certainties were being eroded and displaced, this vigorous and influential system of thought asserted that the meaning of any term and the reality of any object lay in what it could and would do. In short, the importance of ideas lay in their results. William James, a Harvard psychologist and philosopher and brother of the novelist

Henry James, developed the philosophy which would dominate twentieth-century America. Actively positivistic, James declared that in a changing world people could often affect the course of change through bold, creative action. Pragmatism offered reassurance of individuality, free will, initiative, and human spontaneity in opposition to the seemingly helpless position of men and women in the deterministic framework of Social Darwinism. "Believe that life is worth living," James wrote in books like *A Pluralistic Universe* and *The Meaning of Truth* (both published in 1909), "and your belief will help create the fact."

John Dewey, a Columbia University educator and philosopher, went even further than James. In the concept of *instrumentalism,* Dewey held it proper to use the instrument of collective action, whether through private association or through the actions of government, to improve society. Guided by intelligence and employing scientific methods, people, Dewey believed, could intervene purposefully, modify their environment, and improve the quality of their lives and of society itself.

In Support of Intervention

Faith in the marketplace ideal and a self-regulating society was undermined by the rigors of industrialization, but the framework of thought which supported the status quo—natural law, unrestrained individualism, Social Darwinism, and laissez faire—was overturned by a new class of intellectuals, university trained and often academically employed social scientists. They helped overcome traditionalist thinkers who continued to defend the old concepts. Although William Graham Sumner lived until 1910, he and his disciples found it increasingly difficult to deal with the fact that giant businesses were not strictly private but were "affected with a public interest" and, therefore, presumably subject to regulation by the public. Their other problem was the inconsistency of businesspeople who championed laissez faire but wanted maintenance of the status quo—governmental protection in the form of tariffs, patents, aid against labor—for them but not for their adversaries.

Increasing numbers of individuals and groups became impatient at the helplessness of their position as it was reflected in the concept of inevitable, gradual evolution. Through its organization, business had shown how to influence the environment. Evolutionary determinism could be stood on its head. If the environment determined adaptation and other behavior, then by altering the environment for the better, people and society itself might be improved. This kind of "reform Darwinism" gave hope of improvement through manipulation of the environment.

Abandoning mechanistic doctrines and abstract principles, the social scientists of the Progressive Era sought to understand how society really worked so that people could improve its operation. Many attacked the justifications for the status quo. The historian Charles Beard, in *An Economic Interpretation of the Constitution* (1913), undermined the sanctity of the Constitution and the Supreme Court's use of it to thwart reform by unveiling the property interests, and presumably the economic motivations, of the nation's founders. The radical economist Thorstein Veblen, in *The Theory of the Leisure Class* (1899) and later works, differentiated between engineers, who, he claimed, were responsible for mass production, and businesspeople, who were more interested in profit than in production for society. The legal system's emphasis on the need to adhere to absolute principles, with highest priority to laissez faire and the protection of private property, was challenged by Roscoe Pound of the Harvard Law School, who formulated a "sociological jurisprudence." Like pragmatism, it shifted from absolutes to relatives, arguing that the law was dynamic, was a product of experience and could thus be created, and was subject to continuous improvement in the interests of society. "The Fourteenth Amendment," Justice Holmes declared in a famous dissent from the Court's invalidation of a law limiting the working hours of New York bakers (*Lochner* v. *New York*, 1905), "does not enact Mr. Herbert Spencer's Social Statics."

Sociologists like Edward A. Ross also rejected Spencerian sociology and Social Darwinism. Ross helped develop the concept of social control, the use of collective action to control forces threatening to pull society apart. Ross rejected the concept of a self-regulating society in which individuals, following their own interests, contributed to social progress. Rather, in the view of Ross and many others, such individuals posed a social danger.

The Jeffersonian tradition of limited government was addressed directly in a widely read book, *The Promise of American Life* (1909), by Herbert Croly, one of the editors of the liberal *New Republic* magazine. Given the changing nature of society and the growth of industrialization and giant organizations, Croly argued, Jeffersonian, liberal democratic ideals could no longer be attained without governmental action. Croly, like Roosevelt and others, urged the use of strong, positive government to ensure continued progress toward its ideals, to use, in his memorable phrase, Hamiltonian means to achieve Jeffersonian ends.

The conceptualization and intellectual justification of private collective and governmental interference in the functioning of society accompanied the interventionism which was already taking place. The construction of the intellectual argument did not create intervention in the marketplace or cause the erosion of the idea of a self-regulating society. But once it had been formulated in intellectually respectable terms, it provided a powerful justification for these trends and helped stimulate the widespread interventionism of the Progressive Era.

Social Criticism and Individualism

Writers challenged genteel literary strictures and emphasized instead the seamy side of modern society, the despair of the masses, and the impact of impersonal forces on people's lives. Influenced by Émile Zola and other European social critics, American naturalistic writers helped set the stage for social reform. Theodore Dreiser introduced *naturalism* with *Sister Carrie* (1900), which dealt with sexual exploitation. He went on to attack big business in *The Financier* (1912) and *The Titan* (1914). Frank Norris exposed railroad monopoly in *The Octopus* (1901) and the commodity exchange in *The Pit* (1903). Upton Sinclair assailed the meatpacking industry and the capitalist system in *The Jungle* (1906). But while many of the naturalist writers were influenced by Darwinism and the vast, impersonal forces which controlled human destinies, they also emphasized the powerful individual struggling to dominate the environment. Cowperwood, in *The Titan,* is a symbol of force in business and politics, and the larger-than-life protagonists of Jack London's novels, like Wolf Larsen in *The Sea Wolf,* resemble Nietzschean supermen.

In a time of increasing social organization, there was also a countermovement to emphasize the importance of the individual. The individual in mass society was a critical focus of a number of writers, including Ibsen, Bergson, and Nietzsche. Freud, too, contributed to the intuitive probing of inner experience, providing a new appreciation of the need to come to terms with the irrational and the absurd, and the importance of personal integrity, fulfillment, and freedom.

Some of this new individualism appeared in the transformation of art. Modern art, which moved from the social criticism of naturalism to highly individualistic expressionism, arrived in the United States in the first decade of the century. Like the new literature, it repudiated the genteel culture of the Victorian Era. Influenced by romantic realism and French impressionism, painters like George Luks, John Sloan, and George Bellows and the photographer Alfred Stieglitz portrayed the drabness and repressed violence in urban industrial life so forcefully that after their New York exhibition in 1908 critics labeled them the "Ashcan School."

At the New York Armory show of 1913, these artists introduced European modernism, including cubism, expressionism, and other avant-garde schools of painting. The works of Picasso, Matisse, Cézanne, and others emphasized the unpredictable, the unmanageable, and the flux and formlessness of modern life. As such, they challenged the positive optimism of many American intellectuals and progressives. Many traditionalist critics attacked the new movement. One described the cubist Duchamp's "Nude Descending a Staircase" as "an explosion in a shingle factory." Theodore Roosevelt denounced cubists and futurists as "the lunatic fringe."

Cultural Rebels

Emphasis on the creation of a freer, more fulfilling life and repudiation of oppressive, outdated institutions became the focus of a subculture of young cultural rebels who established Bohemian centers in New York and Chicago. To the little cafes of Greenwich Village came

Max and Crystal Eastman and the other editors of the startlingly radical new journal *The Masses*; the poet Edna St. Vincent Millay; the playwright Eugene O'Neill; John Reed, scion of a wealthy Oregon family, former Harvard cheerleader, and radical journalist; and many others. These young people felt keenly the gap between outdated ideas and institutions and new social and industrial conditions. Dissenting from conventional standards and values, outraged by the poverty, injustice, and oppression they saw all around them, they assailed the dead hand of tradition and conscienceless industrialism. "The old world was dying," wrote Floyd Dell, the literary chronicler of Greenwich Village. It could not survive the clash between "utopian ideals and machine-made fact." In one of the first documents of the countercultural tradition, a young Columbia College graduate, Randolph Bourne, published *Youth and Life* (1913) and juxtaposed the spontaneity and daring of youth with the arid conventionality of adulthood, writing: "It is the young people who have all the really valuable experience. . . . Very few people get any really new experience after they are twenty-five. . . . "

"Everywhere new institutions were being founded—magazines, clubs, little theaters, art or free-love or single-tax colonies, experimental schools, picture galleries," the literary critic Malcolm Cowley recalled of the years just before World War I. "Everywhere was a sense of comradeship and immense possibilities for change." The mood of the nation encouraged Americans to assume responsibility for their fate as a people and to do so with an assertiveness that was virtually unprecedented in their history.

CHAPTER 4

Progressivism Arrives

THE GREAT LIGHT

"Slowly as the new century came into its first decade, I saw the Great Light," wrote America's most celebrated small-town newspaper editor, William Allen White. The Great Light he saw was progressivism, a collective effort of millions of Americans to modernize antiquated institutions at the beginning of the twentieth century. "Around me in that day," White recalled, "scores of young leaders in American politics and public affairs were seeing what I saw, feeling what I felt. . . . All over the land in a score of states and more, young men in both parties were taking leadership by attacking things as they were in that day."

Progressivism was the name given at the time to a number of major efforts to reform society through the power of private groups and public agencies. As a nationwide movement, it began to influence events during the 1890s depression and faded after World War I began. Although traces of it lasted nearly thirty years, progressivism became most influential and successful between 1906 and 1916. During that decade millions of people sensed the increased tempo of reform. One progressive, a political scientist, claimed boldly in 1913 that "one of the most inspiring movements in human history is now in progress."

The movement proved both inspiring and confusing because progressive leaders—nostalgic knights of reform—mixed new methods with old visions and often differed among themselves over their goals. Successful political leaders like Theodore Roosevelt and Woodrow Wilson tended to blur the differences among their followers. The tumultuous 1912 convention which gave birth to the short-lived Progressive party* illustrated how different reformers were pulled together by their faith in a progressive spirit and belief in noble leaders.

Modern crusaders swelling with righteousness and hope, the delegates to the Progressive party convention set out to battle the forces of evil. Their champion, Theodore Roosevelt, appealed to them with the shrewdness of a politician and the moralistic fervor of an evangelist: "This new movement is a movement of truth, sincerity and wisdom, a movement which proposes to put at the service of all our people the collective power of the people, through their Governmental agencies." Roosevelt ended his "confession of faith" with a rousing declaration:

> Our cause is based on the eternal principles of righteousness; and even though we who now lead may for the time fail, in the end the cause itself shall triumph. . . . We stand at Armageddon, and we battle for the Lord.

Leaping to their feet, the delegates filled the great hall with applause and responded with choruses of "Onward, Christian Soldiers" and "The Battle Hymn of the Republic." With enthusiasm as their armor, the Progressives marched forth against their foes.

Such displays of mass enthusiasm concealed great differences within the Progressive party and within progressivism as a whole. Among the delegates cheering Roosevelt that day were people as diverse as George W. Perkins, a former Morgan partner and the head of International Harvester Corporation, and Amos Pinchot, a maverick millionaire and socialistic labor lawyer who favored breaking up trusts like International Harvester. Progressives included militarists like Roosevelt, who thrilled to wartime combat, and pacifists like the Quaker settlement house worker Jane Addams, who founded the Women's International League for Peace and Freedom to help abolish war.

* The capitalized *Progressive* refers to the political party which existed from 1912 to 1916. The lowercase *progressive* refers to reformers in the diverse social reform movement regardless of their party affiliations.

In diverse ways and with divergent goals, the progressives sought to modernize American institutions while attempting to recapture the ideals and sense of community which they believed had existed in the past. They battled conservatives, radicals, other reformers, and often each other. But despite their disagreements and difficulties, progressives played a major role in helping Americans adjust to new conditions and create new institutions for coping with the challenges of the time. They took the lead in establishing a social agenda for modern America.

PROGRESSIVES AS INTERVENTIONISTS

Historians have given the label "Progressive Era" to the first two decades of the twentieth century, but they have not been able to agree on the nature of either progressivism or the era. Some, such as Richard Hofstadter, saw it as a movement led by declining gentry and middle-class professionals anxious about their loss of status and the threats to the social order posed by corporate wealth and the industrial masses. Another school of interpretation, led by Gabriel Kolko, asserted that progressivism was conservative and was dominated by the new corporate managers and financiers, who sought to control government. Still others, such as David Thelen, suggested that it was radical in its potential for building coalitions of consumers across class and ethnic lines. Samuel Hays and Robert Wiebe determined that the progressives continued the long-term trend toward rationalization, bureaucratization, and centralization in an industrial society. Stressing the diversity among progressives as an explanation for such widely varying interpretations, Peter Filene concluded that a coherent progressive movement had never existed and that the concept of progressivism should be abandoned as factually inaccurate and analytically useless. In part, the historiographical controversy stems from scholars' focus on the people who called themselves progressives as the agents of social change. In fact, these men and women were only part of the forces for innovation in the Progressive Era.

The concept of interventionism helps clarify the nature of the changes which occurred in the first two decades of the twentieth century. Modernization resulted not only from the progressives' actions but also from initiatives taken by other groups, including many radicals, conservatives, and nonprogressive reformers. The corporate reorganization movement, the labor movement, the women's movement, the agrarian reform movement—all contributed to change. All were willing to intervene in the economy and society, and sometimes world affairs, on an unprecedented scale. The new interventionists—progressives among them—challenged the nineteenth-century belief in an autonomous and apolitical market system, the idea that the economy and society benefited when each individual was free to follow his or her own goals and self-interest with only a minimum of governmental interference. The concepts of laissez faire, unrestricted individualism, and an open, competitive marketplace had been seen as encouraging the development of a vast continent. But the closing of the frontier, the depression of the 1890s, and the transformation of America through massive immigration, rapid urbanization, and sweeping industrialization led many Americans to question the continued usefulness of these traditions without some modification on behalf of the public interest. The faith in natural development fostered by unrestrained individualism and an unregulated marketplace gave way to a fear that blind social forces threatened to transform society without regard to social values and goals. Many feared the destruction of American society.

In the first two decades of the twentieth century, Americans first sought on a nationwide basis to bring industrial change under control. They modified the philosophies of laissez faire, an unregulated marketplace, and unrestricted individualism, and intervened to direct change in what they considered a purposeful and intelligent manner. The leaders of this transformation employed new methods of science and the techniques of modern business organization. The new interventionists formed voluntary associations and other private cooperative groups and, when necessary, expanded the power of government to achieve their ends. They understood that they faced conditions which demanded new responses, and they were willing to create new or reorganized institutions—trade associations, professional groups, chambers of commerce, consumers' leagues, unions, and government regulatory agencies—which would benefit their own particular group and at the same time be consistent with their vision of the national interest.

Some Americans remained anti-interventionists. They continued to believe in classical political economy, laissez faire, the unregulated marketplace, and a mechanistic type of gradual progress through what John D. Rockefeller called "the working out of a law of nature." Progress could not be achieved by legislative fiat. "God Almighty made men and certain laws which are essential to their progress in civilization," the financier Henry Lee Higginson wrote to President William Howard Taft in 1911, "and Congressmen cannot break these natural laws without causing suffering." Progress was possible, but painfully slow. In a 1912 speech Elihu Root, a corporation lawyer and former secretary of state, saw progress as measured "not by days and years but by generations and centuries in the life of nations." The most conservative noninterventionists linked private property with a divine plan. They refused to believe that property rights should be restricted. In a famous declaration against unionization of coal miners, George F. Baer, a mine owner and president of the Reading Railroad, asserted in 1902 that the interests of the miners would be protected "not by the labor agitators, but by the Christian men to whom God, in His infinite wisdom, has given control of the property interest of the country."

Such assertions in favor of complete freedom to use private property without concern for the immediate impact on society were heard less frequently in this interventionist age. Some of the leading nineteenth-century advocates of laissez faire continued to expound it until their death; Sumner died in 1910 and Carnegie in 1919. During the Progressive Era, however, those who espoused such ideas were on the defensive. Even many conservatives realized the need for change. "Every one of us must recognize that the days of pure individualism are gone," Taft's secretary of commerce and labor, Charles Nagel, admitted. Nicholas Murray Butler, president of Columbia University and one of the leaders of the Republican old guard, asserted in 1912 that the "new development is cooperation, and cooperation as a substitute for unlimited, unrestricted, individual competition has come to stay as an economic fact, and legal institutions will have to be adjusted to it."

Despite the breadth of the forces for change in the early twentieth century and the scope of the new interventionism, the Progressive Era cannot be understood without understanding progressivism. It was a crucial part of the new interventionism. A multifaceted reform movement affecting nearly every aspect of American life, progressivism—like its successor, liberalism—was controversial and complex. Millions of people in both major political parties and several other parties and in every region of the country called themselves progressives. But while they all believed in some kind of reform, they differed over the substance and tempo of reform. Progressivism was not a united movement, but a broad and diverse effort for moderate social change within the American tradition. It is best understood as a dynamic general reform movement composed of many specific social movements and shifting coalitions of self-interested groups uniting temporarily over different issues and behind different political leaders. The specific nature of the progressive coalition varied, depending on the issue, the region, and the political leadership. Effective political figures like Theodore Roosevelt and Woodrow Wilson often muted the differences among their followers. They sought to maintain their coalitions by avoiding conflict among their members as much as possible and by promoting conciliation and compromise when disagreements threatened to disrupt the alliance. The fact that so many different people and groups worked so hard for reform in these years gave the era much of its distinctive quality. Progressives established a national reform agenda, helped create widespread support for it, and obtained a significant amount of legislation based on its principles.

Progressives differed from their critics on both the left and the right. Moderate modernizers, they were optimistic about their ability to achieve important, but not radical, change in the social system within a short time. They used collective action, even dramatic governmental intervention, to achieve progress. Yet as reformers, not radicals, they supported only enough change to counteract the ills of what they considered a basically sound, liberal, democratic, capitalist system. "The world moves and we have got to move with it," one progressive editor wrote to a conservative friend in 1912. "So with all that is going on in politics today. . . . It is evolution, and not revolution."

Many conservatives saw such a position as a prelude to disaster. They feared that the progressives were going too far too fast, unduly interfering with liberty and property rights and raising dangerous expectations among the masses. Conservatives considered the social fabric to be a fragile web held together by the stability of institutions and morality under the watchful eye of the judiciary. They warned that the progressives jeopardized the social order. Senator Henry Cabot Lodge protested in 1910 that reformers sought "to bring in laws for everything, for everything that happens, to try and find a remedy by passing a statute, and to overlook the fact that laws are made by men and that laws do not make men."

Radicals devoted themselves to drastic change. Despite the differences among socialists, syndicalists, and anarchists, all radicals considered it impossible to achieve industrial democracy without major deviations from the prevailing capitalist order. Debs, Haywood, Goldman, and scores of other dissenters condemned capitalism and the wage system as inherently exploitative and oppressive.

The largest of the radical groups, the socialists, contained almost as many differences as the progressives. Marxists and non-Marxists, political gradualists and militant extremists, Christian socialists, atheists, and agnostics—all were disillusioned with current institutions. Some came to socialism from the labor movement or from the writings of Edward Bellamy. Many radical tenant farmers of the Midwest and Southwest came to it from populism. To numbers of Jewish Russian and German workers and intellectuals in Chicago, New York, and Milwaukee and to Finnish miners in Minnesota, socialism provided an ethnic bond and an intellectual heritage. Socialists pointed out injustices and proposed alternatives ranging from improved working conditions to public ownership of utilities, transportation, and many basic industries. Their challenges to private property, limited government, and organized religion appealed to several million Americans but frightened many more, including most progressives.

Averse to extreme solutions, progressives nonetheless recognized that solutions of some kind were urgently needed. Like other interventionists, progressives tried to rectify the problems accompanying industrialism and replace drift and indecision with positive, creative direction. But they differed from the others in possessing a unique *progressive ethos,* which combined the nineteenth-century sense of Protestant evangelism with the new methods of science and large-scale organization. Evangelistic modernizers, progressive leaders wedded quasi-religious idealism and scientism in a movement which worked for specific reforms while seeking to restore a sense of community and common purpose to a nation they saw splintering into diverse ethnic and interest groups.

The leaders of progressivism grew up in the late Victorian Era, a period of intense revivalism, evangelism, and affirmation of the cultural and moral values of small-town America: hard work, frugality, self-improvement, decency, and altruism. This moral idealism led younger members of the dominant American elite to try to impose their group's standards on an increasingly diverse society, using new methods learned from science and business. Fired with the passion of moral rectitude, the progressive leaders were also obsessed with efficiency, rationalization, and orderly procedure. "There are two gospels I always want to preach to reformers," Theodore Roosevelt told delegates to a conference on city improvement. "The first is the gospel of morality; the next is the gospel of efficiency. . . . I don't think I have to tell you to be upright, but I do think I have to tell you to be practical and efficient."

But the progressives, like other interventionists, also drew upon science and the corporation. Imbued with faith in predictability and efficiency, they launched a search for systems through which to manage change in an orderly manner. Instead of relying on chance and ad hoc local responses to problems, reformers turned to the methods of medicine and the social sciences. They employed scientific methods of investigation: extensive data gathering, analysis, prognosis, and prescription. Heirs of Darwin, they thought that by manipulating the environment and behavior they could improve the human condition. They gathered extensive statistics to document problems and then sought to alleviate them by educating the public. To produce the desired results, progressives tried to alter attitudes, behavior, and even environmental conditions. In doing so, they were influenced by the model of the large-scale corporation, which showed how thousands of people could be organized and directed efficiently and how the organization's environment could be manipulated. Progressives emulated these organizational and management techniques, particularly specialization, bureaucratization, and expert professional direction. "The trust," Jane Addams explained, "is the educator of us all."

THE PROGRESSIVE AGENDA

As they challenged established policies and officeholders, progressives became key leaders in public and private organizations: political parties, government, the media, and institutions and associations ranging from education to engineering. In these positions they translated the reform spirit into an ideal which could mobilize millions of Americans to participate in campaigns for progress. They helped establish a diffuse agenda for reform which gave some coherence to the myriad efforts for change and provided identifiable dimensions to progressivism in politics. That agenda included four broad categories of issues.

First, the business regulation movement represented an effort to make business more responsible to American values and the public interest. Rejecting the theory of laissez faire and unrestricted individualism, Theodore Roosevelt declared,

> The man who wrongly holds that every human right is secondary to his profit, must now give way to the advocate of human welfare, who rightly maintains that every man holds his property subject to the general right of the community to regulate its use to whatever degree the public welfare may require it.

Although all progressives agreed that there must be some public control of business, they disagreed over the amount of such control, especially with regard to the supercorporations. Some, such as William Jennings Bryan and Wisconsin Senator Robert LaFollette, urged that the supercorporations be broken up into smaller companies to encourage competition and protect the public. They wanted to strengthen the antitrust laws. Others, such as Roosevelt and George Perkins, one of the major financial contributors to the Progressive

party, argued for federal charters and regulations of the giant corporations to sustain them and yet ensure that they operated in the public
interest. "Competition," Perkins declared, "has become too destructive to be tolerated. Cooperation must be the order of the day."

Second, the good-government or direct democracy movement
represented an effort by progressives to capture and reform the
political system. "Give the government back to the people" became a
rallying cry for progressives. They detested the so-called "invisible
government," a system in which nonelected and unaccountable
political party bosses manipulated elected officials and ran city and
state governments. Disdaining legislators as corrupt and captured by
special interests, progressives sought to reduce the power of party
bosses and legislators by increasing the power of middle-class voters
and members of the executive branch of government—mayors,
governors, and the president—as well as nonpartisan experts like city
managers and regulatory commissioners.

Third, the social justice movement sought to aid exploited workers
and the urban poor. The major organizations in this movement were
led by women, who demonstrated their administrative skill and
leadership in efforts to abolish child labor, establish wage and hour
laws for workers and ensure factory safety, alleviate poverty, and
encourage respect for human rights. The women social workers who led
this movement were assisted by Social Gospel clergy and a number of
social scientists. Although they often failed to obtain the backing of
more conservative interventionists, social justice progressives frequently formed a political coalition with labor and foreign-stock urban
dwellers on these issues.

Fourth, the social control movement represented a coercive effort by
old-stock Americans to impose a uniform culture based on their
values. Distressed by increasing cultural and racial diversity, many
progressives joined with large numbers of conservatives to employ
governmental power to impose homogeneous standards of behavior on
the entire population. Directed especially against Catholic and Jewish
immigrants and blacks, the movement took the form of compulsory
education, mandatory Sunday closing of business and entertainment
establishments, prohibition of alcoholic beverages, control of narcotics,
restriction of immigration, and limitation of voting privileges.

Regional differences in progressivism reflected the sectional nature of American society. Reformers in the South often meant demagogic race baiting. Southern progressives rapidly removed blacks from the electorate, using literacy tests and grandfather clauses (which excluded blacks but not poor whites by exempting from property or educational requirements in state suffrage laws those people and their lineal descendants who had the right to vote before 1867, when blacks were enfranchised by the Fifteenth Amendment). Southern whites also employed both rigid new statutes and vigilante terrorism to segregate blacks from white society. The reformers then worked to improve conditions *for whites* in the South through expanded education, prohibition of alcohol, and the establishment of efficient government regulation of railroads and other large corporations.

In both the South and the West, progressives deplored absentee corporate ownership of raw materials and the concentration of economic and political power in the Northeast. After curtailing the rights of Chinese, Japanese, and Hispanic residents, western progressives led in the adoption of direct democracy measures among whites. In the highly urbanized states of the Northeast and North Central regions, progessivism took on an urban cast in its concern for the improvement of the cities. Despite such distinctive variations, progressivism was nationwide in scope, the first general national coalition of reform movements since abolitionism, temperance, women's rights, and a host of other issues fueled the ferment of the Jacksonian Era.

THE DEVELOPMENT OF NATIONWIDE REFORM

In the late nineteenth century two earlier sectional movements— mugwumpism and populism—had heralded the need for reform. The mugwumps, a group of upper-middle-class businessmen and professionals in the Northeast, had bolted from the Republican party in the 1880s over issues of partisanship and corruption. Although critics satirized them as indecisive fence sitters—with their mugs on one side and their wumps on the other—the mugwumps were more generally portrayed as independent civic reformers. Many of the good-government measures of the Progressive Era flowed from the mugwumps' advocacy of nonpartisanship, civil service, and independent voting.

Populism emerged from another side of society, the financially squeezed, discontented dirt farmers of the South and Midwest. By the 1890s it had become a potent agrarian movement attacking high tariffs, deflationary currency, trusts, railroads, and big banks. It merged with the Democrats in William Jennings Bryan's unsuccessful bid for the presidency in 1896. Few Populists became progressives, however. Indeed, most of the leaders of progressivism had been unsympathetic or actively hostile to populism. Nevertheless, agrarians from the South and the West, former Populists as well as non-Populists, later provided an important element in the progressive coalition. They supplied votes and issues such as tariff reduction, business reform, rural credits, and the income tax. As William Allen White put it, the progressives had "caught the Populists in swimming and stole all of their clothing except the frayed underdrawers of free silver."

Narrower movements also paved the way for progressivism. The social justice movement had its antecedents among the settlement house founders, Social Gospel clergy, labor leaders, and socialists of the late nineteenth century. Business regulation had been advocated by agrarians, shippers, some social scientists, and reformer–writers like Bellamy and George. Budding movements against vice, obscenity, alcohol, and immigration, and against political participation by blacks and alien immigrants, laid the foundations for the larger social control movement which would follow. A new urban middle class, produced by the increasingly mass production and service-oriented economy, came to believe that rationality, efficient administration, and manipulation of the environment could be applied to public affairs as well as business.

It took a cataclysmic event like the depression of the 1890s to disrupt society sufficiently so that reformers could begin to forge the separate elements of discontent left from previous decades into the broad-based nationwide movement known as progressivism. Formerly divided along regional, ethnic, or class lines, many disaffected groups were temporarily pulled together by local reformers. Progressive political leaders, especially on the local level, minimized differences among their constituents by stressing their common position as "exploited" consumers. "The people," as the reformers called them, were robbed by "selfish interests" in business and politics. The depression made people conscious of their role as consumers. It helped reformers expose the corporate arrogance by which monopolies like the privately owned gas and electric utilities and streetcar companies maintained or increased rates during the economic downturn without consequent improvements in service. Progressives showed that as local governments raised taxes to meet the higher costs resulting from massive unemployment, wealthy individuals and corporations often dodged taxes through favoritism purchased from governmental officials. Hard times and the exposure of exploitation led many consumers to support radical measures such as progressive taxation, recall of public officials, and public ownership of utilities and streetcar lines. Angered consumers and urban reformers took over some of the utilities and established a form of municipal socialism in more than a hundred cities.

When the depression ended and prosperity began to return in the late 1890s, the reform movement continued. Although many of the temporary consumer alliances split apart, the pressure for reform was sustained among many consumers in middle- and lower-income groups by the new problem of inflation. The period was primarily one of economic growth, and Americans defined themselves less as exploited consumers and more as members of job-oriented groups. The identification of Americans with broad national functional groups—for example, the machinists union, the engineers' association, the national organization of settlement house workers, the National Association of Manufacturers—developed rapidly in the late nineteenth century as urbanization and industrialization uprooted people and replaced small-town loyalties with more segmented economic affiliations.

During the Progressive Era these production-oriented groups, national in scope and organization, continued to increase in number, size, and influence. They lobbied actively to promote their own interests, often identifying these with the public interest. Thus, reform activity, which had begun on the local level to mobilize large numbers of people as consumers during the depression, moved during the subsequent period of economic growth to shifting alliances of organized, producer-oriented interest groups working especially on the state and national levels to protect their own interests. This resulted in the rise of a national political order dominated by an unprecedented variety of producer-oriented pressure groups vying for public protection and favor. Soon Washington was dotted with the headquarters of these groups: the Farmers Union, founded in 1902; the International Brotherhood of Teamsters 1903; the American Federation of Teachers, 1905; the American Institute of Chemical Engineers, 1908; the United States Chamber of Commerce, 1912; and scores of others. But while these job-oriented interest groups helped to give substance to many of the Progressive Era's reforms, they were not responsible for the fervor or the breadth of progressivism.

The spirit of moral indignation and the sense of idealistic purpose came in part from the "muckrakers." Like later investigative journalists, these reporters exposed dishonesty, greed, and corruption throughout American society and helped rouse Americans, especially middle-class readers of the muckraking magazines, to action for reform. The literature of exposure went back to Thomas Nast's cartoons and the press assault on the Tweed Ring in New York in the 1870s and Henry Demarest Lloyd's attack on Standard Oil in the 1890s. But in the first decade of the twentieth century exposure journalism reached an unprecedented scale. In city after city the muckrakers demonstrated the corrupt interrelationships of business and political machines. They showed the American public that business corrupted politics, not merely in a few cities but throughout the nation.

The muckrakers alerted citizens to the national scope of political corruption. Beginning in 1902 with a series in *McClure's Magazine,* Lincoln Steffens documented municipal corruption linked to business interests in St Louis, Minneapolis, and a dozen other cities. His findings were republished as *Shame of the Cities* in 1904. In addition to municipal graft, reporters discovered gouging by oil companies and the railroads, poison dispensed by patent medicine companies, and fraud in high finance. Muckraker Ray Stannard Baker mused forty years later:

I think I can understand now why these exposure articles took such a hold upon the American people. It was because the country, for years, had been swept by the agitation of soap-box orators, prophets crying in the wilderness, and political campaigns based upon charges of corruption and privilege which everyone believed or suspected had some basis of truth, but which were largely unsubstantiated.

The muckrakers provided the facts to substantiate these accusations. However, by 1906, when the exposure movement reached its peak, some reporters were ignoring the need for careful documentation.

Increasing stress on sensationalism weakened the muckrakers' reputation. Conservatives and even many progressives condemned them, and in 1906 President Roosevelt denounced the more sensationalistic journalists by comparing them with the man in Bunyan's *Pilgrim's Progress* who was so busy raking the filth from the floor that he neglected the beauty of the world. By 1912 the muckraking era had passed, terminated by hostile business, which withheld credit and advertising, and by public fatigue. Yet investigative journalism had done much to sustain and direct the reform impulse and, by demonstrating the national scope of corruption between business and politics, had helped create the spirit of indignation necessary for a broad reform movement in favor of honesty, democracy, and accountability in American institutions.

VOLUNTARISM AS A MIDDLE WAY

Progressives and conservatives did not always turn directly to government to adjust institutions or gain control over the powerful forces of industrialism. Concerned with establishing the antecedents of the liberal activist state, many historians have oversimplified progressives' positions regarding the expansion of governmental power. Subsequent political figures like Franklin D. Roosevelt, seeking to legitimize the New Deal through historical continuity, also contributed to the conception of progressivism as a major step toward the welfare state. But the traditional focus on the progressives' proposals to expand the powers of government to deal with new problems, while partially warranted, distorts the greater complexity of the progressives. They generally acted first through private associations and saw voluntary cooperative effort as an essential part of the progressive impulse. This area is generally ignored by historians, who concentrate on advocates of governmental intervention like Roosevelt and Herbert Croly.

Traditional interpretations often neglect progressives like Jane Addams and Oswald Garrison Villard, who remained deeply suspicious of giving too much power to the government. Indeed, many progressives continued to fear that business would corrupt politics and bureaucracy as well, and that big government under the control of big business would be a threat to American democracy. Large numbers of progressives, and other interventionists, believed primarily in collective action in the private sector as a means of directing change. "Our national idea is not a powerful state, famed and feared for bluster and appetite," the muckraker David Graham Phillips asserted in 1905, "but manhood and womanhood, a citizenship ever wiser and stronger and more civilized—alert, enlightened, self-reliant, free."

Voluntarism offered a device which could mediate between social demands and the American traditions of individual autonomy, privatism, and cooperative groups. Progressives sought to use voluntary associations as effective instruments of reform. To do that, they patterned their organizations to some degree after the corporation, with boards of directors, expert administrators, hierarchical chains of command, and multiple branches and field offices. Through carefully defined goals, precise rules and regulations, and adequate coordination, such organizations could function effectively on a national scale. Progressives believed that through intelligence, will, and proper organization and techniques they could manipulate society and the environment for the betterment of all.

The settlement house movement typified that optimistic belief. "Life in the Settlement discovers above all what has been called 'the extraordinary pliability of human nature,'" said Jane Addams, the founder of Hull House in Chicago, "and it seems impossible to set any bounds to the moral capabilities which might unfold under ideal civic and educational conditions." At Hull House and at other settlements in Boston, New York, and elsewhere, reformers established private, voluntary institutions to give advice, education, and care to the immigrant poor in the ghettos. The profession of social work, an outgrowth of the settlement house movement, departed from the nineteenth-century reform emphasis on saving individuals. It focused instead on changing the environment, which was seen as responsible for the plight of both the individual and the family.

The women's consumer movement also demonstrated the role of cooperative action in the private sector to ameliorate conditions. The National Consumers' League, organized in 1899, grew out of an effort by upper- and middle-class New York City women and a number of clergymen to improve the working conditions of saleswomen in the city's department stores and of the women who toiled in the garment factories and sweatshops. The league, which within a decade had twenty-five chapters in nearly a dozen states, attempted to organize the power of women as consumers to improve working conditions for women and children. According to Florence Kelley, the head of the league, organized consumerism—through selective purchasing and, when necessary, boycotts—could protect both the workers and the consumers from exploitation. Increasingly, however, it was the mass production companies and advertising agencies that manipulated consumer tastes and habits. The National Consumers' League turned to programs of education and lobbying to ensure passage and enforcement of legislation regulating the wages, hours, and working conditions of women and children, a significant part of the social justice movement.

Like settlement house workers, many physicians encouraged efforts to improve the environment and the standard of living. Together with social workers they played leading roles in a number of reform movements. They participated prominently in the campaign against tuberculosis, the "white plague," which was a major killer, especially in tenement districts. The antituberculosis campaign offers a specific model of the organized reform movements of the Progressive Era. When medical researchers identified the tuberculosis bacillus and learned that, though communicable, it was not hereditary (as people had believed for years), reformers set out to educate the public in the proper treatment of the disease and to establish sanitary measures to combat its spread. To do so, they had to overcome a tradition which considered tuberculosis, like venereal disease, a forbidden subject. Through local and state antituberculosis societies and, after 1904, the National Tuberculosis Association, the reformers educated other physicians and the public in the new findings, helped discourage public acceptance of spitting (spittoons began to disappear), began registering cases of TB, and increased the number of public sanitariums. Within fifteen years the mortality rate from tuberculosis had dropped 30 percent as a result of both the antituberculosis crusade and a higher standard of living. The movement's success, like that of many other reform movements, encouraged progressives to believe they could manipulate society and the environment in beneficial ways and curtail many of the hazards of urban industrial society.

During the Progressive Era the general concern with public issues led many professionals—physicians, lawyers, professors, and others—to examine the operation and organization of their professions in an attempt to gauge their responsiveness both to society's interests and to their own needs for standards and authority. For example, by the turn of the century the emergence of the new corporate law firms had transformed the legal profession. Small-town and country lawyers still constituted the majority of the practitioners of law, with the new immigrant solo practitioners at the bottom level in terms of income and prestige. Desiring cohesion and control within such a divided profession, prominent lawyers established bar associations in every state and major city and sought to standardize training and licensing requirements. To provide at least some legal services to the urban poor, attorneys and other reformers founded more than forty legal aid societies in the first two decades of the century.

Another important effort to defend the profession against charges that it was dominated by the corporate interests came from the professors at the law schools which were replacing the old system of "reading law" in the offices of practicing attorneys. Legal scholars like Roscoe Pound, Felix Frankfurter, and Thomas Reed Powell portrayed themselves as keepers of the professional conscience and neutral social scientists who could evaluate data and produce legal solutions to social problems. In their sociological jurisprudence (which stressed social context and not just legal precedent), the law could be used as an instrument of social engineering and progressive reform in the public interest.

Engineers also transformed their conservative group of professional associations during the Progressive Era. Traditionally, the societies for civil, mechanical, electrical, and mining engineers had served as gentlemen's clubs for elite engineer–entrepreneurs like the Roeblings, who built the Brooklyn Bridge. They ignored the large numbers of engineer-technicians and showed virtually no interest in public policy. Consequently, progressives charged them with shirking their social responsibilities, noting especially their failure to do anything about the problem of air pollution in the cities, which had become even more serious after the massive switch to soft coal following the anthracite strike of 1902. Under pressure, the engineering societies abandoned their traditional laissez-faire attitude and began to establish codes and standards for boilers, electrical generators, and other devices. "The golden rule will be put in practice through the slide rule," the president of the American Society of Mechanical Engineers optimistically predicted in 1912.

Converting from elite clubs to mass membership bodies, the engineering societies democratized their organizations. By the end of the Progressive Era they included a majority of the engineers in America. By linking citizens living in different areas through their common occupational roles, the engineering societies, although still led by elites, took on new roles as modern functional associations.

Conservatives as well as progressives established professionally directed organizations in the private sector to help guide change in appropriate directions. Andrew Carnegie and John D. Rockefeller, for example, created giant philanthropic foundations to work for the improvement of humankind. In the process they transformed the nature of philanthropy and produced a truly unique American contribution to modern social organization—the modern giant philanthropic foundation, a large, autonomous organization formed to use private wealth for public purposes. Andrew Carnegie, whose concept of the stewardship of wealth led him to consider it a disgrace to die wealthy, gave more than $330 million to funds for education, peace, pensions, libraries, and heroism. The largest, the Carnegie

Corporation of New York, was established in 1911 with a grant of $135 million. Two years later John D. Rockefeller created the Rockefeller Foundation with a grant of $242 million "to promote the well-being of mankind throughout the world." Rockefeller's philanthropies, which totaled nearly $500 million, encouraged medical research, education, and a major program to combat hookworm, malaria, pellagra, tuberculosis, and other diseases in the rural South. As the United States lagged behind Europe in accepting the idea of a welfare state, philanthropists consciously created alternative private mechanisms for social improvement to help deter the governmental planning of the socialistic state they feared. In so doing, they created the largest foundations the world had ever seen.

In the field of labor relations, conservative interventionists also established a private-sector mechanism for encouraging cooperation among contending groups. The National Civic Federation (NCF), organized in 1900, included representatives of the new supercorporations, labor leaders like Samuel Gompers, and public representatives such as ex-president Grover Cleveland. Opposed to both laissez faire and governmental ownership and control, the NCF advocated a number of moderate social reforms, such as workmen's compensation. It played an important role in educating many businesspeople, professionals, labor leaders, journalists, and officials to the need for cooperation instead of conflict between management and labor.

The National Civic Federation was only one of many private voluntary associations through which interventionists—progressive and conservative—sought to reorient society, educate the public to new attitudes and modes of behavior, and provide mechanisms for managing relations in a new enlightened manner. It was part of the organizational revolution of the time, and was spurred by the belief in the ability of people to apply scientific knowledge to improve their environment and their lives. The list of organizations of this type founded in the Progressive Era includes chambers of commerce, community chests, the Boy Scouts of America, and the Institute for Government Research (now the Brookings Institution), a private association set up to promote efficiency and economy in government, as well as the Women's International League for Peace and Freedom, the American Civil Liberties Union, and hundreds of other groups. In this manner interventionists employed cooperative effort to guide the direction of change and progress in industrial America.

URBAN REFORM

Despite the efforts of progressives in the private sector, it was in the political arena that progressivism emerged as a most clearly identifiable movement. There, progressive reformers led a significant attempt to oust incumbent politicians and restructure the political system to make it more efficient and capable of managing the conflicting needs of various groups while upholding the ideal of a single public interest for the entire community. This difficult task began in the cities.

The depression of the 1890s struck the cities especially severely. Local revenues plummeted, and many urban social services failed to meet the needs of millions of jobless residents. Many reformers blamed the urban crisis on corrupt, inefficient boss government. Swayed by nativist agrarian prejudices, many Americans were quick to view the urban situation in terms of good and evil. "Sometimes, I think they'se poison in th' life in a big city," the political satirist Peter Finley Dunne had Mr. Dooley say. "The flowers won't grow there. . . ."

Critics often ignored the difficulties of controlling urban growth and minimized the informal social services provided by the political machines. Instead, they emphasized the "corruptible vote of the city," the millions of immigrants, many of whom were recent arrivals permitted to vote under alien suffrage laws which gave immigrant men the right to vote as soon as they officially declared their intention of becoming American citizens. Reformers considered new-stock residents ignorant of American ways and easily misled by demagogic bosses. "Saloons and gambling houses and brothels," one Baltimore reformer charged, "are the nurseries of [urban] statesmen."

In the depression of the 1890s progressives brought together the separate elements of discontent from previous decades into a nationwide urban reform movement. Hard times led many people who had formerly been separated by class or ethnic differences to unite behind particular political leaders because of their common interests as "exploited" consumers. In addition, numerous citizens' and taxpayers' associations demanded tax reduction through honest and efficient government. Reformers, often uniting upper- and middle-income old-stock residents from the suburban wards with urban immigrant voters, led this protest beyond mere tax cutting or economizing into a broader movement for both structural reform and policy changes in the nation's cities. The first step was to win control of City Hall. This was done by exposing municipal corruption, personal graft, protection peddling, contract padding, and collusion between city officials and utilities, streetcar companies, and other firms doing business with the city. Progressive mayors won office in New York, Chicago, Baltimore, and other cities and began reform programs.

While they controlled City Hall, progressive reformers sought to end forever the potential for "machine politics" by restructuring municipal government. The structural reforms of the good-government movement drew upon many of the administrative techniques used by business corporations, as suggested by the National Municipal League's model program, developed in 1894. Although they emphasized efficiency, honesty, and democracy, reformers often sought to take control of city government away from the alliance of companies doing business with the city and the representatives of lower-income immigrant groups who controlled the political machines. To lodge power in their own hands, reformers revised city charters to end the decentralized system in which each ward elected representatives to the city council. Reformers replaced this system with a "strong mayor," city councils, and boards of education elected by the city as a whole. Urban reformers also expanded the use of appointed administrators and career civil servants in City Hall and helped bring modern methods of accounting and management to city government.

On a hot summer night in 1900, a giant tidal wave created by a hurricane in the Gulf of Mexico smashed down on the port city of Galveston, Texas. The flood waters killed one out of every six people in the city. When the municipal government proved unable to respond to the disaster, leading citizens replaced it with a special commission in which each commissioner headed a particular city department. So effective was the city commission plan of government that Galveston's ad hoc response to crisis was adopted in Houston, Des Moines, and a number of other cities. It was soon refined by the city manager plan, in which a single trained administrator, appointed by the city council, exercised all administrative authority. First adopted in Staunton, Virginia, in 1908, the city manager plan gained acceptance after Dayton, Ohio, adopted it in 1914. The idea of centralized planning by a unified board and efficient administration by a chief executive officer came directly from the corporate model. Indeed, the president of the National Cash Register Company, who helped establish the city manager system in Dayton, described the ideal city as "a great business enterprise whose stockholders are the people." Hundreds of small and medium-sized cities, especially in the South and Midwest, adopted the new forms of city government during the Progressive Era.

It took more than efficiency to meet urban problems. "The challenge of the city," Cleveland reformer Frederic C. Howe explained in 1906, "has become one of decent human existence." Some reform mayors, such as Hazen Pingree of Detroit and Samuel "Golden Rule" Jones in Toledo, tried to go beyond good government and structural reform to broad social programs which they hoped would retain the allegiance of the majority of urban voters, especially the working classes. Speaking for "the people" as consumers, they battled "the interests," particularly the privately owned utilities and transit companies, seeking reduced rates and improved services. They supported the construction of public parks, playgrounds, schools, and municipal hospitals to provide a better standard of living. They tried to provide some work relief during the depression. Pressed by angry taxpayers, they tried to redistribute the tax burden more equitably by reducing tax evasion. Bowing to indignant consumers, mayors and councils in more than a hundred cities established municipally owned gas and water companies and in some cities public electric companies and city-owned transit companies as well.

Thousands of people joined in crusades for urban reform during the Progressive Era; yet for all their effort they left a divided legacy. Reformers won elections and produced new forms of city government which consolidated upper- and middle-class rule. But although they captured City Hall, they failed to reduce taxes, which increased at unprecedented rates during the period. Rising municipal costs resulted less from inefficiency and waste than from inflation and the long-term trend of expanding urban services. Indeed, the municipally owned utilities slowed cost-of-living increases by keeping their rates lower than those of private utilities. They were one of the reformers' most lasting and most radical legacies, surviving various changes in government. Especially in the metropolises, the old bosses maintained or quickly regained power. For virtually a generation Charles Croker and Charles Murphy of Tammany Hall ran New York City's government. The Republican William Vare dominated Philadelphia. William Crump's Democratic machine presided over Memphis, and the Democratic Pendergast brothers ruled Kansas City.

Although they helped make the cities cleaner and healthier, on the whole the reformers proved more successful at arousing indignation and protest than at maintaining effective government and substantially ameliorating urban problems. Many of the difficulties of the cities persisted, but the progressives and others had established an agenda of municipal reform—more efficient government, nonpartisan social services, zoning, planning, public ownership of some essential services, and improved standards of health and housing—which would influence urban politics for the next half-century.

PROGRESSIVISM IN THE STATES

"Whenever we try to do anything, we run up against the charter," the reform mayor of Schenectady complained. "It is an oak charter, fixed and immovable." Since the charters which spelled out the cities' powers were granted by the states, reformers soon discovered that they needed to capture the state governments to achieve their goals. Furthermore, the states set the requirments for suffrage, regulated business and labor conditions, and legislated to enforce morality. When they looked into the State House, reformers found as much corruption and intransigence as they had found in City Hall. Muckrakers and progressive politicians exposed alliances between powerful business interests—expecially the railroads—and state party bosses, who represented the big-city political machines or rural county courthouse rings and actually ran the state governments.

Reform

Attacking collusion among the political bosses and "the special interests," progressive reformers overwhelmed many state machines in the first decade of the century and captured dozens of governorships. Robert La Follette, a small-town lawyer and former congressman, led the movement in Wisconsin. During his three terms as governor, "Battling Bob" modernized the state government through what came to be known as the "Wisconsin idea." This state reform program included direct party primaries, an improved civil service, a graduated state income tax, a corrupt-practices act prohibiting direct corporate contributions to political parties, labor legislation, and a strengthened railroad regulatory commission. Other Republican reformers in the Midwest, such as Albert Cummins of Iowa, copied La Follette's program.

In the South the revolt occurred within the Democratic party. Progressives like James Vardaman of Mississippi and Hoke Smith of Georgia led white farmers against alliances of wealthy, conservative Democrats (who were called Bourbons), the railroads, timber companies, and other large corporations. Before adopting much of the "Wisconsin idea," southern progressives disfranchised black voters, who they claimed were a source of Bourbon Democratic support. Using literacy tests, grandfather clauses, and sometimes terrorism, they purged blacks from the rolls. In Louisiana, for example, the number of registered black voters dropped from 130,000 in 1896 to 1,000 in 1904. Once in power, the insurgents adopted many of La Follette's programs. In addition, prohibition of alcohol was a strong component of southern progressivism, with its emphasis on rural Protestant morality and its antipathy toward the multiethnic, economically powerful urban Northeast.

The movement for progressivism in the states came late to the Northeast and Far West. In the East, it was largely a continuation of the urban reform movement, but many of La Follette's measures were also adopted. After exposing abuses in the life insurance field, the attorney Charles Evans Hughes became the progressive Republican governor of New York in 1906. He established stricter supervision of insurance companies and instituted a state public service commission to regulate utilities. Woodrow Wilson, president of Princeton University, won the governorship of New Jersey on the Democratic ticket in 1910 and began a program of progressive reforms similar to the "Wisconsin idea." On the West Coast, attorney Hiram Johnson campaigned against the dominant position of the Southern Pacific Railroad and entered the governor's mansion in 1911 with a slate of reforms. Oregon, which had adopted the first maximum-hour law for women workers, elected the insurgent Republican William U'Ren to the governorship; he introduced a number of reform bills. Not since the burst of activity which had occurred in the 1830s had so many state governments been so strongly committed to reform.

Once in control of state governments, progressives in every region began far-reaching reforms by changing both electoral procedures and the scope of the electorate. Progressives wanted to create a political process which would break up the coalition between government and business and would make government responsive to the people and the new pressure groups. Progressives and others believed the problem was that the party system was hierarchical, dominated by bosses at the top. Many of the progressive political reforms were based on the idea that ways must be found to remove the bosses or limit their power. Through direct primaries the progressives took the nominating procedure away from party bosses, who had controlled it through their grip on local nominating conventions. They also sought to reduce the voting base of the machines. In the South, this meant disfranchising blacks. In the North, it meant eliminating alien voters through increased residency requirements, thereby restricting suffrage to native-born or fully naturalized citizens. Except in the South, which resisted vehemently in part because it might lead to enfranchisement of blacks, progressivism came to mean expanding the vote by including women, whose ballots were expected to aid the reform movement.

Having "purged" the electorate, progressives enacted a number of "direct democracy" measures designed to increase the power of the remaining voters by allowing them to override legislators. By means of petitions voters could introduce legislation through the initiative, repeal legislation through the referendum, and call for a vote to remove elected officials through the recall process. Progressives also expanded home rule for the cities and, in state governments, helped centralize administrative responsibility and modernize the budgetary process. Many of the progressive governors moved to the U.S. Senate near the end of the first decade of the century. But before they left for Washington, they helped reform groups pass significant social and economic legislation in their states.

As a means of curtailing favoritism toward special interests and mediating conflicts among competing interest groups, most progressives and many conservative interventionists put their faith in the independent regulatory commission. Like the city managers, the commissioners were supposed to remove politics and "special deals" from administration and use the power of government to ensure that the economic system worked in the public interest. The regulatory commission was seen as a moderate alternative to both an unrestricted marketplace and government ownership and operation. Unfortunately, however, progressive legislators provided little guidance for the regulatory commissions on how to determine the public interest.

Not surprisingly, the legacy of the state regulatory commissions was ambiguous. For example, the railroad commission found itself confronted by the contending interests of carriers and shippers, rather than that of the public. The commissioners tried to derive compromises that were satisfactory to the major parties, that is, the railroads and the shippers. Many citizens, who had hoped that the railroad and other commissions would find that rates were generally inflated and would sharply reduce transportation costs and consumer prices, were disappointed. They claimed, with much justification, that the commissions had become responsive to the interests of the industries they were supposed to regulate.

The Wisconsin Railroad Commission demonstrated the complexity of the situation. Created in 1905 as part of La Follette's campaign against "the interests," the commission failed to find the widespread injustices which the reformers claimed existed. By 1910, having dropped all pretense of battling the railroads, which originally opposed its creation, the commission sought instead what it called fair or "scientific" rates, a moderate program of piecemeal rate adjustment based on compromise. The regulatory commission worked primarily to reduce open conflict and remove the issue of railroad rates from popular politics. Two months before the first commissioners took office, the editor of the *Wisconsin State Journal* predicted such a result:

> The commission once in operation, its chief value will be in abating discontent. It is doubtful if the rank and file of us will know, by any marked reduction in prices of commodities, that anything has happened. But the distrust and suspicion born of secrecy and unqualified power will be relieved, for there is appeal to the commission.

As the editor prophesied, the state regulatory commissions proved a victory more for orderly management and adjustment to the new industrial system than for consumer interests, becoming one of the new mechanisms for managing change in twentieth-century society.

Under pressure from various private interventionist groups and from progressive governors and legislators, many states also adopted measures to reduce the harshness of industrial work. Workmen's compensation was the most widespread of these reforms. Both workers and employers argued against the common-law assumption that employees willingly took on the risks of work and could collect compensation for accidents only if they could prove the employer negligent. Because of this assumption, most victims had received nothing while a few particularly grisly cases had won extremely high settlements. Maryland adopted the first workmen's compensation law in the United States in 1902, and by 1916 most other states had adopted employer liability and workmen's compensation laws. Workmen's compensation, with its predictable but limited awards, conformed to the desire of conservative and most progressive interventionists for systematic and moderate solutions to social problems.

Social justice progressives and their organizations were less successful at obtaining and enforcing other legislation to assist industrial workers. The National Consumers' League led the drive for maximum-hour and minimum-wage legislation modeled on that of Australia and New Zealand. American judges proved willing to uphold such laws only as relating to women workers. They were impressed by arguments made by the League's attorney, Louis D.

Brandeis, in *Muller* v. *Oregon* (1908) that long hours were dangerous to women's health and morality and, thus, to the future of society. Nearly two-thirds of the states adopted maximum-hour laws, and a dozen states enacted minimum-wage protection for women. In a more difficult battle the National Child Labor Committee obtained laws in most northern and western states prohibiting the employment of children under 14, but it failed to convince the legislators of southern states. On the whole, state labor legislation, although it was an improvement over the past, left much of the progressive agenda unfulfilled. Even where progressives and their allies succeeded in obtaining satisfactory legislation, they often failed to secure provisions or appropriations for adequate enforcement.

Social Control

Under pressure from a variety of citizens' groups, the states also increased their powers of social control during the Progressive Era. Rising rates of violent crime, combined with the period's belief in human malleability, led to a number of changes in the criminal justice and penal systems beginning in the 1890s. Reformers attempted to make these systems more effective and humane.

Many states converted from hanging to electrocution in the belief that the new technology of the "electric chair" would reduce the number of mishandled and prolonged executions and that the specter of death by electric shock would deter potential criminals from committing capital crimes. For criminals who were convicted but not sent to prison, the suspended sentence was generally replaced by supervised probation. In addition, legislatures authorized judges to hand down indeterminate sentences, the ultimate decision on a convict's release being relegated to newly formed parole boards acting on the basis of their view of the convict's rehabilitation. Extensive systems of probation and parole bureaucracies were established to monitor the behavior of convicted criminals so as to ensure their readjustment to society.

In addition, through the work of judges like Benjamin Lindsey of Denver and Julian Mack of Chicago, a new system of juvenile courts was set up to deal with youthful offenders on the basis of circumstances and promise as well as guilt and innocence. A recent study of the origins of the juvenile court and the industrial school for delinquent boys in Pittsburgh showed that, despite their creators' desire to encourage moral reform and internalization of American middle-class values among the convicted youths, the managers of the "reform school" emphasized control rather than reformation. By the end of the first decade of the century, the institution had become primarily custodial and punitive in nature. To a great extent, the form of the criminal justice system for both juveniles and adults in the twentieth century is a product of the Progressive Era.

One of the most widespread state attempts to control behavior and instill uniform social standards was the prohibition of the manufacture and sale of alcoholic beverages. Many progressive and conservative interventionists joined in this crusade to improve social conditions by dictating moral standards. In many ways prohibition was a cultural issue, for the saloons and the drinking habits of many urban immigrants appeared alien to nativist, evangelistic Protestant Americans, who were concerned with the transformation of America which was already under way. Sentiment for prohibition was strongest among evangelical Protestants in the rural areas of the country, especially the South and West. It seems to have reflected in part these agrarians' antipathy to the growing dominance of the city. However, many within the urban middle class also reacted to the changing nature of the city by supporting prohibition.

The issue of the "wets" versus the "drys" split the progressives. Many supported prohibition, but many others, especially those who identified with urban-labor-immigrant elements, fought against it. The eastern-dominated Progressive party convention of 1912 opposed prohibition. So did labor, immigrants, Catholics, and many Episcopalians, Lutherans, and other Protestants.

The Anti-Saloon League, founded in 1893, mobilized the forces of evangelical Protestantism to promote abstinence and sobriety as public ideals and made prohibition a national issue. The league isolated itself from the broad social reform programs of the more established Women's Christian Temperance Union and the third-party tactics of the old Prohibition party. Instead, it focused on the eradication of the working-class saloon and used the new pressure-group politics on the two major parties. The campaign worked. Between 1906 and 1917, twenty-one states, mostly in the South and West, passed prohibition laws. In 1913, the league obtained from Congress the Webb-Kenyon Act, which banned the transportation of intoxicating beverages into "dry" states. This was the movement's first major national legislative victory.

Prohibitionists pointed to the increase in the per capita consumption of alcohol, which had risen from 2 gallons per person in 1900 to 2.6 gallons by 1911, as a sign of the increasing danger to American society. They argued that the liquor interests demoralized and corrupted American politics and that alcoholism impeded workers, ruined increasing numbers of families, and filled taxpayer-supported poorhouses and prisons with its victims. When the United States entered World War I, the Anti-Saloon League associated prohibition with winning the war, and in 1917 Congress sent to the states the Eighteenth Amendment which prohibited the "manufacture, sale, or transportation" of intoxicating liquors for beverage purposes. By the time the Eighteenth Amendment was ratified in 1919, more than half the American population already lived in areas which had proclaimed themselves "dry" with the approval of their state legislatures. Prohibition was indeed one of the legacies of the Progressive Era.

Because narcotics addiction was not regarded as so great a threat to society as alcoholism, the movement for narcotics control was not as widespread as that for prohibition. Nevertheless, the narcotics control movement emerged in its modern form during the Progressive Era. The use of narcotics—primarily opium, morphine, and cocaine— increased steadily during the nineteenth century. By the turn of the century the United States had a comparatively large addict population of approximately 250,000 persons. Diluted quantities of opium were widely prescribed by physicians and were included in patent medicines like "Mrs. Winslow's Soothing Syrup" as analgesics for crying babies and others suffering from gastrointestinal illnesses. Cocaine was popular for treated sinusitis and hay fever, and as a general tonic. Coca-Cola contained small doses until 1903. Only gradually did the medical profession agree that narcotics were too readily prescribed by physicians, that the inclusion of narcotics in patent medicines should be curtailed, and that addiction was a substantial and harmful possibility.

States began to enact narcotics legislation in the 1890s and continued to do so into the early twentieth century, but by the Progressive Era the major effort to curtail narcotics use had moved to the national level as a result of the interplay of both domestic and foreign forces. Progressive reformers exposed the dangers of improperly labeled patent medicines, many of which contained narcotics. As a result of lobbying by the General Federation of Women's Clubs, the American Medical Association, and the federal government's chief chemist, Dr. Harvey Wiley, the Pure Food and Drug Act, passed in 1906, banned mislabeled or adulterated drugs.

Other Americans became more concerned with the narcotics addicts, especially when addiction was identified with groups which were already feared and repressed. Opium smoking was associated with the Chinese on the West Coast and the use of cocaine with blacks in the South. Southern newspapers printed widespread but unsubstantiated rumors of "cocainomania" among blacks. Many white southerners feared that the euphoric properties of cocaine might stimulate a black rebellion against white society. Thus, during the first decade of the century a significant body of opinion grew to support federal action to control the use of narcotics. This movement coincided with efforts to back the Chinese government's attempts at international narcotics control, and in 1909 the United States prohibited the importation of smoking-opium. Influenced also by reformers in the American Medical Association and the American Pharmaceutical Association, Congress adopted the Harrison Narcotics Control Act of 1914, which prohibited the dispensing and taking of narcotics for other than medicinal purposes. The belief that drug use threatened to disrupt American society led authorities to dismiss suggestions for wider toleration.

THE PROGRESSIVE IMPULSE

Even before it dominated politics on the national level, progressivism emerged as the most pervasive political reform effort since the pre–Civil War period. Combining the efforts of various disaffected groups in the depression of the 1890s, it soon became a widespread movement for the reorganization and improvement of American life.

As part of the "new interventionism" private groups intruded into the marketplace or sought governmental intervention for their own benefit and presumably for society's as well. Outside of progressivism, corporate reorganizers, trade unions, and feminist groups sought to direct the marketplace. Radical interventionists wanted to expand government ownership and control of industry. Conservative interventionists, while balking at such a threat to private property, were often willing to have the government control labor or immigration or maintain dominant cultural standards through prohibition of alcohol, Sabbatarianism, or other forms of "Americanization." Different groups used interventionism in different ways. But all of them reflected the widespread disillusionment with unrestricted individualism and an unregulated marketplace. These interventionists included many of the various groups which historians have identified as progressives—the anxious old middle class and gentry, the confident new professionals, the business and academic elites, the corporate managers and financiers, and the ethnic and working-class leaders. However, the members of each of these groups supported only part of the progressive reform agenda. Progressivism was a series of shifting coalitions of various interventionist groups coming together behind particular issues and political candidates.

Despite the diversity of its component groups, progressivism had qualities which made it distinct from other movements. Progressives combined religious fervor with an optimistic belief in the methods of science and organization. This made them particularly evangelistic modernizers. The combination of moralism and pragmatism also produced the progressive ethos, which characterized the leadership of the most readily identifiable progressives.

The progressive leaders who headed reform groups in various parts of the country in social work, philanthropy, medicine, public health, and other areas had good informal communication ties with one another. Although the specific reform movements were often backed by different sets of supporters, their leaders tended to use the same kinds of educational and political tactics and similar justifications on idealistic, practical, and social grounds.

In politics, progressive leaders throughout the country, like their opponents, came primarily from upper-middle- or upper-class families. On the average, the progressive political leaders were substantially younger than the conservatives and other party regulars. In many ways progressivism represented a movement led by younger members of the American elite, whose sense of power to change the world was different from much of the pessimism or belief in automatic progress which characterized the last third of the nineteenth century.

Like many conservatives, progessives wanted to rid the country of the notion that there were different social classes. The hero of one of Harold Frederic's novels hoped that "the abominable word 'class' could be wiped out of the English language as it is spoken in America." Progressives insisted that there must be an organic community with common interests and values, with a single public interest. "We have come to the time," Harry Garfield, the president of Williams College, said in January 1917, shortly before joining the Wilson administration, "when the old individualistic principle of competition must be set aside and we must boldly embark upon the new principle of cooperation and combination." The progressives' refusal to accept the concept of conflicting and competing groups and classes was ironic, since they helped construct some of the most effective pressure groups. In their search for a larger public interest, progressives inadvertently contributed to the growth of the interest-group democracy they bemoaned.

Their belief in private initiative led many progressive as well as many conservative interventionists to develop voluntary assocations as alternatives to continued expansion of government power. The heritage from the Progressive Era includes scores of voluntary associations for civic improvement, social betterment, and economic advancement, many of which continue to play an important role in American society.

Despite their emphasis on private initiative and associationalism, progressives and other interventionists expanded the functions of government and laid the groundwork for the regulatory and administrative state. Progressives recognized the need for expanded governmental power in a nation of corporate and other private power centers. But they sought only enough state power to establish the public interest as a vital counterweight to more parochial private interests. They did not want to end the community's primary reliance on private, voluntary action and initiative. In government, progressives relied not on legislators but on strong executive leaders and expert nonpartisan administrators, authorities who could help the community avoid the pitfalls of lethargy and parochial selfishness. Progressives believed in leadership as an antidote to the tyranny of change.

For all their talk of "the people" and popular democracy, most progressive leaders, like many conservatives, believed that leadership was the province of an educated elite. Such a view clashed with the concepts of democracy and the distrust of experts and bureaucrats widely held by Americans, including many Jeffersonian agrarians and members of organized labor. In trying to balance the American ideal of democracy with their own belief in elite expertise, progressives suggested that the role of the people was to elect good leaders, but that the leaders and their subordinates should then find and follow the general public interest unfettered by direct influence from the masses. "Our aim must be to give [wider] scope to the wise administrator," admonished the economist Richard Ely.

The progressives' faith in leadership for the entire community, their search for a general public interest, and their challenge to established power holders ultimately led them to Washington. In the nation's capital a new era began with a boisterous young politician who came to symbolize progressivism for millions of Americans. His name was Theodore Roosevelt.

CHAPTER 5

The Washington Whirligig

THE DEATH OF A PRESIDENT

In September 1901, President William McKinley took a few days' respite from his official duties in Washington to attend a public reception at the Pan-American Exposition in Buffalo, New York. Unaware of impending danger, the president shook hands in a receiving line. Moving toward him was a man with a bandaged hand. The white wrappings concealed a tiny pistol. As the president extended his hand in mechanical greeting, the assassin thrust his arm forward and pulled the trigger, firing two shots into McKinley's chest. The president staggered and slumped to the floor. McKinley's murderer was a 28-year-old unemployed laborer and anarchist from the slums of Pittsburgh and Cleveland. Embittered and alienated, Leon Czolgosz sometimes used the alias Fred Nieman—Fred Nobody. He had acted alone, but he had shot the president, he said, on behalf of the poor, the forgotten, and the exploited. "I didn't believe one man should have so much service, and another man should have none." McKinley died after lingering for eight days. Following a two-day trial Czolgosz was sentenced to death. He was executed in the electric chair a month later.

In an era in which the forces of radicalism and reform gained strength throughout the country, the national government was led not by the lackluster McKinley but by one of the most colorful, dynamic political personalities of the century: Theodore Roosevelt. A former governor of New York, the aggressive young politician had felt stifled as vice-president. Now he responded candidly to McKinley's death: "It is a dreadful thing to come into the presidency this way; but it would be a far worse thing to be morbid about it." The youngest man to become president of the United States (he was 42),* Roosevelt set actively to work. Neither the Executive Mansion, which he officially renamed the White House, nor the country would ever be the same again.

THEODORE ROOSEVELT: THE MAN AND THE SYMBOL

For millions of Americans, Theodore Roosevelt has symbolized the Progressive Era. Personifying the vigorous, assertive leadership acclaimed by progressives, Roosevelt appeared a strong-minded hero to a generation of Americans. TR, as the press called him, acted the part well. He was constantly in motion, his face and gestures continually animated. When he spoke, his toothy grin, framed by his bushy mustache, stretched nearly into a grimace. He flailed about when driving home his points. Fists clenched, arms pumping up and down, he resembled a human windmill. "The President," journalist Ray Stannard Baker concluded, "ran full-speed on all the tracks at once."

Evangelist and Activist

As evangelistic as any progressive, Roosevelt summoned the country forward while seeking to rejuvenate traditional values. An active moralist, he lectured the American people on the proper code of life. In these secular sermons the president preached the need to maintain

* In 1960, at the age of 43, John F. Kennedy became the youngest man to be *elected* president.

the virtues of hard work, self-control, duty, honesty, sobriety, and courage. Like many other eastern patricians, Roosevelt feared that changes in American life—the ending of the frontier, the influx of immigrants, and the urbanization of the country—were softening Americans and weakening their ability to compete as individuals and as a nation. Roosevelt's moralism came both from his desire to re-infuse direction and purpose into the American people and from his own peculiar personality.

From his youth, Roosevelt displayed the strenuous and flamboyant activism, intensive moralism, and desire for order which he exemplified as president. Born into a comfortable old New York mercantile family in 1858, he was sickly, asthmatic, and nearsighted. But under his father's tutelage he built up his strength through rigorous exercise and boxing lessons. He learned to master his emotions as he mastered his body. When his father died, the 13-year-old boy buried himself in his studies to avoid feelings which he considered weak and maudlin.

After attending Harvard College and Columbia Law School, Roosevelt entered politics as a New York State assemblyman from Manhattan. In 1884, when his wife perished in childbirth and his mother died on the same day, he insisted on rigid self-control. Three days after the double funeral he returned to his seat in the Assembly. When the session ended, he headed west and spent the next two years running a ranch in the Dakota Territory, submerging his anguish in the hardships of the frontier. Although he eventually remarried, he never mentioned his dead wife again, not in his autobiography nor even to their daughter. Roosevelt had pushed himself beyond self-control to obsessive self-denial. Throughout his life he maintained his rigid determination to hold in check potential chaos in both private and social experience.

Roosevelt's insistence on order and his admiration for vigor, bold leadership, and martial virtues endeared him to many progressives and conservatives, but these qualities also led him to extremes. He viewed warfare as a test of character and a means of advancing civilization. During the Spanish-American War he thrilled to combat and bragged, "I killed a Spaniard with my own hand." By the outbreak of the war he had risen within the Republican party from U.S. civil service commissioner and New York City police commissioner to assistant secretary of the Navy. Resigning this last position, he had formed the

1st U.S. Volunteer Cavalry Regiment, a collection of eastern aristocrats and western cowboys known as the Rough Riders. A successful—and well-reported—charge up San Juan (actually Kettle) Hill in Cuba made him a war hero. When he returned home the young colonel was elected governor of New York. Two years later he became the vice-presidential candidate and the following year the "damned cowboy," as McKinley's campaign manager called him, was president.

Steward of the People

In the White House Roosevelt initiated the modern presidency. Conceiving of the chief executive as "a steward of the people," he argued that the president had the right to do anything the nation needed unless it was specifically forbidden by law or the Constitution. "There adheres in the Presidency," he asserted, "more power than any other office in any great republic or constitutional monarchy of modern times." He broadened the power of the executive by greatly contributing to the modern roles of chief legislator, molder of public opinion, and world leader.

Previous presidents had outlined their goals through speeches to the country and messages to Congress. Roosevelt went beyond these methods by sending drafts of bills to Capitol Hill and lobbying for his legislation both privately and publicly. In dealing with Congress Roosevelt moved boldly. He deliberately exceeded congressional authorization in withdrawing public lands for conservation purposes. He personally revived the Sherman Antitrust Act, thereby thrusting the executive branch into the corporate economy. In foreign policy he seldom waited for congressional approval before taking aggressive action. "I did not usurp power," Roosevelt explained later, "but I did greatly broaden the use of executive power."

Sensing the popular hunger for leadership and a sense of participation, Roosevelt fed the public's interest in the presidency. He encouraged people to expect the president to speak and act on matters of importance. From his "bully pulpit" he cultivated public opinion by using the mass media. He gave information to selected reporters and provided the first White House press room. Together, TR and the press personalized the presidency. His active life made exciting copy.

Roosevelt became the first president to play tennis, ride in an automobile, fly in an airplane, and submerge in a submarine. Reporters scrambled after him as he hiked through Rock Creek Park in Washington and hunted bears in the mountains of the West. A news story of the president protecting an infant bear warmed the hearts of millions. It led an enterprising New York toy maker to create a stuffed honey-colored cub, which he promptly named the Teddy bear.

In his seven years as president Roosevelt encouraged a positive role for the federal government in managing the direction of modernization. The president, he believed, should intervene in the economy when necessary to contain the more destructive aspects of assertive wealth and provide some protection for its victims. Without strong presidential leadership and some reforms, mounting discontent might explode into widespread militance and even class conflict. Roosevelt wanted to preserve American corporate capitalism as it was evolving by regulating it in the public interest. He had little patience with radicals, whom he called "the lunatic fringe," or with reactionaries who sought to block his reforms. "The friends of property," he told his attorney general, a wealthy corporation lawyer, "must realize that the surest way to provoke an explosion of wrong and injustice is to be shortsighted, narrow-minded, greedy and arrogant." Roosevelt was a reformer because he was basically a conservative.

THE SQUARE DEAL, 1901–1909

Roosevelt had not been elected president, so his primary political aim during his first term was to build up the strength and reputation to win election in 1904. The task did not seem easy. None of the four previous vice-presidents who had succeeded to the presidency upon the death of the incumbent had even won renomination.* The conservative Republican old guard, which dominated the party and Congress, distrusted Roosevelt as impetuous and unpredictable. "Go slow," the GOP national chairman advised him. "I shall," Roosevelt replied.

* They were John Tyler, Millard Fillmore, Andrew Johnson, and Chester Arthur.

Although he began by assuring Americans that he intended to continue McKinley's popular policies, Roosevelt quickly established his own program.

He started with the trusts. In his first inaugural adddress he picked up McKinley's theme, the need for publicity to expose any evils resulting from the recent corporate consolidation movement. Roosevelt went beyond his predecessor, however, when he insisted that the federal government should have the power to deal with big business:

> The great corporations which we have grown to speak of rather loosely as trusts are the creatures of the State, and the State not only has the right to control them, but it is in duty bound to control them wherever the need of such control is shown.

Roosevelt was not antibusiness. He thought the new supercorporations were inevitable and even beneficial. He believed they could produce goods more cheaply and abundantly and that they could compete more effectively with the powerful European cartels. Nevertheless, he sought to apply his standards of moral conduct to them. He opposed rebates, watered stock, unfair competition, and the corruption of public officials. Thus, he considered the behemoths to be "good trusts" or "bad trusts," depending on their practices rather than their size.

In Roosevelt's view government should discover what the trusts were doing and then negotiate with the corporate managers to end improper practices. If the heads of the corporation proved recalcitrant, the president could, if necessary, expose them to adverse publicity and even antitrust prosecution. During his first administration Roosevelt overcame opposition to active governmental intervention from conservatives like John D. Rockefeller and his son-in-law, Nelson Aldrich, the powerful old guard senator from Rhode Island, and forced Congress to establish a Bureau of Corporations with the power to investigate the giant interstate corporations. Despite Roosevelt's bellicose posturing, however, he took a relatively moderate position. As Mr. Dooley, the fictitious character created by satirist Peter Finley Dunne, recognized:

> Th' trusts, says he, are heejoous monsthers built up be th' enlightened intherprise iv th' men that have done so much to advance progress in our beloved country, he says. On wan hand I wud stamp thim undher fut; on th' other hand not so fast.

The early and somewhat misleading reputation Roosevelt acquired as a "trust buster" derived from the actions he took in 1902 against the Northern Securities Company, a projected railroad monopoly in the Northwest, and also against the beef trust. In a surprise move Roosevelt ordered the Justice Department to file suit to dissolve the enormous railroad holding company created by Morgan, Hill, Harriman, and Rockefeller. The government charged that the proposed consolidation was an illegal restraint of trade. It also contended that nearly one-third of the company's capital stock represented an unwarranted profit to the organizers and that it would lead to higher freight charges. While Wall Street gasped, most of the country cheered Roosevelt's resurrection of the moribund Sherman Antitrust Act. A few months later Roosevelt's suit against the big meat packers of Chicago delighted eastern consumers and western farmers. Modifying its previous position, the Supreme Court supported the government in both cases.

Stunned, Morgan hurried to the White House. "If we have done anything wrong," Morgan reportedly told the chief executive, "send your man [meaning the attorney general] to my man [naming one of his lawyers] and they can fix it up." "That can't be done," Roosevelt replied. "We don't want to fix it up," the attorney general, Philander Knox, added. "We want to stop it." Although he considered the antitrust approach an antiquated idea, Roosevelt wanted to show that the supercorporations would have to reckon with the federal government. Although the Morgan-Hill railroad combination was barred from selling stock, the stock already issued was returned to the individuals who had conspired to restrain trade. Thus, while the gambit was blocked, the individuals involved were not penalized. Most corporate leaders worked out "gentlemen's agreements" with Roosevelt under which they consented to provide the president with information about their companies and make whatever reasonable changes he suggested.

A few months after filing his first antitrust suits, Roosevelt intervened in a lengthy strike in the anthracite coal fields of Pennsylvania. Early in the winter of 1902 the strike threatened the Northeast with a critical fuel shortage. Roosevelt invited both sides to the White House, becoming the first president to try personal mediation rather than using federal troops to protect property and crush the strike.

When the owners refused to meet with the union leaders, the irritated chief executive threatened to seize the mines and use soldiers to produce coal. Roosevelt may have been bluffing, but his ploy worked. J. P. Morgan and other financiers induced the mine owners to agree to arbitration by a presidential commission. The commission authorized both wage and price increases and averted the fuel crisis. Through his bold and unprecedented use of the presidency to help mediate industrial relations in the national interest, Roosevelt reinforced the idea that he would act to curb the excesses of big business while giving labor and capital "a square deal," as he called his program.

Election Strategy

By the 1904 election Roosevelt had strengthened both his personal position and that of the Republican party. Despite the animosity of some conservatives, the president received widespread popular acclaim for his forceful policies. Wooing recent immigrants with praise and some patronage, he had also tried to reduce the GOP's nativist image and expand its constituency among workers. He enlisted the support of southern blacks because they made up the majority of southern Republicans and the South elected nearly one quarter of the delegates to the Republican national convention. In fact, Roosevelt was the first president to invite a black man to the White House. Booker T. Washington joined him for lunch in 1901, evoking a howl of protest from much of the white South. Yet Roosevelt's southern strategy mixed expediency with principle. Like many other white Americans, he held a stereotypical view of "the Negro." In 1906, for example, he dishonorably discharged three entire companies of black soldiers because a few unidentified soldiers had retaliated with violence against racial slurs in Brownsville, Texas.

Roosevelt's efforts to cultivate support within the Republican party proved successful, and in 1904 he won the nomination for president without serious challenge. Winning nomination was virtually tantamount to being elected, since the GOP remained the majority party and the dominant force in national politics for nearly forty years, from the depression of the 1890s to the Great Depression of the 1930s.

McKinley and Roosevelt had identified the GOP as the party of strong national leadership by actively promoting prosperity and national greatness. They had broadened its appeal to a wider range of ethnic groups than its traditional native Protestant base.

The Democrats, on the other hand, were still discordant and faction-ridden. They could not find a leader who could unite the party's two constituencies: the southern and western wing, which was composed of rural, prohibitionist, native white Protestants, and the northern wing, which was made up of a few wealthy conservative businesspeople and a number of city machines based on urban, antiprohibitionist, foreign-stock Catholics and Jews. The bastion of the Democratic party was the deep South. That region's racism and ruralism encouraged a program of states' rights and limited government and reinforced the party's notorious parochialism. The leader of the party's southern and western wing, William Jennings Bryan, ran for president in 1896, 1900, and again in 1908. But in 1904 the Democrats put forward a representative of the eastern conservatives: Alton Parker, a colorless New York judge.

Roosevelt whipped Parker in the most decisive victory since Andrew Jackson defeated Henry Clay in 1832. A personal triumph for Roosevelt, the election also indicated a popular demand for innovation. In addition, it raised the issue of campaign contributions by giant corporations, which, it was later confirmed, contributed 70 percent of the $2 million raised by the GOP National Committee that year. (Three years later Congress prohibited contributions by national banks and corporations—but not by their officers as individuals—to the election campaigns of federal officials.) In 1904, to the dismay of conservatives and many progressives, Eugene V. Debs, the nominee of the Socialist Party of America, multiplied his vote from 88,000 in 1900 to 400,000. Undeterred, Roosevelt basked in his personal victory. He was, he bragged to his wife, "no longer a political accident."

Roosevelt's Second Term

An astute politician, Roosevelt understood the increasing sentiment for new policies demonstrated by the growing success of progressive reformers on the local and state levels. During his second term he became more progressive. But recognizing the power of the conservative old guard Republicans in Congress and desirous of easing the growing split between progressive and conservative factions of the party, Roosevelt followed a middle path.

Moderate, not radical, reform was what Roosevelt favored, and his position on railroad regulation shows how he worked within the center of a debate to achieve a practical solution. The railroad problem was old and complex, but at the turn of the century new difficulties stemmed from the consolidation of hundreds of smaller lines into half a dozen major rail systems. Consolidation may have curtailed rate wars and brought stability to the carriers, but it also increased the railroads' indebtedness and contributed to higher freight rates, which were then passed on to consumers by shippers in the form of higher prices. Southern and western shippers, especially, feared that Wall Street, once it controlled what had formerly been local or regional railroads, would neglect the needs of their commerce. Even the railroads themselves complained, since big shippers like Standard Oil often forced them to give major discounts or rebates. In 1903 the railroads, with Roosevelt's endorsement, therefore sponsored the Elkins Anti-Rebate Act, which sought to prevent the loss of railroad revenues from such rebates by declaring them illegal. However, the problems of consolidation, collusion, monopolistic rate fixing, and other discriminatory practices continued and led to mounting public discontent. Concluding after the election that further action was inevitable, Roosevelt decided to lead the movement toward moderate goals.

Theoretically at least, a number of alternatives existed for dealing with railroad problems. Some conservative anti-interventionists wanted to end governmental regulation and return to *laissez faire and the free-market system*. Radical antitrust advocates urged the government to *break up the giant consolidations* and go back to many smaller lines. Socialists and some progressives advocated *government ownership* of what they called natural monopolies, including the railroads, which in Germany were government owned and operated. Most people probably supported increased *governmental regulation,* but they differed on its nature. Since the Interstate Commerce Commission was ineffective, radical progressives like Senator La Follette, who wanted strong national supervision, urged a new agency which could both prevent excessive rates and enforce adequate service. However, moderates like Roosevelt suggested only that the ICC be strengthened so that it could prevent discriminatory rates. Battling radicals, conservative senators, and railroad interests, which blocked such changes for two years, Roosevelt and congressional moderates finally won approval for a compromise measure through a combination of accommodations and coercion. The commission was given increased powers, but to satisfy conservatives it was left to the courts to determine how broad their review powers would be.

Despite its mild nature, the Hepburn Act of 1906 re-invigorated the ICC. For the first time, the commission obtained authority to set rates. Soon its power expanded as the courts limited themselves to narrow procedural review and Congress, in the Mann-Elkins Act of 1910, authorized the ICC to act on its own initiative instead of waiting for a shipper to file a complaint.

During the Progressive Era the strengthened ICC acted against inflation and kept freight rates down by repeatedly denying railroad applications for increases. Despite greater traffic, the carriers found it harder to obtain capital investment from their cash flow or from the stock market. Instead, they increased their sale of bonds. Although railroad managers and some revisionist historians have blamed government regulation for this financial squeeze, the railroads themselves also bore major responsibility for their difficulties. Their reputation for financial manipulation and overcapitalization made many investors reluctant to buy their stock. As some reformers, like Brandeis, suggested, the railroads might have increased their cash flow through more efficient operation.

As a result of legislative action in the Progressive Era, the federal government greatly increased its intervention into the transportation sector of the economy. It moved beyond its old promotional role and acted as a negative regulator of the railroads, keeping down their rates in the larger public interest. Not until after World War I did it make a positive attempt to foster a sound, adequate national railroad system. That and a number of other efforts failed, however, and over the years the railroads became a "sick industry." By the 1970s the United States had evolved a mixed system of profitable private lines in the

South and West and publicly owned unprofitable carriers in the Northeast.

In the area of consumer protection, Congress, under pressure from consumer groups and other associations, adopted two moderate reform measures to help protect the public against unhealthy food and drugs. Muckrakers like Upton Sinclair, in *The Jungle* (1906), his exposé of the meatpacking industry, helped raise public fears about diseased meat. Although some conservatives opposed it, the Meat Inspection Act passed that year was shaped to a large degree by the big packers, who wanted to quiet public concern. Also, governmental inspection and certification would drive many of the smaller firms out of business. Roosevelt lacked enthusiasm for the second of the legislative enactments in this field, the Pure Food and Drug Act of 1906. Nevertheless, legislation forbidding adulterated or fraudulently labeled food and drugs was supported by the government's chief chemist, Dr. Harvey Wiley, physicians and consumer organizations, and large food and pharmaceutical firms, which sought to curtail patent medicine companies and the adverse publicity they generated. Although he did not initiate either of these pieces of legislation, Roosevelt characteristically received credit for both.

During his second term Roosevelt applied the antitrust laws more vigorously than in his first term. Despite the fact that the Rockefeller and Morgan companies had contributed substantially to his election campaign, the president filed suits against American Tobacco, DuPont, Rockefeller's Standard Oil, and Morgan's New Haven Railroad. Roosevelt believed in regulation rather than antitrust action, but he relied on what he called "the foolish antitrust law" because Congress refused to enact his recommendations for federal licensing and regulation of interstate corporations.

The Wall Street panic of 1907 and the consequent short-lived but severe recession strained relations between the president and the business community even further. Although a temporary overextension of credit probably caused the recession, business blamed the uncertainty on Roosevelt's antitrust policy. In order to save one of the major brokerage houses and avoid a sharper market break and intensified economic contraction, the president subsequently gave tacit approval to U.S. Steel's acquisition of a competitor, Tennessee Coal & Iron Company. More significant, he had the Treasury pump $150 million in bonds into the credit resources of the national banks, an action which helped stem the decline. Angered by the attacks on him, Roosevelt lashed out against "certain malefactors of great wealth," who he charged had intensified the panic in order to discredit the government's policies. He named Standard Oil and the Santa Fe Railroad as examples of "predatory wealth." This most slashing assault on business by any president since Andrew Jackson showed Roosevelt's ability to direct public attention against "the interests." So did the conservation movement.

The Conservation Crusade

The modern conservation movement began during the Progressive Era. Not as simple as Roosevelt often portrayed it, the movement demonstrated the tensions engendered by modernization. Industry's rapid consumption of natural resources and the Census Bureau's 1890 announcement that the frontier had come to an end caused Americans to worry that unbounded expansion had reached its limits. Economic growth had expanded opportunity and ameliorated social conditions. Now many Americans argued that it would be necessary to conserve resources in order to maintain that tradition. Progressives and many other interventionists asserted that the federal government should encourage rational, planned management through regulation to ensure wise and efficient utilization of resources.

Sensing a growing popular issue, Roosevelt took over the leadership of the movement and developed the comprehensive policy which gave conservation its particular character. He rejected as impractical the goals of preservationists like the naturalist John Muir, who wanted to maintain the forests untouched so that people could enrich their spirits through contact with the beauties of nature. Instead, Roosevelt supported the program of Gifford Pinchot, chief of the U.S. Forestry Service, for federally regulated use of certain coal and mineral lands, forests, oil reserves, and water power sites. During his administration Roosevelt quadrupled—to 200 million acres—the land taken out of the public domain and put into government reserves.

Progressives spoke of conservation as a battle between "the people" and "the interests," which they identified as the big mining, timber, and oil companies that exploited the country's resources. In reality, conservation was less a grassroots popular movement than an attempt by eastern modernizers to make the federal government a mechanism to administer natural resource development. The majority of westerners—those who were or wanted to be ranchers, miners, or lumbermen—opposed this limitation on the tradition of exploiting the public domain, a tradition which had been one of the main avenues to wealth in the West.

In practice, conservation did maintain resources, but it also caused much hardship. It drove small operators from government land. Big companies continued to work there under lease, but they complained of bureaucratic interference. New federal conservation agencies were underfinanced and often relied on the companies to police themselves. Before long the companies and the agencies developed working relationships which limited the effectiveness of regulation.

The Roosevelt Legacy

Seven years in office left their mark on Roosevelt and the country. By the time he left office in 1909 to spend a year hunting big game in Africa, the president felt the strains of growing congressional discontent with his forceful actions and the widening breach between conservatives and progressives within the GOP. He had avoided prickly issues like currency and the tariff, the latter of which raised prices and cost consumers hundreds of millions of dollars each year. Nevertheless, Roosevelt had joined the growing movement for change. Putting the presidency behind the moderate reform wing of the GOP, he dramatized the progressive movement and helped raise some of its issues to the national level.

Despite his rhetoric and activist image, however, Roosevelt was often less progressive than he sounded. More assertive reformers like Senator La Follette expressed disillusionment with the former Rough Rider:

> [Roosevelt's] cannonading filled the air with noise and smoke, which confused and obscured the line of action, but, when the battle cloud drifted by and the quiet was restored, it was always a matter of surprise that so little had really been accomplished.

Still, Roosevelt had achieved some results. He had pulled his party and the government along with him on the path toward moderate reform and interventionism, and he had strengthened the executive branch of government so that it might be a source of strong leadership.

TAFT IN THE WHITE HOUSE, 1909–1913

Inheriting a difficult situation, Roosevelt's hand-picked successor, William Howard Taft, made the worst of it. Faced with mounting pressure for action, Taft sought to slow and consolidate change. The tide of reform overwhelmed him. Although historians were too quick to judge Taft a weak president, they correctly assessed him a failure. He failed to mobilize the people or keep his party intact. In the end the electorate repudiated him.

The Jurist as President

Taft was not the man for the presidency. He lacked the imagination and ability to manage contending political forces. He preferred the calmness of the courtroom. Born into a moderately wealthy Cincinnati family, Taft had become a lawyer, then solicitor general and a federal judge before Roosevelt selected him as the first American governor-general of the Philippines. He returned to the United States to become secretary of war. Taft did not want to be president so much as chief justice, a position he obtained in the 1920s. Sitting in the White House in 1909 after defeating Bryan and Debs, Taft said he felt "like a fish out of water."

Although he greatly admired Roosevelt, Taft proved incapable of imitating his predecessor. He did not have the personality for bantering with the press or the magnetism to rouse the public. In the White House he felt misunderstood by the people outside pressing for action. The kindly, 350-pound executive was slow moving and somewhat indecisive. "The truth is," he wrote sadly to his wife, "it is not the height of my ambition to be popular." Despite his admiration for

Roosevelt, Taft was too strict a constitutionalist to emulate TR's bold political ventures and too conservative to go along with continued sweeping reform. He could, however, be an activist president for conservative reasons—battling Congress to establish a budget for the federal government, vetoing actions of reformers in Congress, and dispatching Marines to Nicaragua without congressional consent. Trying to bring under strict control the movement for an expanded role for the federal government in social and economic areas, Taft believed his primary task was to integrate Roosevelt's reforms into the legal system and return society to stability.

In his first two years as president, Taft dissatisfied both progressives and conservatives within his party. Republican insurgents became angered by Taft's refusal to support their efforts to reduce the dominance of the powerful speaker of the House, "Uncle Joe" Cannon. Taft also mishandled the tariff issue. True to his campaign pledge, he sought lower rates, thereby angering protectionists. But when conservatives maintained control of Congress and enacted the high Payne-Aldrich Tariff of 1909, Taft embittered insurgents by refusing to veto it. The measure did move toward flexible tariff schedules by authorizing maximum and minimum rates for each item, the rates to be determined by the administration. But Taft further alienated its opponents when he reportedly praised it as "the best tariff act" ever passed.

Hardly had the tariff row ended when Taft stumbled into an even more vehement conflict with progressives, and eventually a battle with Roosevelt himself. The Ballinger-Pinchot controversy of 1909–1910 exploded from an administrative dispute into a cause célèbre. It raised serious questions about the administration's support of conservation and demonstrated widespread public suspicion that big business was corrupting the federal government.

The controversy began when a young special agent for the Interior Department, Louis Glavis, and Chief Forester Gifford Pinchot publicly accused Secretary of the Interior Richard Ballinger of weakening the conservation program in order to aid corporate interests. A Morgan-Guggenheim syndicate had been organized to mine government coal reserves in Alaska, and Ballinger was accused of aiding the giant combine. With tremendous lack of judgment, Taft took a narrow procedural view and decided that the matter was merely an interdepartmental squabble. He failed to recognize that the matter involved larger issues of conservation and public policy. Carefully examining the technical aspects of the case, he ruled in favor of his secretary of the interior and discharged Glavis and eventually Pinchot.

Progressives immediately raised a cry of outrage. A congressional investigating committee dominated by the old guard agreed with Taft and exonerated Ballinger of charges of fraud and corruption. Nevertheless, most Americans, including former President Roosevelt, continued to believe that Ballinger was guilty of working with giant corporations against conservation and the public interest. Convinced of Ballinger's innocence, Taft refused to sacrifice him for political gain. As the president complained to a friend in 1910,

> If I were to turn Ballinger out, in view of his innocence and in view of the conspiracy against him, I should be a white-livered skunk. I don't care . . . how it affected the administration before the people; if the people are so unjust as this, I don't propose to be one of them.

Long after Ballinger had become a political liability, Taft stood by him out of a sense of justice. Even the fact that Taft put more land into government reserves than Roosevelt had failed to win the support of progressives.

Taft also disturbed many conservatives by supporting some progressive reforms during his first two years in office. The president helped strengthen the ICC and supported the enactment of a postal-savings bank system. Although he joined in defeating the provision for an income tax attached to the Payne-Aldrich Tariff, he concurred in sending the federal income tax amendment (the Sixteenth Amendment) to the states for ratification. Characteristically, Taft received little credit from progressives, who disdained his attempts to moderate the legislation. Unlike Roosevelt, Taft proved unable to gain credit for legislation passed during his term in the White House.

The election of 1910 made Taft's situation more difficult. Progressive insurgents unseated many conservatives and party regulars. Aided by divisions within the GOP, the Democrats won control of the House of Representatives for the first time since 1895. Confronted with a hostile and reform-minded Congress, Taft tried to appear as the leader of progressive forces and restore harmony to his party. He supported several kinds of factory safety legislation and endorsed the U.S. Children's Bureau. Despite these actions, Taft angered progressives by his vehement opposition to the recall of judges and by his lack of enthusiasm for another direct democracy measure— the Seventeenth Amendment, which provided for the direct election of U.S. Senators.

While alienating progressives, Taft also dissatisfied many conservatives by waging the most active antimonopoly campaign of the era. Taft filed more than seventy antitrust suits. Acting on his own belief that there was no halfway position (such as governmental regulation) between competitive capitalism and socialism, Taft sought to restrict major consolidations in order to restore the mechanism of the marketplace.

The Supreme Court, however, supported Roosevelt's more flexible approach, judging consolidation and monopoly not on the basis of its existence but, rather, by whether its behavior was acceptable or not. In the *Standard Oil* case (1911), for example, it ordered the dissolution of Rockefeller's giant holding company as an "unreasonable" restraint of trade. In enunciating this "rule of reason," a majority of the justices fundamentally altered the Sherman Antitrust Act. They implied that the Court would accept a reasonable restraint of trade, which it eventually did in 1920, when it upheld the dominant position of U.S. Steel.

The administration's antitrust suits failed to satisfy most progressives. The more extreme antitrust advocates, such as La Follette and Bryan, wanted to break up the big combines by outlawing specific actions, providing for criminal prosecution, and taxing them out of existence. Other progressives, business regulators like Roosevelt, favored giving the federal government the power to charter big business and regulate its behavior, even to the extent of regulating prices and wages. Taft's antitrust campaign challenged these progressives as well as conservatives who supported the regulatory system which Roosevelt envisioned.

The suit against United States Steel, filed by the Taft administration, had little impact on the structure of the steel industry, but it had a disastrous political effect upon the GOP. A major part of the government's case rested on U.S. Steel's acquisition of Tennessee Coal & Iron Company, which had been approved by Roosevelt to help stem the Panic of 1907. In 1911 the Justice Department suggested that Roosevelt had been duped by the industrialists. The administration seemed blind to the implications of this action, which contributed directly to Roosevelt's decision to challenge his former friend for the Republication presidential nomination.

The Election of 1912

One of the most dramatic elections in American history, the political battle of 1912 temporarily split the Republication party and put a Democrat in the White House for the first time in twenty years. Although Roosevelt won most of the dozen state primaries, the incumbent president influenced the majority of state delegates, who had been elected without primaries, and easily won renomination. But it proved a hollow victory. Refusing to wait until 1916, Roosevelt decided to bolt the GOP and run at the head of the Progressive party, which was being organized by La Follette and other insurgents.

The election of 1912 dramatized the Progressive Era's emphasis on the politics of personality rather than party. All the major candidates stressed their own leadership styles and philosophies, a far different approach from that of nineteenth-century presidential candidates, who emphasized their party and often hardly campaigned at all. The main contenders, especially insurgents, appealed to voters through vigorous personal campaigns and the mass media, asking for support on the basis of their dedication and programs.

Voters listened to four different philosophies in 1912 as part of the new, issue-oriented politics of the age. Taft, the regular Republican candidate, expected to lose, but he hoped his defeat would discipline the insurgents and re-create a unified and conservative GOP. At the head of the Progressive party, Roosevelt wooed voters with a "New Nationalism." A program of broad social and economic reform, it included a call for national incorporation and regulation of interstate business, income and inheritance taxes, compulsory investigation of major labor disputes, limitation of labor injunctions, an eight-hour work day, and workmen's compensation. The Progressive party program would thrust government directly into the economy to benefit business and industrial workers. After much wrangling the Democrats nominated Woodrow Wilson, a southern-born educator and the progressive governor of New Jersey. Attacking Roosevelt for catering to the trusts, Wilson called for a "New Freedom," encouraging the restoration of competition in the marketplace and opportunities for small entrepreneurs. The tariff needed to be reduced, Wilson said, and the antitrust laws and banking system improved in order to limit consolidation. In contrast, the Socialist candidate, Eugene V. Debs, summoned Americans to make drastic changes. He advocated restriction of capitalism through government ownership of railroads, grain elevators, mines, and banks. He called for unemployment insurance, old-age pensions, and a restructuring of government to include the elimination of the U.S. Senate, an end to judicial review by the Supreme Court, and limitation of the presidency to one term.

The Republican party split apart, thus enabling Wilson to win the presidency. More than one out of every ten GOP voters from 1908 sat out the 1912 election. Those Republicans who voted were divided almost equally between Taft and TR, but Roosevelt and his program of business regulation and protection for workers proved particularly popular in the cities, where he drew the votes of large numbers of first- and second-generation immigrants. Of all those who voted in 1912, 27 percent cast their ballots for the Rough Rider. Taft received 23 percent of the popular vote, which, if combined with Roosevelt's, showed that the Republicans remained the majority party when united. Debs won 900,000 votes, which was 6 percent of the total and the highest number ever received by the Socialist ticket. Wilson won a plurality—42 percent—of the popular vote by lining up the support of the South and the West. Aided by the division of the GOP, Wilson won a clear majority of the states. The electoral college gave him 435 votes to 88 for Roosevelt and 8 for Taft. Wilson thus became the first Democrat to sit in the White House since 1897.

Wilson's sectional victory meant that, while the Democrats held power, southerners would dominate the executive and legislative branches of the federal government for the first time since before the Civil War. But this shift in control of the national government would be only temporary. In the long run the election of 1912 proved to be an aberration and failed to produce any fundamental realignment of voter allegiance. The GOP remained the majority party, the choice of most registered voters. It regained control of Congress in 1919 and of the White House in 1921, and it maintained that control until the Great Depression.

Identified as a symbol of standpattism, Taft was repudiated by the voters. An inept politician, he failed as a leader of the traditionalists, who tried to fight a rear guard action against the mounting demands for reform. He never grasped the dynamics of pressure groups or understood how to balance reformers against reactionaries. He could not, like Roosevelt, play off interest groups, work one side and then the other, and gain credit by convincing a majority that he had obtained all that was politically possible. Taft failed to see the dangers in refusing to help unseat Speaker Cannon and in his positions on the Payne-Aldrich Tariff, the Ballinger-Pinchot controversy, and the suit against U.S. Steel.

Taft did expand executive power, however. He terminated private oil exploration on government oil reserves. He inaugurated a budget for the executive branch which temporarily brought business methods to the government before it was terminated by Congress, which was suspicious of centralized budget making (the concept of a unified federal budget was not adopted until 1921). He contributed to the dissolution of a number of corporate consolidations, including Edison's Motion Picture Patents Association, the so-called "movie trust." He nullified treaties without asking Congress, and he sent Marines into Nicaragua without legislative approval. Nevertheless, Taft was a political failure. Trying to be a harmonizer when most people wanted a fighter, he alienated progressives, conservatives, interventionists, and traditionalists. In the end he retreated into a defense of conservative constitutionalism, spending most of his last year in office vetoing reform legislation passed by a hostile Congress.

WILSON: THE SCHOLAR AS PRIME MINISTER

"I have no patience with the tedious world of what is known as 'research,'" a young Princeton professor once confided to a friend. "I should be complete if I could inspire a great movement of opinion." This young scholar, Woodrow Wilson, got his wish. He left the academic world to become one of the most important presidents in the nation's history and a leader of movements for progressivism and international peace. Working with a progressive-minded Congress, he signed more reform legislation into law than Roosevelt and Taft combined. He also pursued an active foreign policy. His response to the events of World War I made him one of the world's leading statesmen.

A forceful leader, Wilson nevertheless differed sharply from Roosevelt in personality and style. Slim and unbending, with a long, angular face and cold, steely eyes peering through pince-nez glasses, Wilson looked and acted like a schoolmaster to the nation. Reserved, aloof, and austere, he lacked TR's animation, exuberance, and camaraderie. "I have a sense of power in dealing with men collectively," he confessed, "which I do not feel always in dealing with them singly." He lectured the public and won its loyalty through his eloquent appeals to moral principles and ideals.

A long-time admirer of the parliamentary system, Wilson helped transform the presidency into an instrument of party leadership and a vehicle for directing legislation. Acting like a prime minister, he boldly led Congress into enacting his proposals. He acted without hesitation. Upon taking office he summoned the lawmakers into special session and then drove to Capitol Hill, becoming the first chief executive to appear before Congress in more than a century. He and his advisers drafted reform legislation and worked closely with Democratic congressional leaders to get it enacted. Wilson coaxed, persuaded, threatened, and pressured. He appealed directly to the public when he thought it necessary. He also realized that he could help define the issues for newspaper readers. Expanding on TR's use of the mass media, Wilson held the first general presidential press conference. In his substantive policies he understood that the country wanted reform and that the Democratic Congress was prepared to act. "We are greatly favored," he remarked early in his administration, "by the circumstances of our time."

Although he was an effective and courageous leader with great skill and inspiring strength and purpose, Wilson was in many ways his own nemesis. His character was that of the protagonist in a Greek tragedy, a heroic figure containing the seeds of his own destruction. The problem stemmed partly from his divided personality. "There are two natures combined in me," Wilson confided to his private secretary in 1912, "that every day fight for supremacy and control."

> On the one side, there is the Irish in me, quick, generous, impulsive, passionate, anxious always to help and to sympathize with those in distress. . . . Then, on the other side, there is the Scotch—canny, tenacious, cold and perhaps a little exclusive. . . . When these two fellows get to quarreling among themselves, it is hard to act as umpire between them.

Compulsively ambitious, Wilson channeled his driving energy and rigid self-discipline into effective leadership. When he exerted it in behalf of worthy causes with widespread backing, he obtained significant results. But when his forceful leadership was applied to projects without such broad support, effective opposition triggered anxiety and ire and frequently led him into dogmatic, self-defeating behavior. At those times the flaws in his temperament—pride, ambition, overconfidence, stubbornness, and intolerance—often changed differences over issues into bitter personal quarrels. This problem was exacerbated by a cerebrovascular disease which afflicted him with a number of strokes, including a particularly severe one in 1906 and a massive, crippling one in 1919. A combination of recurring physical disability, aggressive overconfidence, and impatience could lead this man, who could compromise on other issues at other times, to become petty, vindictive, intractable, and ultimately self-destructive.

The personality traits of political leaders like Wilson do not alone cause the outcomes of actions and events. Results also derive from the situation itself. Many of the difficulties Wilson faced would have confronted anyone who occupied the executive mansion at that time. Yet Wilson's personal values, motives, dispositions, and physical condition were important. They helped shape his perception of the situations confronting him, and they helped determine which course of action he chose from among the available alternatives.

Each of the three executive positions Wilson held during his long career produced a similar cycle: initial reform achievements were followed by insurmountable obstacles and intense personal frustration. It began at Princeton University. A circuitous path led Wilson there. The son of a leading Presbyterian minister, he had grown up in Virginia and Georgia during the Civil War and Reconstruction periods. Following a brief stint as a lawyer, he became a political scientist and historian, eventually teaching at Princeton. He became president of the university in 1902. A leading educator, he instituted a number of reforms but was defeated in his attempt to abolish elite eating clubs and integrate the graduate school into the college campus. Embittered, Wilson left to run for governor of New Jersey in 1910. Once in office he rammed through a progressive program until the Republicans regained control of the state legislature and brought his success to an end. Then he went to Washington. In the White House Wilson would again accomplish significant reforms, but he would ultimately suffer a great defeat as his opponents blocked his proposal for American participation in a postwar League of Nations.

In his political thought Wilson was a curious paradox, for he combined a conservative background with willingness to lead the country along progressive lines. Originally a conservative eastern Democrat, he publicly repudiated his early sponsors, embraced progressivism, and helped make reform a moral crusade. Wilson began his presidency as a Jeffersonian states-rights Democrat favoring only enough expansion of national governmental power to prevent special privilege. Yet in the White House he proved flexible enough to meet changing conditions and political needs. Realizing the widespread support for expanded governmental intervention, he adopted much of Roosevelt's "New Nationalism" and increased federal power far more than his predecessor had. His use of active intervention by the government both in the marketplace and in international affairs demonstrated that interventionism could stem from both conservative and progressive origins.

THE NEW FREEDOM, 1913–1916

Wilson launched his administration with a sweeping series of reforms. This legislation resulted from the interaction of the president, Congress, and nationally organized pressure groups. However, Wilson skillfully maintained his leadership in managing the bills through the compromises of the legislature. Working with key congressional leaders and private advisers, the chief executive threw the weight of the presidency behind reform proposals which had been hammered out in Congress so that they would satisfy a wide range of interest groups and constituencies. Although it resented such strong assertion of presidential power, Congress enacted a reform program which in most of its aspects conformed to Wilson's wishes, a legislative record unequaled at any time between the Civil War and New Deal eras.

In his first address to Congress Wilson called for a general lowering of tariff duties. In doing so, he could count on support from farmers and consumers who wanted lower prices for manufactured goods. Many businesspeople were willing to lower America's protective barriers in order to open up markets abroad through reciprocal tariff reductions. When protectionists opposed him, Wilson beat them down by publicly denouncing the "industrious and insidious" lobbyists of the trusts. The Underwood Tariff passed by Congress in 1913 was the first significant reduction in the protective tariff since before the Civil War. But, despite the major political victory it represented, the Underwood Tariff had little effect on the economy. Within a year World War I interrupted normal trade patterns, and in the 1920s, Republicans restored protective barriers.

A new federal income tax had a greater impact. Empowered by the Sixteenth Amendment, ratified in February 1913, Congress adopted a graduated personal income tax, in part to compensate for the loss of federal customs revenue which would result from lower tariff duties. A moderate tax, it applied only to the 5 percent of the population which earned more than $4,000 a year, and its highest rate was only 7 percent. Nevertheless, the income tax of 1913 set an important precedent. It began to shift federal revenue from its nineteenth-century base—public lands and customs duties—to its twentieth-century foundation—personal and corporate income. Widely extended in future years, it would provide the basis for financing expanded social services and massive military costs.

Almost everyone agreed that the country needed banking and currency reform, but when Wilson turned to these issues, he found an array of conflicting proposals and interest groups. Inflation-minded farmers in the South and West argued that currency based solely on gold and U.S. government bonds was too limited. After the Panic of 1907, most of the business and financial community agreed that the money supply was too inelastic to respond to changing demand. Nevertheless, interest groups differed over an appropriate basis for the currency. The financial community was divided: Urban bankers wanted to add commercial paper; rural bankers sought to use commodity notes as well.

Interested groups also differed over the best means of coordinating the reserves of the nation's 7,000 banks and mobilizing them in a financial crisis. Unlike European nations, the United States had lacked a central bank since Andrew Jackson destroyed the Bank of the United States nearly a century earlier. Beginning in the 1890s J. P. Morgan and other major New York bankers had provided limited private, centralized direction. Now they proposed a formalized, private central bank, controlled by them, which could issue currency and determine interest rates. This proposal was opposed by smaller local and regional bankers in the South and West. They also wanted a privately owned and controlled system but not one dominated by Wall Street. Instead, they recommended a decentralized system of regional banks run by local bankers. In the most extreme proposal left-wing progressives and Bryanite Democrats suggested that the government own and control both the banking system and the currency. Recognizing the lack of consensus, Wilson, assisted by Carter Glass of Virginia, the head of a House banking subcommittee, used the fragmentation of opinion over this complex issue to press successfully for a compromise which all the major interest groups could accept.

Overbilled as a democratic reform which curtailed the power of Wall Street, the Federal Reserve Act of 1913 aimed primarily at providing a more orderly, coordinated system to aid the banking and business communities and the nation's economy. It combined private direction with some public regulatory supervision. The Federal Reserve System contained twelve regional Federal Reserve banks which held reserves for commercial banks. Each was privately controlled by a board of local business and financial people but was supervised by a public body, the Federal Reserve Board in Washington. The system could regulate the credit supply by raising or lowering the rediscount rate it charged commercial banks to borrow from it or by buying or selling government bonds in the open market. The new currency, backed by at least 40 percent in gold, consisted of Federal Reserve notes based on government bonds and commercial paper. (Agricultural paper was added later.) Like the Interstate Commerce Commission, the Federal Reserve Board was designed to act as a nonpartisan mechanism to mediate among contending interest groups and help manage a crucial section of the economy in the public interest while allowing initiative and responsibility to remain in private hands.

Wilson reversed himself on the trust issue. During the campaign he had emphasized the need to curtail monopolistic consolidations and to restore competition. But once in the White House he departed from his antitrust position. Bryanite agrarian Democrats introduced bills to break up supercorporations through punitive taxes, federal regulation of the stock exchanges, and a legal limit to the share of the market any one company could control. But Wilson gave only mild assistance to the Clayton bill, which in its first versions prohibited specific monopolistic practices. Many businesspeople and a number of progressives had protested that such extensive government prohibitions would hamper all entrepreneurs and that monopolists would find new ways to achieve their goals. When the president lost interest in specific prohibitions, opponents were able to dilute the bill significantly. As enacted in 1914, the Clayton Antitrust Act outlawed price discrimination, exclusive selling agreements, holding companies, and interlocking directorates among competing firms *only* when the government could prove a tendency toward monopoly. It failed to declare these practices illegal in themselves. "When the Clayton bill was first written, it was a raging lion with a mouth full of teeth," one senator mused. "It has degenerated to a tabby cat with soft gums, a plaintive mew, and an anemic appearance."

Advised by Louis D. Brandeis, who had also reversed his position, Wilson turned instead to favor continuous federal regulation of big business. Some interest groups wanted a weak governmental commission empowered to investigate but not regulate business activities. Others, such as Morgan partner George Perkins, favored a strong commission authorized to advise corporations of acceptable behavior and then immunize them against antitrust proceedings. Taking a middle position, Wilson came out for a moderately strong Federal Trade Commission (FTC), which would oversee business activity and could prevent illegal suppression of competition. The FTC, created in 1914, had the power to investigate corporations and issue restraining orders to prevent "unfair trade practices." Antitrust sentiment was too strong to give the FTC authority to immunize business from governmental prosecution. But to assuage the doubts of those traditionalists and other conservatives who had opposed such a potentially powerful agency, the president agreed to support broad judicial review of FTC orders and appointed a number of businesspeople as commissioners.

Having decided on federal regulation rather than active dissolution of the trusts, the Wilson administration made only modest gestures toward the antitrust tradition. Although it initiated some suits, it announced that corporations could seek advice from the Justice Department in assessing and rearranging their corporate structure. Beginning with American Telephone and Telegraph Company, the Wilson administration accepted consent decrees as a means of obtaining modification of monopolistic behavior. Under these court rulings—a kind of corporate plea bargaining—an indicted corporation could comply with government recommendations and thus avoid possible conviction for restraint of trade, and the penalty of triple damages as well. In return for some corporate concessions, the Justice Department would drop its suit.

The most unfortunate aspect of the Wilson administration's record lay in yet another area, namely that which involved black Americans. Racial segregation was a part of the southern progressivism that the Democrats brought to Washington. In 1912 Wilson had appealed for black support, urging blacks to give up their historic allegiance to the Republican party. Some, like W. E. B. DuBois, had campaigned for

Wilson. Once in office, however, Wilson allowed southerners in his administration to dismiss many black civil servants and to initiate official segregation—Jim Crow, as it was called after a nineteenth-century blackface minstrel song—in federal offices, shops, restrooms, and restaurants. Like many other southern whites, he argued that segregation was in the blacks' own best interests. Vigorously dissenting, northern newspapers like *The New York World,* which ardently supported Wilson's "new freedom" program, labeled segregation "a reproach to his Administration and to the great political principles which he represented."

At the end of 1914 Wilson announced that his domestic program of reform had been adopted. But if Wilson seemed satisfied with his reform package, many Americans were not. The editors of *The New Republic,* a recently founded journal of progressive opinion, chided the president as follows:

> Any man of President Wilson's intellectual equipment who seriously asserts that the fundamental wrongs of a modern society can be easily and quickly righted as a consequence of a few laws . . . casts suspicion either upon his own sincerity or upon his grasp of the realities of modern social and industrial life.

A Second Burst of Reform

Wilson's original, limited aims gave evidence of the conservative nature of his brand of interventionism, but political realities eventually forced him to champion additional reforms. With the Republicans reunited, the Democrats fared poorly in the 1914 congressional elections. As the 1916 presidential contest approached, Wilson resumed his leadership of the progressive program and endorsed increased governmental activism and intervention in the economy. During the first three years of his administration, the president had been reluctant to support legislation benefiting specific interest groups as opposed to a wider national interest. In 1916, however, he modified this position and gave valuable support to groups of farmers, businesspeople, and wage workers seeking beneficial legislation.

The president won over many workers and reformers with his increased activism in their behalf. He nominated Louis D. Brandeis, the "people's lawyer," to the Supreme Court in 1915. A campaign against Brandeis was mounted by conservatives and by anti-Semites, who were outraged by the first nomination of a Jew for the high tribunal. Wilson nevertheless obtained Senate confirmation of Brandeis's appointment. Also, despite his reluctance to aid particular interest groups, Wilson signed the La Follette Seamen's Act, which provided federally guaranteed rights and greatly improved living and working conditions for merchant seamen. Abandoning his earlier opposition, Wilson also helped secure passage of the Keating-Owen Child Labor Act (later declared unconstitutional) and workmen's compensation for federal employees. Just before the election he intervened to avert a threatened nationwide strike of railroad workers and, despite great personal reservations, signed the labor-supported Adamson Act, in which the government ordered that the regular work day be reduced to eight hours on the nation's railroads.

Business also benefited from the actions of the Wilson administration. The president appointed businessmen to many federal regulatory boards. In 1916, as a result of wartime changes in trade patterns, Wilson abandoned his attachment to free trade and endorsed protection against postwar dumping of goods in the United States. In addition, he helped establish a permanent U.S. Tariff Commission in an attempt to remove tariff rate making from politics and provide flexible schedules determined by experts. To aid American business abroad, he tried to amend the antitrust laws to allow manufacturers to form cartels for foreign sales, a proposal which Congress finally enacted in 1918.

Previously Wilson had blocked a movement to offer rural credits to farmers in the South and West, arguing that the federal government should not aid special interest groups. By 1916, however, he had changed his mind. His support proved decisive in securing the Federal Farm Loan Act and the Warehouse Act, which provided farmers in these credit-tight regions with long-term, federally supported, low-interest loans based on the value of the farmer's land and crops. Agrarians also benefited disproportionately from the Federal Highway Act of 1916. This economic promotional legislation in the tradition of nineteenth-century governmental support for railroad construction was one of the first examples of a "new federalism" in which the national government gave substantial grants-in-aid to the states to spend for specific developmental purposes. It marked the beginning of federal intervention in support of an extensive highway network.

The Election of 1916

By the 1916 election Wilson and the Democratic Congress had enacted much progressive and special-interest legislation. The president campaigned for re-election on a platform of peace, progressivism, and prosperity. Aided by his incumbency and the foreign policy issues raised by World War I, Wilson effectively mobilized many new voters. The Republicans had bypassed the rambunctious Roosevelt and nominated an associate justice of the Supreme Court and former progressive governor of New York, the austere Charles Evans Hughes. Without Roosevelt, the Progressive party died.

Despite the GOP's re-unification after the 1912 split, one out of ten Republicans—especially social justice progressives and antiwar Republicans—voted for Wilson. In the 1916 election Wilson added many urban workers and social justice progressives and some socialists to his original coalition of agrarians from the South and West. The president won re-election with 277 electoral ballots and 49 percent of the popular vote compared to Hughes's 254 and 46 percent. The Socialist candidate, A. L. Benson, won only 600,000 votes, 3.2 percent of the turnout. Wilson had forged a coalition which combined several urban eastern states with the agrarian South and West. More than any previous Democratic candidate, he had been able to unite and expand the two wings of the party. But the coalition would not hold together. It broke apart during World War I and was not fully resurrected until the 1930s.

POLITICAL MODERNIZATION

Progressivism was the most important new force in American politics in the early twentieth century. It helped change the nature of politics and the relationship between political leaders and government on the one hand and the public on the other. It infused a new spirit into the national government, rekindling public faith in Washington's ability to respond to national problems. "Democracy is now setting out on her real mission," William Allen White wrote in 1910, "to define the rights of the owner and the user of private property according to the dictates of an enlightened public conscience." Progressive leaders like Roosevelt and Wilson encouraged capable, idealistic people to go to work in Washington. They helped displace the late nineteenth-century view of government as corrupt and ineffective and replace it with a new belief that a responsible and expert, democratically based government could be an effective instrument of continued progress.

In little more than a dozen years, progressives and other interventionists greatly strengthened the role of government. They began to create regulatory machinery and, unwittingly, the broker state. The progressives' belief in a common public interest prevented most of them from acknowledging the emerging role of the federal government as a mediator or broker among various interest groups. But with the nationalization of issues many new pressure groups emerged on the national level. Bodies like the U.S. Chamber of Commerce, the National Consumers' League, the National Civic Federation, and a host of others lobbied actively for governmental action to protect and improve their position, and the various agencies of government responded to them. New political leaders like Roosevelt also recognized that they had to show some of the people who had been hurt by the forces of industrialism that government could be responsive to them. Despite their aversion to parochialism and interest-group politics and their search for a larger public interest, progressives found themselves pressured into creating a broker state as a replacement for the self-regulating marketplace. As Herbert Croly asserted in 1909:

> Reform is both meaningless and powerless unless the Jeffersonian principle of non-interference is abandoned. The experience of the last generation plainly shows that the American economic and social system cannot be allowed to take care of itself, and that the automatic harmony of the individual and the public interest, which is the essence of the Jeffersonian democratic creed, has proved to be an illusion.

It was not only progressives who pressed for government action. Conservative interventionists also played major roles in the enactment of legislation dealing with railroad regulation, currency and banking reform, and consumer protection through meat and drug inspection and labeling. They were the most important force in achieving social control legislation involving alcohol prohibition, narcotics control, and immigration restriction and in expanding the armed forces. Organized labor supported governmental intervention to benefit unions and direct federal guarantees of worker rights, including pay raises, for seamen and railroad workers. Agrarian interventionists obtained a system of federal extension agents from land grant colleges to provide advice and, more important, a federally supported system of rural credit.

The new interventionists established a major role for the federal government in the economy and society. They created a regulatory state and established the federal income tax to pay for it. The new system emphasized executive, nonpartisan, expert mediation by government bureaucracies whose role was to balance the demands of contending interest groups in the larger public interest. Congress authorized, and the Supreme Court upheld, most of the new departures which were designed to provide mechanisms for government to regulate important areas of the economic system while keeping primary initiative and responsibility in the hands of individuals and groups in the private sector.

The single most important innovation of the Progressive Era was the creation of the modern presidency. Activist and reform minded, Roosevelt and Wilson drew upon constitutional and latent powers to serve as effective national leaders. To an extent unheard of in the late nineteenth century, they outlined major programs, mobilized public opinion, lobbied bills through Congress, and took bold executive action in support of labor when industrial disputes threatened to jeopardize the public welfare. Most important, they portrayed the chief executive as the only political leader who represented the American people as a whole. Thus, the Progressive Era presidents reached for and often obtained new power to deal with national domestic problems and, increasingly, to assert actively American interests abroad.

CHAPTER 6

Taking the Flag Overseas

THE ROAD TO INTERVENTIONISM

Like a young giant flexing new-found muscles, the United States swaggered onto the center of the world stage in the early years of the twentieth century. The rapidly industrializing nation expanded its economic interests and began a policy of diplomatic and military intervention abroad. This new international activism moved beyond America's traditional foreign policy of reacting to events. Policy makers now sought to exert some control over external forces of change. They began to use American power to shape the international environment, protect American interests, and encourage progress in international relations.

Throughout most of its existence the American republic had been sheltered from the need to engage in extensive diplomacy and substantial military defense. It enjoyed what one historian has called an "era of free security." During most of the nineteenth century the country benefited from a stable balance of power in Europe and the significant obstacle to invasion presented by the breadth of the Atlantic and Pacific Oceans. As the French ambassador declared around the turn of the century, the United States was blessed by having relatively weak neighbors on the north and south and "on the east, fish, and on the west, fish."

173

Although Americans had for generations sent their commodities and ideas overseas, the nation had remained politically and militarily aloof from foreign entanglements. The government adopted a policy of neutrality toward wars outside the Western Hemisphere and of isolationism from many events abroad. Convinced of its own rectitude and pursuing a policy of limited objectives overseas, the United States had pictured itself as a moral exemplar to the world rather than as a nation actively engaged in influencing international events. Even within the New World, American expansion had been primarily across the continent. The Monroe Doctrine proclaimed U.S. opposition to new European colonies in the Western Hemisphere, but it was seldom confronted in the nineteenth century.

The growth of American economic and military power, burgeoning national pride, and new international developments challenged this self-imposed curtailment. A limited number of Americans interested in foreign policy sought to establish new mechanisms to control developments and create an international order favorable to the United States. They wanted to influence events rather than merely react to them; they wanted to have the nation act as a world power. The United States, according to Theodore Roosevelt, could no longer renounce the obligations of a great power and avow itself "merely an assemblage of well-to-do hucksters who care nothing for what happens beyond [their borders]." As one expansionist senator asserted at the outbreak of the Spanish-American War, "there is no such thing as isolation in the world today."

The world changed quickly. Industrialism stimulated competition among the great powers. It also provided new weapons: steel warships, airplanes, long-range cannons, and rapid-fire artillery and machine guns. Armed with these, the imperialist nations—Britain, France, Italy, Russia, Japan—plunged across the globe in search of markets, raw materials, enhanced security, and greater national glory. By 1900 they had conquered and carved up Africa and much of Asia, squashing local resistance and occasionally skirmishing among themselves.

Great Britain had already entered a period of long-term decline, and the less satisfied industrializing nations—Germany, Russia, Japan—had begun to challenge the nineteenth-century world order.

World War I, which lasted from 1914 until 1918, was the first general European war in a century. It ended nineteenth-century diplomacy and the balance of power. In doing so, it began the military challenges between conflicting alliances which dominated the first half of the twentieth century, although the devastation which resulted shifted the locus of international power away from Europe.

American Activism

Amid international rivalry and expansionism American foreign policy entered one of its most formative periods. During the Progressive Era policy makers sought to influence the international environment through active interventionism. They abandoned hemispheric isolation, built an island empire, and expanded American interests throughout the world. Beginning in the late 1890s the United States moved beyond mere trade expansion and limited commercial arrangements. In the wake of the war with Spain, the U.S. government made unprecedented new strategic and economic commitments in the Caribbean and the Far East to protect American possessions there and to pledge support for the administrative and territorial integrity of China. The ease with which the United States had successfully intervened in Cuba, Puerto Rico, the Panama Canal Zone, and the Philippine Islands helped create the illusion that such commitments could be made without great costs. In the first two decades of the twentieth century, the United States concluded the aftermath of the Spanish-American War and put down resistance in the Philippines. It sent military expeditions to several other countries, suffered several war scares, and finally marched into World War I. At the same time, Americans made major diplomatic efforts to establish a stable and peaceful world order. Private groups helped expand trade. The peace movement encouraged legal mechanisms like arbitration, mutual disarmament, and world government. American presidents became significant figures in international diplomacy, and their names were associated with dynamic new foreign policies: Roosevelt's Corollary to the Monroe Doctrine, Taft's "dollar diplomacy," and Wilson's Fourteen Points.

Until the outbreak of World War I, the U.S. government focused primarily on the Caribbean and to a lesser extent on the Far East. American interest and involvement in these areas were intensified by the acquisition of colonies and protectorates there following the Spanish-American War. By 1900 the United States had acquired the territories of the Philippine Islands, Samoa, Guam, Hawaii, and Puerto Rico. It dominated Cuba as a protectorate through financial control and occasional military intervention. In the early years of the century, the United States established protectorates in Haiti, the Dominican Republic, Nicaragua, and Panama. In Panama, Americans built a major interoceanic canal which transformed the Caribbean from a drowsy backwater area into an international crossroads. In the Caribbean and the Far East, the conflicting aims of many of the big powers affected American economic, political, and strategic interests. With regard to these areas the U.S. government saw America as both a beneficiary and a protector, and it began to try to influence events there in favor of the United States.

During the Progressive Era American economic interests expanded dramatically. The United States had always been a major exporting nation, but in the two decades before World War I U.S. exports doubled. More important, in 1905, for the first time in American history, manufactured goods surpassed agricultural commodities as the major items being shipped abroad. Crates filled with tractors, typewriters, automobiles, phonographs, and similar products illustrated the nation's industrial progress. The United States had also been a major importer, especially of investment funds from Europe. But Americans' growing wealth enabled them to quadruple their own investment in Europe and elsewhere; this figure reached $3.5 billion in the two decades before 1914. During World War I the United States replaced Britain as the world's leading creditor.

In these years American industrialists established the multinational corporation as a major private sector mechanism for managing economic interests abroad. Spurred by the depression of the 1890s, American corporations turned to foreign markets and sources of raw materials to supplement their domestic activities and began to establish sales offices, plants, and other facilities abroad. The names of these early multinationals became a familiar sight overseas: Singer Sewing Machine, American Tobacco, Armour Meat, Eastman Kodak,

General Electric, Ford Motor Company, Standard Oil, and eventually the ubiquitous Coca-Cola. Although some corporations sought raw materials, especially in Latin America, most engaged in selling American manufactured goods in wealthier consumer nations like Canada and the countries of Europe.

Through such expansion U.S. multinational corporations began to shape the economic development not only of smaller countries in Latin America but also of major nations like Canada and Britain. By 1907 the British claimed that some 2,000 American firms in London dominated many of their industries and were reshaping aspects of life in Britain. Europeans, like others, were ambivalent about this process. They wanted American goods and investment funds but not American influence and control. The turn of the century saw them warning of the "American menace" and the "Americanization" of Europe.

Except in the Caribbean and the Far East, U.S. governmental policies and actions had only a small impact on this pattern of economic growth. The corporations took the initiative in expanding into foreign markets and sources of raw materials. They negotiated concessions from foreign governments or individuals. They established mines and smelters, railroads and port facilities. They opened up sales outlets and constructed factories. When they encountered problems abroad, they often dealt with them by admitting local elites into the management or financing of the operation or by hiring foreign nationals as workers. Sometimes they joined with European companies in international cartels which fixed prices and divided world markets.

The protective tariff had been the U.S. government's primary instrument for assisting business in the international marketplace. But in the early twentieth century the government began to change the way it used this device. Many people believed that the tariff had outlived its usefulness and was being turned against the United States. They urged the government to negotiate reciprocal tariff reductions with other nations to open up markets for American goods. President McKinley confided to one friend that his "greatest ambition was to round out his career by gaining American supremacy in world markets." He and his successors sought to open up areas abroad for U.S. investment and trade through reciprocal or unilateral tariff reduction.

American Attitudes

As the United States became increasingly involved overseas through economic, diplomatic, and strategic interests, many Americans re-examined their attitudes toward world affairs. They wanted a foreign policy which would protect the nation's interests in a changing world and also reflect its traditions. Not surprisingly, they differed over what was the best solution.

Traditionalists continued to accept basic policies which had been employed for generations. They believed in political isolationism. They supported a policy of staying out of foreign quarrels in Europe or Asia. They endorsed the Monroe Doctrine. To protect American security they relied on the barriers provided by the great oceans, reinforced by coastal fortifications, mines, and a defense-oriented navy composed of submarines, gunboats, and destroyers. As for land forces, traditionalists supported a small Regular Army, which could be augmented in an emergency by the National Guard and citizens who would enlist in the regiments of the U.S. Volunteers. This policy emphasized America's natural security and its role as an exemplar to the world. Sentiment for it was strongest among the rural folk of the South and Midwest, especially the followers of William Jennings Bryan.

Modernizers in foreign policy considered many of the nation's traditions inadequate for the new international circumstances. Those who sought new directions concurred on the necessity for greater activism, but they disagreed on the form it should take. *Militant expansionists* like Theodore Roosevelt, Admiral Alfred Thayer Mahan, and General Leonard Wood, military governor of Cuba and later army chief of staff, wanted to commit the United States to active use of diplomatic, economic, military, and naval power in pursuit of broadened goals. They argued that the United States should secure a dominant position in the Western Hemisphere to prevent the incursion of expanding European nations, especially Germany. In addition, the United States should vigorously pursue prestige and commercial opportunities abroad. Militant expansionists emphasized *Realpolitik*, the use of force and the balance of power to achieve the nation's aims. They advocated a large, modern high-seas fleet and an efficient, expandable army with large numbers of trained reservists. Believers in a kind of international Darwinism, militant expansionists saw international competition and war as inevitable and sometimes beneficial. The nation, they argued, should prepare for such struggles.

Reform internationalists were also modernizers who wanted to change American foreign policy. But they placed greater emphasis on the improvement of international relations. Seeing war as anachronistic, they hoped to curtail or even eliminate the use of armed force. Among them, the *legalists*, like William Howard Taft, Woodrow Wilson, and Elihu Root, Roosevelt's secretary of state, advocated arbitration, mediation, adjudication, and the use of a world court or international parliament. *Pacifists* or *communalists* like Jane Addams and Oswald Garrison Villard agreed, but in addition they emphasized the need to eliminate the causes of war by actively working toward equity, humanity, and justice in international development.

There was considerable overlap among traditionalists, militant expansionists, and reform internationalists as they sought appropriate foreign and defense policies. Although progressives tended to be modernizers in foreign policy, they could be found among both militant expansionists and reform internationalists. All three groups included conservatives, moderates, and radicals, Republicans and Democrats. Such diversity confirmed the lack of consensus on the proper course for America.

Within this broad discussion the president and his chief advisers played the most important role in determining foreign policy and the manner in which the United States responded to specific events. The chief executive's leadership stemmed from his constitutional authority and his latent powers as party leader and spokesman for the nation. His power increased as a result of the country's growing strength and larger role in world affairs.

But there were limitations on the president's power in foreign affairs. He was constrained in part by the growth of national interest groups concerned with events abroad. Business associations, ethnic groups, and ideological societies, such as peace groups and the Army and Navy Leagues, kept track of foreign developments and sought to influence U.S. policy. Presidents also found themselves restrained by political realities and the continued widespread popularity of political isolationism. Furthermore, the United States' role abroad was limited by the activities of other powerful nations.

Despite these limitations, the chief executives in the Progressive Era helped modernize American foreign and defense policy. They greatly expanded the power of the president as an international manager. Using executive power boldly, they promulgated doctrines which defined national interest and policy. They sent delegates to international conferences, broadened the use of executive agreements as substitutes for formal treaties, and unilaterally dispatched the Navy and the Marines to countries in the Caribbean and the Far East. Expanded activity in foreign affairs proved to be one of the foundations of the modern presidency.

TR AND BIG-STICK DIPLOMACY

Theodore Roosevelt thrived on power. He used it to help lead the United States into the international arena and to educate Americans to the responsibilities of great-power status. He relished the role of innovator, modernizer, and international statesman. His personal and activist diplomacy stemmed in part from his own vigorous style of life as an outdoorsman, amateur athlete, and sometime soldier. A vociferous moralist, the former Rough Rider expressed his views frequently and forcefully. He urged Americans forward into world affairs. "If we shrink from the hard contests," he warned, "then the bolder and stronger people will pass us by. . . . Let us therefore boldly face the life of strife."

From the White House Roosevelt watched the changing nature of international relations. He realized that Germany, Russia, and Japan had begun to challenge the stability of the nineteenth-century world order. He watched the contests of the imperialist nations with concern. He also worried about instability in the less developed regions. Influenced by the pseudoscientific racism of the time, he considered it the responsibility of the so-called civilized nations to ensure order and gradually "uplift" people in what he called the world's "wasted spaces."

As an apostle of *Realpolitik,* Roosevelt sought to protect the United States' national interests. Admiral Mahan and others taught him to think of those interests not only in racial and geographic terms but in strategic and commercial terms as well. Roosevelt became convinced that the United States had to be strong and purposeful in order to protect itself and its areas of prime concern, such as the Caribbean. Fearing that Germany would challenge U.S. interests in Central and South America and that Japan would threaten the Open Door policy in China and the security of the Philippines, he worked to protect American interests in those areas.

Roosevelt loved the spotlight. Conducting a personal brand of diplomacy, he communicated directly with other heads of state and with friends in foreign governments. In the nation's capital he led panting diplomats on brisk hikes through Rock Creek Park or on horseback rides through the countryside. He personally negotiated the settlement in the Russo-Japanese War after both sides accepted his offer of mediation. During lulls in the conference the president practiced jujitsu with Japanese instructors. TR knew how to capture the public imagination through personal deeds or colorful phrases. When asked about his foreign policy, he liked to quote an old African proverb: "Speak softly and carry a big stick." Roosevelt believed in active diplomacy and seeking a balance of power which would use nations to offset each other. He also favored having military and naval forces ready in case they were needed, and he tried to link foreign and defense policy. "I utterly disbelieve in the policy of bluff . . . or in violation of the old frontier maxim, 'Never draw unless you mean to shoot,'" he told his successor. "I do not believe in our taking any position anywhere unless you mean to shoot."

In relations among nations, as among individuals, Roosevelt was convinced that power commanded respect and that, as a rich and expanding country, the United States needed force to protect its interests. He launched America into the naval arms race which was developing among Britain, Germany, and Japan. During his two terms as president he doubled the size of the Navy. Although Congress reacted to the high cost of navalism and curtailed his battleship-building program in 1907, it had already authorized an expanded, modern high-seas fleet second only to that of Great Britain.

Roosevelt also reorganized the military establishment to guard the new American territories and to be ready for major action abroad. Like Root and General Wood, Roosevelt admired the European system of mass conscript armies based on universal military training and directed by experts in a general staff. National conscription was too repugnant to American traditions to be obtained in peacetime, but the military modernizers did establish a general staff and several Army war colleges for advanced training for the officer corps. They also more than tripled the size of the Regular Army, which grew from 25,000 before the Spanish-American War to 85,000 by 1902. Modernizers reorganized the National Guard, increasing the amount of federal funding and control and authorizing these state forces to be used outside the continental United States.

Sentiment against a large standing army was part of the American tradition, and many people feared the growth of professional military power and influence. In addition, organized labor warned that the troops might be used against strikers. Although some federal troops were deployed in labor disputes, the Army's main role was to garrison the American territories and protectorates in Cuba, Puerto Rico, the Philippines, and the Panama Canal Zone.

CARIBBEAN CLIENT STATES

It was in the Caribbean that Roosevelt intervened most boldly. The centerpiece of his policy and of U.S. national interest was a canal between the Atlantic and Pacific Oceans. Like many other Americans, he considered an interoceanic waterway essential to increased trade and to more effective protection of the U.S. coastline and the sea lanes. The two-month voyage of the battleship *Oregon* around Cape Horn during the Spanish-American War had convinced many people of the need for a shorter route between the East and West Coasts. During his administration Roosevelt obtained the canal site and established American hegemony in the Caribbean.

The Panama Canal

Of the two possible canal routes, Roosevelt and Congress at first favored the one leading across Nicaragua. The Panamanian route was shorter but more expensive, since the French Panama Canal Company wanted $109 million for its rights to the route. The U.S. government agreed to the more expensive route, however, partly as a result of extensive lobbying by the French company and partly as a result of the dangers illustrated by a volcanic eruption in Nicaragua. In 1902, after the French company had cut the asking price to $40 million, Congress approved the Panamanian route.

Because Colombia controlled Panama, the United States negotiated with the Bogotá government to build and operate a canal. However, the Colombian senate rejected the Hay-Herran Convention of 1903, which provided a payment of $10 million and an annual rental fee of $250,000 for the canal zone. Apparently, the lawmakers thought that by deferring action until after the French company's franchise expired in the following year Colombia might receive a substantial part of the $40 million which Congress had authorized for the canal company's rights.

Outraged, Roosevelt refused either to wait or to renegotiate the price with the Colombians. Nor would he return to the Nicaraguan route. Confronted by what he considered blackmail from a minor and "less civilized" nation, the president denounced the Bogotá legislators as "bandits" and "corruptionists" who were blocking the progress of civilization. "You could no more make an agreement with the Colombian rulers," he said later, "than you could nail currant jelly to a wall." Recklessly, he considered seizing Panama. Instead, his purposes were served by a revolt there which was instigated by foreign promoters and native elites led by the former chief engineer of the French company, Philippe Bunau-Varilla. He had met with Roosevelt in the White House less than a month earlier and learned that the president was dispatching U.S. warships to the area. As Roosevelt later admitted, Bunau-Varilla "would have been a very dull man" if he had been unable to "guess" that the United States would respond favorably to his revolution. On the day the U.S.S. *Nashville* arrived, the Panamanian revolt began. The presence of the U.S. Navy prevented Colombia from landing forces to suppress the revolt, and three days later the president recognized the new Republic of Panama.

Within two weeks Bunau-Varilla arrived in Washington as the Panamanian minister and signed the Hay–Bunau-Varilla Treaty. It gave Panama the sums rejected by Colombia. In return the United States received, in perpetuity, the use and control of a canal zone ten miles wide and the right to intervene in Panama if its independence was threatened by Colombia or by any other country. The treaty was ratified in 1904 and the Panama Canal opened in 1914 after a decade of construction costing $374 million.

Roosevelt's actions represented an extreme form of the new American activism abroad. They were controversial from the start. Acting precipitously, with little regard for law or morality, he had encouraged revolution and infringed upon Colombian sovereignty. He justified his high-handed action by claiming that immediate construction of the canal was vital to the United States and in "the interests of civilization." Later he boasted, "I took the Canal Zone and let Congress debate; and while the debate goes on, the Canal does also." Roosevelt's nationalism proved popular with many Americans, but others abhorred it as disreputable and unnecessary. In 1921, after Roosevelt's death, the United States paid $25 millioto Colombia to make amends and obtain oil concessions there. Half a century later Panamanians forced the United States to renegotiate the treaty and provide, in 1979, for increased annual payments and for transfer of the Canal Zone to Panama in the year 2000.

Caribbean Protectorates and the Roosevelt Corollary

Throughout the Caribbean, Roosevelt extended American power and hegemony. Partially to prevent possible German expansion, the United States annexed Puerto Rico as a territory in 1898. Cuba, governed by the American military from 1898 to 1902, remained a protectorate under the Platt Amendment, which authorized U.S. military intervention when necessary "for the preservation of Cuban independence" and "the maintenance of a government adequate for the protection of life, property, and individual liberty." Under its provisions American troops occupied the island from 1906 to 1909 and from 1917 to 1923. American economic investment in Cuba grew from $50 million in 1898 to $500 million in 1920. By the time the Platt Amendment was abrogated in 1934 as part of the "good neighbor policy," Cuba had become an economic dependency of the United States.

Roosevelt's Caribbean policy, designed to establish stability and U.S. hegemony in the region, received its clearest and boldest justification in the 1904 presidential pronouncement known as the Roosevelt Corollary to the Monroe Doctrine. The Corollary grew out of the attempts of

European governments to force debt-ridden Latin American nations to pay their creditors. In Africa and Asia this kind of action had often led to European occupation and colonization. In 1902, British, German, and Italian warships bombarded Venezuelan ports until the creditors obtained satisfaction. Two years later, when the Dominican Republic defaulted, French and Italian cruisers trained their guns on Santo Domingo. To prevent possible European military incursion into the Caribbean, Roosevelt decided that the United States should intervene. Thus he unilaterally expanded the Monroe Doctrine from a prohibition against additional European colonization in the Western Hemisphere to an authorization for pre-emptive U.S. intervention. The United States became the policeman of the Caribbean. "If we intend to say 'Hands off' to the powers of Europe," Roosevelt told his secretary of state, "then sooner or later we must keep order ourselves."

The president had as little desire to *annex* the Dominican Republic as a "boa constrictor might have to swallow a porcupine wrong-end to." Instead, he established a customs receivership protectorate there. With American warships in the harbor, the president's representative obtained an executive agreement with the Dominican government authorizing the reorganization of the nation's debt and shifting it from European to American creditors. The United States also took over management of the customs house, through which the nation's exports flowed and its revenues returned. The customs receivership ensured repayment of the debt from current export revenues. Thus, through the use of American economic and military power, Roosevelt began to establish U.S. hegemony in the Caribbean and Central America, a policy his successors pursued in varying degrees for the next two decades.

ACTIVISM IN THE FAR EAST

Roosevelt also pursued his active diplomacy in East Asia. But in that area of the world his policy proved neither as decisive nor as successful as it was in the Caribbean. In the Far East the United States faced the great powers which competed for the spoils offered by the approaching collapse of the Manchu dynasty and central authority in China. The situation there was much less open to U.S. influence and less important to most Americans than Caribbean affairs.

The United States was in a weak position to achieve its Far Eastern goals, which Roosevelt defined as protection of the Philippines and maintenance of the Open Door in China. The Open Door policy was "an excellent thing" on paper, but Roosevelt warned his successor that it "completely disappears as soon as a powerful nation determines to disregard it, and is willing to run the risk of war." Furthermore, the Philippines, more than 7,000 miles from the United States, would be virtually impossible to defend against a concerted Japanese attack. Once an ardent champion of their annexation, the former Rough Rider later acknowledged that the islands were "our heel of Achilles." Without American support for the use of military force in East Asia, Roosevelt sought other ways to maintain U.S. commitments.

The president tried to balance Russia and Japan against each other. The interests of the two major Asian powers clashed in the iron- and coal-rich Chinese province of Manchuria. When the Japanese launched an attack on the Russian holdings there in 1904, Roosevelt privately cheered them on, but a year later he expressed concern over the increasing magnitude of their victories. Both sides were, however, drained by the war, and they accepted the president's offer to mediate. In Portsmouth, New Hampshire, at the last of the personally managed peace conferences that had characterized the nineteenth century, Roosevelt sought a compromise which would keep each side in a position to check the other. The Treaty of Portsmouth recognized Japan's dominant rights in Korea and split both Sakhalin Island and the railroad rights in Manchuria between the two powers. For his part, Roosevelt won the Nobel Peace Prize and a reputation as the first American president to play such a significant mediating role in world affairs.

Afterwards Roosevelt conciliated Japan, which emerged from the war as the strongest naval power in the Pacific. When the Japanese public grew incensed over a San Francisco School Board order segregating Oriental children, the president fumed at the "infernal fools in California" and finally persuaded the school authorities to rescind the order. In the following year, 1907, he reached a "Gentlemen's Agreement" with the Japanese government, which promised to prevent agricultural laborers from emigrating and competing with American workers. In the Root-Takahira Agreement of 1908, Roosevelt placated the Japanese by recognizing their hegemony over Korea and Formosa, which they had captured in the Sino-Japanese War of 1895. In exchange, the emperor's government renounced any interest in the Philippines and affirmed the Open Door policy in China. Support for the "existing status quo," however, left ambiguous the question of whether the United States accepted Japan's paramount economic and strategic interests in southern Manchuria. Roosevelt sought both to conciliate and to impress the Japanese. Before he left office, he sent sixteen U.S. battleships—the "Great White Fleet"—on a round-the-world voyage which began with a ceremonial visit to Tokyo Bay.

Despite Roosevelt's actions in the Far East, he was unable to ensure stability there. The difficulty stemmed not from his policy but from the fact that the United States lacked the will or the power to prevent the instability caused by the disintegration of the Chinese Empire or to deter the rivalry of the great powers in China. The U.S. commitment in the Far East had overreached the means to sustain it.

INVOLVEMENT IN EUROPE

The United States' new role in world affairs led to increased involvement in the shifting power relationships of Europe. While in the White House, Roosevelt encouraged the growth of Anglo-American friendship, one of the most important diplomatic developments of the period. Despite the traditional hostility of many Americans toward Britain, elites in both countries brought about a *rapprochement* in the two decades between the war scare with Britain over the Venezuelan border dispute in 1895 and the American entry into World War I on the British side in 1917. In the meantime the United States joined its new power to what perceptive observers like Roosevelt saw as Britain's declining strength in an effort to maintain a stable Anglo-American world order in the face of aggressive challenges from Germany, Russia, and Japan. As TR put it, "Together . . . the two branches of the Anglo-Saxon race . . . can whip the world."

The British acquiesced in American dominance of the Western Hemisphere. London was convinced that the United States would maintain order there and prevent German expansion into Latin America. Cultivating American support, Britain retreated before U.S. claims regarding Venezuela, Panama, and the Dominican Republic. Furthermore, the British delegate to an international arbitration commission voted against Canada and endorsed the U.S. claims to the harbors of the Alaskan panhandle, which commanded the water routes to the Klondike gold fields.

In his role as world statesman Roosevelt often sided with the British. He favored the Anglo-French alliance formed in 1904 as a restraint on Germany. When Germany and France became embroiled in a dispute over which would control Morocco, Roosevelt initially did not want to get involved. "We have other fish to fry," he told his secretary of war. Nevertheless, he soon resolved to "keep matters on an even keel in Europe" and sent American delegates to the 1906 Algeciras Conference in Spain with instructions to support the French rather than the German claims. The president's involvement in the multinational conference enhanced his international prestige, but it also broke a century-old American tradition of nonintervention in European affairs.

An alternative to Roosevelt's *Realpolitik* was put forward by the peace movement, which contributed greatly to the effort to improve international relations. After years of relative lethargy the American peace movement grew dramatically during the first decade and a half of the new century. Since its inception during the reform outburst of the 1830s, the movement had been composed primarily of Quakers and other religious pacifists and a handful of New England reformers. Beginning around 1905, under the pressure of events and changing attitudes, an influx of new members transformed the traditional peace movement. Many believed that war had become an anachronistic and inefficient way of settling disputes. At the same time, concern over the naval arms race between Britain and Germany and the bloodiness of the Russo-Japanese War intensified the search for new forms of international relations by demonstrating the costs of modern war. Under pressure from a number of peace advocates, including several members of Congress, President Roosevelt called, during the 1904 election campaign, for a second international disarmament conference, to be held at The Hague in 1907.

Plans for that conference helped expand the peace movement, which swelled in the following decade. The number of American Peace Society chapters grew from seven to thirty-one. The expansion of traditional peace groups was matched by the creation of new organizations to curtail war. The publisher Edwin Ginn left $1 million to set up the World Peace Foundation, and the steel maker Andrew Carnegie gave $10 million to establish the Carnegie Endowment for International Peace. As a result of attending the Hague Disarmament Conferences of 1899 and 1907, the United States agreed to participate in the Permanent Court of International Arbitration, the so-called Hague Tribunal. Peace advocates urged further steps: a world court, the development of an international common law, arbitration of disputes between nations, multinational disarmament conferences or unilateral abolition of armaments, and even a world parliament. Jane Addams, the social worker and founder of the Women's International League for Peace and Freedom, proposed the creation of an international welfare community as a substitute for war. As early as 1904 she suggested that the labor movement, with its ideal of human solidarity, and the social reform movement, with its trust of the masses, could serve as moral substitutes for international conflict.

So popular was the idea of arbitration that Roosevelt felt compelled to sponsor several treaties requiring the United States to arbitrate certain limited kinds of international disputes. After carefully exempting disputes involving vital U.S. interests, the Senate approved them. Roosevelt agreed with the Senate's limitations, for he viewed arbitration as applicable only to minor issues and as a way of retreating from an embarrassing position without lost of prestige.

When Roosevelt left the White House it was a greater center of international influence than it had been when he entered it. As an international manager TR played a major role in settling conflicts at the conferences at Portsmouth and Algeciras. He encouraged the *rapprochement* with Britain. He sought to coopt Japan into recognizing American interests in the Far East. He forcefully asserted American predominance in the Caribbean in a policy based on protecting the Panama Canal and maintaining American hegemony in the region. Roosevelt stretched presidential power and developed mechanisms for asserting American influence in world affairs. Always an activist, the former cowboy and Rough Rider placed his brand on America and the world and defined policies which the United States would follow for more than a generation.

TAFT AND DOLLAR DIPLOMACY

Roosevelt expected his hand-picked successor, William Howard Taft, to stick closely to his policies, but in foreign affairs as in domestic politics the two presidents differed significantly. Both agreed on fundamentals—U.S. predominance in the Caribbean, preservation of American interests in the Philippines and the Open Door in China, and continuation of the Anglo-American *rapprochement*. Both also saw the need to protect expanding U.S. commerce abroad. They differed on methods, not goals. With his emphasis on peaceful and legalistic means, Taft wished to avoid Roosevelt's bellicose posturing and bold assertion of power. Seeking to abandon strident rhetoric, exaggerated executive action, and the use of force, the former jurist looked for more orderly, cooperative, and constitutional means of pursuing U.S. interests.

But once again Taft failed. He did not win overwhelming support for his policies, and his methods did not always achieve results. Taft lacked the political skill to overcome many of the difficulties he faced. Ironically, he had more foreign experience than most presidents. He had served as the first U.S. governor-general of the Philippines. Then, as secretary of war, he had overseen the colonial administration from the War Department in Washington. Yet Taft's temperament and political acumen did not match his travel and administrative experience. In his kindly but often overly-cautious manner, he found himself hampered by his inability to heal the bitter divisions within the Republican party or inspire the American people. Neither he nor his secretary of state, the corporation lawyer Philander Knox, could win major support for his foreign policies.

"Dollar diplomacy" (the term was coined by the Taft administration) stressed economic policy as a means of influencing international affairs in the interest of the United States. Taft encouraged active private economic intervention in order to maintain stable, pro-

American governments in the Caribbean and China. His aim was one of avoiding military incursion, "substituting dollars for bullets." As Secretary Knox explained in 1910:

> True stability is best established not by military, but by economic and social forces. . . . The problem of good government is inextricably interwoven with that of economic prosperity and sound finance; financial stability contributes perhaps more than any other one factor to political stability.

Nevertheless, when economic solutions failed, the Taft administration did not rule out the use of military force. In fact, Taft sent the Marines into more Caribbean countries than Roosevelt had.

The Caribbean

The difficulties arose from Washington's attempts to achieve hegemony in the Caribbean through direct intervention and control of small underdeveloped nations. Taft and Knox, along with many others, argued that such intervention not only guarded U.S. interests—prevention of European incursion and protection of the Panama Canal—but brought benefits to the "client states" as well. In theory, the local population would benefit from the peace, prosperity, and improved social conditions which should result from the introduction of American dollars and the assurance of internal stability.

Despite the rhetoric, in practice U.S. policy meant control so as to ensure stable, pro-American governments. It did not mean economic and social reform to eliminate massive poverty. The United States embroiled itself in situations which it might control in the short run but did not, or could not, influence in the long run. Admittedly, the situation resisted change. For in most of the Caribbean countries, a small, powerful elite dominated masses of peons in virtually feudal societies. Governmental change occurred either through so-called reform movements, in which one upper-class faction fought against another, or occasionally through revolution by the masses. The U.S. government generally opposed such mass revolution, and it attempted to use its influence among jostling elite groups to ensure pro-American regimes.

Pursuing dollar diplomacy, Secretary of State Knox ventured beyond the Roosevelt Corollary and invited American investors into Caribbean countries. Knox argued that the way to achieve stability there was for

Americans to refinance the debt of an unstable country and manage its customs house. Increased revenue from honest and efficient administration, he suggested, would provide funds for desperately needed reforms. Knox dealt with Caribbean nations as he would with ailing corporations: by adding new capital and reorganizing the management. Thus, when he learned that overindebtedness in Honduras and Nicaragua might lead to instability and revolt, he encouraged American bankers to supply additional credit and appointed a U.S. representative to manage the customs house.

U.S. intervention in Nicaragua provides a case study of dollar diplomacy and military intervention in action. When a revolt broke out in 1909 against the anti-American head of state José Zelaya, State Department representatives on the scene supported the rebel leader Adolfo Díaz. Earlier Díaz had told American diplomats that "Nicaragua is rich in natural resources and under proper administration would be a credit to the Americans and a field for American commerce, instead of a pest under your nose." With American support, Díaz won control of the government. But when the legislature balked at U.S. management of its customs house and refinancing of its debt, the United States withheld recognition and dispatched a warship to wait offshore until the lawmakers changed their minds. Thereafter the pro-American government became increasingly unpopular, and in 1912 the "Zelayistas" launched a counterrevolution. Taft, who had vowed to maintain order in Central America even if he had to "knock their heads together," sent in the Marines and suppressed the revolt. For the next dozen years, until they left in 1925, the Marines kept the minority party in power. Military control, not social and economic improvement, kept Nicaragua stable and pro-American. It was an ironic finale to the diplomacy of an administration that sought to demilitarize American foreign policy.

The primary aim of dollar diplomacy was always to maintain American hegemony in the Caribbean. It did expand U.S. power there and, like foreign aid after World War II, it helped link underdeveloped nations to the United States both economically and strategically. But there was not enough private investment to accomplish major changes, and the haughty use of dollar diplomacy proved highly unpopular in Latin America.

China

Financial diplomacy succeeded in extending American control in the Caribbean, but it failed in China. There Taft and Knox tried to use American capital to build up a counterweight to Russian and Japanese expansion. The former consul general in Manchuria, Willard Straight, a New York banker, called dollar diplomacy the financial expression of the Open Door. He predicted that it would help protect and guide China along its road to modernization. Taft agreed: "The more civilized they become, the more active their industries, the wealthier they become, and the better market they will become for us." Reversing Roosevelt's strategy, Taft and Knox decided to strengthen China rather than conciliate Japan.

Taft's attempt to apply financial leverage in the Far East encountered major obstacles. Russia and Japan resisted it, and Britain proved unwilling to alienate the two countries which had become its allies. American financiers did not respond enthusiastically to their government's invitation to invest heavily in China. They considered the situation there uncertain and risky; they could earn higher returns on their investments at home.

Undaunted, Taft and Knox plunged ahead. The president sent a personal appeal to the Chinese regent to persuade an international banking consortium to allow American bankers to participate in arrangements for the Hukuang loan to build railroads in south-central China. Once admitted to the consortium, an American banking syndicate headed by J. P. Morgan & Co. and the Rockefeller-influenced National City Bank agreed to supply capital. Nevertheless, the ill-considered project was never completed, for foreign penetration of southern China helped trigger the Chinese Revolution in 1911. Whereas Roosevelt had tacitly acquiesced in the economic division of Manchuria between Russia and Japan, Knox suggested loans to China to enable it to buy and neutralize the Manchurian railroads. Russia and Japan responded by concluding a treaty which staked out their spheres of influence in the province, closing the Open Door there in Knox's face. In a final gesture Taft encouraged the formation of an international consortium to underwrite a loan for Chinese currency reform and industrial development.

Although the consortium was organized in 1913, American bankers declined to participate when the Japanese and Russians objected strenuously to the proposal.

Aggressive financial diplomacy in the Far East had foundered. Timidity by American bankers hampered Taft's policy, and the determined opposition of other major powers halted it. The United States did not increase its influence in China. Rather, it alienated Japan and Russia and heightened suspicion of American motives among all the powers.

The United States further irritated Japan when the Senate, in a rare foreign-policy initiative, sought to prevent Japanese expansion into the Western Hemisphere. When a Tokyo-based company started negotiations to buy land around Magdalena Bay, a natural site for a naval base in Mexico, the Senate adopted the Lodge Corollary to the Monroe Doctrine, which expressed U.S. disapproval of the transfer of strategic spots in the Western Hemisphere to non-American companies or nations. The extension of the Monroe Doctrine to Asian as well as European nations demonstrated a new concern about the growing power of Japan.

Other Disappointments

Another major setback for the Taft administration's economic diplomacy came in its dealings with Canada. Pursuing expanded markets, the U.S. government negotiated a reciprocity agreement in 1911 to reduce the tariff barrier between the United States and Canada. The Senate approved it, but Canadian nationalists rejected the treaty when they learned that some congressmen viewed it as the first step toward annexation of Canada. The administration's embarrassment was not overcome by Taft's successful settlement of sealing and fisheries controversies with the Canadians.

Finally, the Senate challenged Taft's attempt to establish arbitration as the basis for the peaceful settlement of international disputes, even those involving national honor and vital interests. When the Senate began to amend and dilute his arbitration treaties into general statements which did not commit the United States to any specific action,

Taft took his case to the public. Stumping the country to deliver speeches in favor of the arbitration treaties, Taft became the first president to appeal directly to the American people on a foreign policy issue. Undaunted, the Senate watered down the treaties. The frustrated chief executive rejected the amended versions of the treaties he had obtained, and nothing was accomplished.

   Taft left office a deeply disappointed man. Most of his foreign policy initiatives—in the Far East, in Canada, and in the field of arbitration—had failed. Only in the Caribbean had he extended American power. There his dollar diplomacy was linked so closely with the interests of American banks and corporations that his successor, Woodrow Wilson, formally dissociated himself from it as soon as he took office. The Taft administration proved unable to overcome most of the obstacles it faced, and unable to inspire the American people to support the new interventionism.

AN EXPANDING WORLD ROLE

Early in 1901 a foreign diplomat remarked that during his brief residence in Washington he had observed two different nations, the United States before the war with Spain and the United States after the war with Spain. Although this picture exaggerates the suddenness with which the United States became an expansionist world power, it accurately reflects the belief of many contemporaries that America's relationship with the world was changing drastically within their lifetime. The United States had begun the transition to a new age of bold international engagement. It began to engage in active intervention beyond its borders in an attempt to shape events to American interests. John Bassett Moore, a leading international lawyer and the assistant secretary of state, concluded that in less than a decade the United States had moved "from a position of comparative freedom from entanglements into the position of what is commonly called a world power."

An American Empire

The United States emerged from the Spanish-American War with an unprecedented series of responsibilities and commitments overseas. American activism and interventionism led to a host of territories and protectorates in the Caribbean: Cuba, Puerto Rico, Panama, Nicaragua, Haiti, and the Dominican Republic. The United States also acquired a chain of stepping stones across the Pacific: Hawaii, Wake, Guam, Samoa, and the Philippine Islands. Acquisition of the Philippines gave the United States a stake in the Far East. As the disintegration of central power in China threatened that vast future market, Washington became increasingly concerned about maintaining the Open Door. In 1905 President Roosevelt believed the Russo-Japanese War over Manchuria so important that he personally mediated its conclusion to keep the two powers balanced against each other. Although Roosevelt viewed the new situation more realistically, many Americans agreed with Senator Albert Beveridge of Indiana, one of the leading progressive expansionists, when he invoked divine mission:

> God has made us the master organizers in the world to establish system where chaos reigns. . . . He has marked the American people as his chosen nation to lead in the regeneration of the world.

As a major power in an age of expansion, the United States became an imperialist nation, but its colonialism was different from that of the British, French, Germans, Russians, Italians, Dutch, Belgians, and Japanese. Since the United States had emerged from a colonial past, Americans made different assumptions regarding imperial responsibility. Unlike the British, who thought in terms of an empire lasting a thousand years, Americans were unwilling to view colonial dependency as more than a passing phase. They attempted to make their possessions into self-governing republics, not permanent colonies. As a result, they demanded rapid "Americanization" of institutions and an intensive kind of cultural imperialism.

On the whole, the United States did not keep its captive peoples in thrall as long as other imperialist powers did. Except for Hawaii, all its colonial possessions had belonged to other nations and had not been independent states. No European power gave any of its colonies independence before World War II, but the United States released Cuba from administrative dependency in 1934 and in the same year promised the Filipinos the independence which they achieved in 1945. Puerto Rico became a self-governing commonwealth in 1952, and Alaska and Hawaii became states in 1959. Congress extended full citizenship to the Puerto Ricans in 1917, to the Virgin Islanders (whose territory had been acquired from Denmark in 1917) in 1927, and to the Guamanians in 1950. Furthermore, the American empire was the only one besides that of Russia to form a single economic system. Alaska and Hawaii came under the American tariff upon annexation, Puerto Rico in 1900, and the Philippine Islands in 1909. The advantages of such a system accrued almost entirely to the colonies, for all were producers of raw materials which might have found their chief markets in the United States anyway. In expanding its empire the United States enlarged its trade and strategic interests, often at the expense of the lives and autonomy of other peoples, but it established primarily an economic and cultural empire rather than a permanent system of colonies.

The acquisition of a colonial island empire proved to be an aberration for the United States. Except for the Virgin Islands, which were annexed primarily so that they would not fall into German hands, the United States acquired no additional territory after 1903. The costs of suppressing the Filipino rebellion, disappointing economic benefits from the Philippines, and the strategic vulnerability of the islands led even ardent imperialists to grow less enthusiastic about the annexation of new territories. As the political commentator Walter Weyl recalled, the urge for colonies had been "an unripe imperialism" with shallow roots.

Cuba, not the Philippines, became the model for future American expansion in underdeveloped regions. The protectorate, not the colony, was the form developed in the Caribbean. Instead of acquiring new territories, the United States expanded its economic, strategic, and diplomatic influence without the costs of actual colonial administration and responsibility. Informal influence replaced formal empire as more compatible with American needs and traditions.

An Illusory Transition

Witnessing the new international activism of Presidents McKinley, Roosevelt, and Taft, most Americans thought the country could enlarge its global role without rejecting its traditional foreign policy. Expansion in Latin America and the Far East had come at such little cost that many Americans believed that moral rectitude was sufficient to ensure the triumph of U.S. policy. Yet others tried to establish a realistic relationship between aims and commitments and the means to obtain them.

Instead of the old policies of reacting to events or merely offering a moral example to the world, the U.S. government and private groups like those in the peace movement attempted to devise new mechanisms to shape the international environment. Multinational corporations and business associations moved beyond the old policy of trade expansion through limited commercial arrangements to active industrial and financial penetration of other countries. Despite these developments, public debate was often couched in moralistic terms which frequently were unrelated to the immediate concerns of national interest and power relations. Former Secretary of State Richard Olney declared cynically at the turn of the century that the United States was "a nation of sympathizers and sermonizers and swaggerers," too immature for a policy of self-interest based on power.

In the first decade and a half of the twentieth century, Americans found it possible to possess overseas colonies and protectorates and still adhere to their traditional principles of isolationism and neutrality and to the Monroe Doctrine. Despite the perversion of the Monroe Doctrine and the violation of historic noninterventionism, the costs of expansionism seemed small because in the main area of American concern, the Caribbean, the only major competing power, Great Britain, decided not to challenge U.S. actions. Thus, the United States could expand with relatively little immediate costs to itself and little disturbance to its primary concern with domestic issues. Traditional American parochialism counterbalanced the new outward thrust. Not until the outbreak of World War I was the United States confronted with the first real test as well as the major costs of its new international position.

CHAPTER 7

The Redeemer Nation:
The Road to World War I

WILSONIAN FOREIGN POLICY

"It would be the irony of fate if my administration had to deal chiefly with foreign affairs," Woodrow Wilson told a friend in 1913 as he headed for Washington to launch a program of domestic reform. From the beginning, however, the new president had to deal with international crises. Placing greater emphasis on idealism than his predecessors had done, Wilson encouraged Americans to think of foreign policy in terms of morality and mission. He grafted the active new interventionism onto Americans' traditional sense of national rectitude and their evangelistic mission to improve humanity, thereby enabling many previously skeptical Americans to endorse the new departures in foreign affairs as consistent with the country's traditions.

Wilson's idealistic justification of America's international activism derived in large part from his own personality and political style. He had an abiding faith in the righteousness of Calvinistic Christianity and believed strongly in God and in a moral law that ruled people and nations. He also believed in individualism, Jeffersonian democracy, and free-trade capitalism. The United States, he held, was responsible for the moral leadership of the "backward peoples" of the world, since its institutions ensured liberty, opportunity, and continual progress.

"We created this Nation," Wilson asserted, "not to serve ourselves, but to serve mankind."

In his emphasis on American morality and mission, Wilson was not utopian. He understood the country's strategic and economic needs and the realities of international relations. He accepted the widely held theory that the closing of the western frontier meant that America would have to find a new frontier of expanding exports and investments abroad.

The Wilson administration laid the foundations of modern American international economic policy. In doing so it emphasized that a humane, reformist capitalism could serve as the economic arm of an expanding democracy that would benefit entrepreneurs, workers, and consumers at home and abroad. Wilson encouraged American expansion and competition in an open world marketplace and opposed the traditional European systems of colonial control or exclusive foreign concessions in which investors were virtually sovereign. To open up Latin American and other markets, he encouraged tariff reduction, prodded banks and businesses to establish overseas branches, and subsidized the growth of the merchant marine. During the Wilson administration Congress suspended the antitrust laws as they applied to American exporters so that these businesses could jointly compete with German, Dutch, British, and French cartels. As a result of Wilson's activist economic policy and the dislocation of European trade and finance during World War I, the United States achieved an economic predominance in Latin America which it never lost. Between 1915 and 1920 the nation's share of goods imported into South America leaped from 16 to 42 percent. "There is nothing in which I am more interested," Wilson told a delegation of American businessmen in 1914, "than the fullest development of the trade of this country and its righteous conquest of foreign markets."

Wilson's idealistic, reformist diplomacy blended with the progressive interventionist impulse. The successes of reform at home suggested that a combination of moralistic fervor and pragmatic activism might be applied abroad. The urge to replace drift and mere response to events with mastery and direction led modernizers to seek new policies and institutions and attempt to create a more favorable environment for American interests. In a world of great international change Wilson offered a middle path between oppressive colonial imperialism and violent revolution. He urged the promotion of international peace and orderly development through democracy and liberal capitalism. Although he did not seek to prevent change, he often failed to understand how it could come about. With his idealized concept of democracy and capitalism, he had more faith than the future would justify in the sustained evolutionary reduction of inequities and injustice.

Like many Americans, Wilson adopted a universalistic approach, believing that American standards and values of stability, democracy, and liberal capitalism could be applied to countries with divergent cultural traditions and national aspirations. He tried to impose democratic solutions in Latin America and later in Russia, where liberal democratic, capitalistic concepts were not widely accepted and could not be imposed from the outside. As a statesman Wilson sought an Americanized world order, and his self-righteousness and periodic rigidity sometimes led him to oversimplify issues and act too hastily.

In his conduct of American foreign policy, Wilson employed a highly personal and single-handed diplomacy. He insisted on taking charge not only of large issues but of minute details, even typing out many of his diplomatic dispatches. Bypassing diplomats, he often dealt directly with other heads of government. When he needed an emissary, he frequently relied on Colonel Edward M. House, a Texas rancher and unofficial political adviser. Quiet, attentive, yet drivingly ambitious, Colonel House became the president's closest confidant. Yet Wilson did not allow either House or the secretaries of state, William Jennings Bryan and later Robert Lansing, to determine policy.

After spending many years as a teacher-scholar, thinking, writing, and lecturing, Wilson preferred to make decisions without outside interference. In part, his diplomatic style stemmed from his personality traits. He was stiff, formal, and aloof as well as high minded and idealistic. Convinced of his own ability and rectitude, he frequently became intolerant of dissent. He distrusted professional diplomats and the State Department. This opinion was not without foundation, for in this period the State Department suffered major inadequacies. Comparable in size to a Latin American chancellery, it lacked good systems for gathering or evaluating intelligence. Several foreign service officers were incompetent political hacks, and some, like Walter Hines Page, the ambassador to Great Britain, worked against Wilson's policies. Yet the president erred in limiting U.S. diplomacy largely to his own efforts, for he narrowed his own perspective, weakened morale in the State Department, and unwittingly prompted secret efforts to undermine his most important aims.

As president, Wilson strengthened recent developments in American foreign and defense policy. After initial misgivings he acknowledged at least temporary responsibility for existing overseas territories as a consequence of American growth. He accepted Roosevelt's expansion of the Monroe Doctrine and proved willing to use force to ensure U.S. hegemony in the Caribbean. He actively encouraged American economic expansion overseas and tried to maintain the Open Door in China. After some hesitation he came to support enlargement and modernization of the armed forces. Wilson went beyond his predecessors in leading the United States into active participation in world affairs, urging the creation of a new framework of international relations, a league of nations. Emphasizing the country's historic mission and idealistic aims—its role as a redeemer nation—he tried to adjust Americans to an active interventionism befitting a great power.

MISSIONARY DIPLOMACY

In his policy toward Latin America and the Far East, Wilson publicly dissociated himself from his Republican predecessors. He denounced Roosevelt's aggressive use of force and Taft's dollar diplomacy and pledged, "The United States will never again seek one additional foot of territory by conquest." As an alternative mechanism for international relations, Wilson in 1915 drew up a Pan-American pact which included many of the ideas he later wrote into the Covenant of the League of Nations. In addition, Secretary of State Bryan signed "cooling-off" treaties with two dozen nations. These provided a means for referring international disputes to a permanent investigating commission and prohibited armed conflict until the commission submitted its report. Wilson's alternative, however, fell victim to his military interventionism in the Caribbean. Despite his original hopes, Wilson came to adopt "moral imperialism" which led him to use more military force in the Caribbean countries than either Roosevelt or Taft. Nevertheless, because of Wilson's stress on educative and uplifting goals and his stated desire to encourage "the development of constitutional liberty in the world," his policy became known as "missionary diplomacy."

Missionary diplomacy often led to military intervention. When an unpopular Haitian president was murdered in 1915, Wilson sent in the Marines to suppress revolution. The leathernecks easily put down the rebellion, but in 1918 they killed more than 2,000 Haitians to crush a second revolt. For nearly twenty years the Marines remained in Haiti maintaining stability and U.S. control. The long period of U.S. military rule had unintended effects on the island. Opposition to the occupation and accompanying racial discrimination generated a new sense of Haitian national pride and emphasis on the French and African heritage of the islanders.

Military or economic intervention soon became the standard means for maintaining U.S. dominance in the Caribbean. When a number of revolts threatened stability in the Dominican Republic, where Americans already controlled the customs house, the United States took control of its finances and its police force. When the Dominicans resisted, Wilson established a U.S. military government, which governed the island from 1916 until 1924. Fearing that the Germans might try to acquire the Danish West Indies (renamed the Virgin Islands), the United States bought them in 1917. By the end of the Wilson administration, the United States had a firm hold on the Caribbean, with territories in Puerto Rico, Panama, and the Virgin Islands and troops in Nicaragua, Haiti, and the Dominican Republic. Cuba remained an American protectorate.

Revolution in Mexico

In Mexico Wilson's combination of missionary diplomacy and military force led him into a morass. American meddling in the Mexican Revolution, which broke out in 1910, demonstrated what could happen when moral diplomacy collided with political realities, indigenous nationalism, and intractable local problems. Wilson found that he could neither easily shape events abroad nor readily remove the United States from such situations once he had committed American influence.

Mexico began nearly a decade of intensive revolution and civil war when a rebellion led by an aristocratic liberal, Francisco Madero, overthrew the aging dictator Porfirio Díaz in 1910. U.S. corporations had invested $1 billion in Mexican mining, railroad, and other facilities, and they soon became distressed by Madero's reform program, which was directed against the government, the army, the Roman Catholic church, and foreign economic involvement. In 1913 Victoriano Huerta, one of Madero's generals, had the new president assassinated. Many foreign investors supported the would-be dictator as a conservative strongman, and most European nations recognized Huerta's regime. Wilson, however, refused, despite pressure from business, arguing that Huerta had seized power illegally and did not represent the Mexican people. "I will not recognize a government of butchers," he declared.

In refusing to recognize a government in power, Wilson broke a century-old American tradition, but he did so in the name of constitutional principles and human rights, raising his action to a high moral plane. Wilson thus became the first president to use nonrecognition as a diplomatic tactic. In 1917 he applied the nonrecognition doctrine to the Bolsheviks when they seized power in Russia; later presidents also adopted it. When he enunciated this doctrine, Wilson said that his object was "to help the [Mexican] people to secure liberty." He hoped, he told a British diplomat, "to teach the South American republics to elect good men." But Wilson went beyond nonrecognition to achieve his purpose; he engaged in active interventionism in Mexico.

During the civil war which followed Huerta's *coup d'etat,* Wilson used American power to depose the general and replace his regime with a liberal, pro-American, constitutionalist government. The president began by establishing an embargo of American arms and credit. Then he blockaded foreign munitions. Finally he authorized outright military intervention. In 1914 a petty incident involving alleged disrespect for the U.S. flag served as a pretext for Wilson to order American sailors and Marines to capture Mexico's main port, Vera Cruz, to prevent a shipload of German weapons and ammunition from being delivered to Huerta. Although Wilson had anticipated a bloodless occupation, 19 Americans and 126 Mexicans were killed in the fighting. But the gambit succeeded. Cut off from his sources of military supplies and besieged by the troops of the Constitutionalist party leader, Venustiano Carranza, Huerta fled the country. Then, in a major blunder, Wilson chose to back not Carranza, who had condemned the American occupation of Vera Cruz, but Francisco "Pancho" Villa, a dashing, peasant-born general who had broken with Carranza. Not until the fall of 1915 did Wilson reverse himself and give *de facto* recognition to the Carranza government. But this alienated Villa, who then turned against Wilson as well as Carranza.

To embarrass and discredit the Carranza government, Villa recklessly sought to force U.S. intervention in Mexico. In 1916 "Villistas" raided border towns in Texas and New Mexico, burning buildings and killing nearly two dozen Americans. Posting the National Guard to protect the border, Wilson ordered a "punitive expedition" into Mexico to try to capture Villa. Led by General John J. Pershing, some 12,000 U.S. Army troops trekked more than 400 miles into northern Mexico following the elusive Villa. But the Americans' advance roused Mexican nationalism. A skirmish between Pershing's and Carranza's troops almost led to a full-scale conflict between the two countries. War was averted through the peace organizations, which bolstered Wilson's reluctance to fight. Facing the prospect of entering the European war, the president withdrew the expeditionary force early in 1917, and later that year, after the Mexican Constitution was proclaimed and Carranza formally elected president, he finally extended *de jure* recognition to the Carranza government.

Wilson's policies had aided the Mexican Revolution, but at great cost. Alone among Western leaders he had refused to recognize Huerta and had helped the Constitutionalist reformers force him out. But his heavy-handed meddling had caused several armed clashes, and his numerous errors in judgment left the Mexicans resentful of his moralistic paternalism and interventionism. This increased anti-American sentiment in Mexico and prevented Wilson from receiving credit for his accomplishments.

The Rising Sun in the Pacific

In the Far East Wilson found that he could not influence events as he could in the Caribbean, but he tried to make U.S. influence felt. When he took office, he officially terminated Taft's policy of dollar diplomacy. He withdrew government support for American participation in an international banking consortium to grant developmental loans to China, whereupon American bankers withdrew from the project.

But Wilson did not abandon China. In his first year in office he recognized the new republican government which had overthrown the crumbling Manchu dynasty. He protested when Japan, taking advantage of the international situation during World War I, gobbled up Germany's Pacific colonies in the Mariana, Caroline, and Marshall islands and the German leasehold on China's Shantung Peninsula, and issued the "Twenty-one Demands" which would have made China virtually a Japanese client state. In response to American and British complaints, Tokyo modified its ultimatum, at least temporarily. Wilson then sought to prevent the new Chinese republic from becoming dependent on Japan for investment funds. Reversing his earlier policy, he encouraged the formation of an international consortium of bankers to help finance modernization in China.

The events of World War I, however, forced Wilson to return at least partially to Roosevelt's policy of conciliating Japan. When the Japanese threatened to make a separate peace with Germany in the fall of 1917, the Wilson administration concluded the Lansing-Ishii Agreement. In return for Japan's endorsement of the Open Door and a pledge not to take advantage of the war to infringe on the rights of other powers in China, the United States recognized Japan's "special [although not "paramount," as the Japanese had wanted] interests" in China. Wilson viewed the ambiguous document as a stopgap measure designed to prevent full recognition of Japan's expanding position in Asia.

Wilson sought to maintain the Open Door and the integrity of China without the use of military force. To do so, he first repudiated and later encouraged investment there. Like Roosevelt, he recognized Japan's growing power and tried, through executive agreements, to integrate the Japanese into a structure of power that would maintain at least some opportunities for Americans in China and some protection for the Philippines.

WORLD WAR I: U.S. NEUTRALITY, 1914-1916

The greatest test to active internationalism and American attempts to improve the world order during the Progressive Era came in World War I. The conflict among the great powers of Europe split the stillness of August 1914 like rolling thunder. Millions of men marched onto the battlefields in the giant struggle between the Central Powers—Germany Austria-Hungary, and Turkey—and the Allies—Britain, France, Russia, and eventually Italy. Americans looked upon the carnage with disbelief and disdain. Europeans had lapsed into "savage tribes," *The New York Times* declared; statesmen behaved like "chieftains clad in skins and drunk with mead." Yet within three years the United States, for the first time in its history, sent American troops to the battlefields of Europe.

The Wilson administration responded to the fighting by declaring the United States legally neutral, but the president went beyond tradition and asked Americans to be "impartial in thought as well as in action." It proved an impossible task. Although most Americans wanted the United States to remain out of the war, they favored one side or the other. The heterogeneous American population included nearly 8 million people from German or Austrian ethnic backgrounds, as well as several hundred thousand Russian Jews who despised the anti-Semitic Czarist regime. Nearly 5 million Irish-Americans hated the British government. The South and West had long viewed Britain with suspicion as the center of the gold standard and the world's moneyed interests. Despite this sizable opposition, however, the majority of Americans probably sympathized with the Allies. The British had strong ethnic and cultural ties to the Americans, and the French drew upon American gratitude for their assistance during the American Revolution.

Both sides competed for American public opinion, but the British and French won. London dominated the trans-Atlantic channels of communication. Its propaganda agency disseminated reports of German illegalities and atrocities. The official report of Lord Bryce's Commission, for example, certified rumors that German troops had been guilty of rape and pillage, had stabbed babies with bayonets, and had crucified Canadian soldiers on crosses. The Germans were stereotyped as "Huns." Only after the war did Americans learn that the Bryce Report had been based largely on unsubstantiated rumor and secondhand testimony. German propaganda, on the other hand, emphasized British violations of international law which involved seizing neutral ships, landing troops in Greece despite Greek protests, and blocking shipments of food to Germany in an attempt to starve the Germans into suing for peace. Many Americans came to view Germany as the aggressor and as a threat to world order. The Germans unwittingly contributed to that impression. The callous manner in which the Kaiser's government dismissed as merely "a scrap of paper" the treaty guaranteeing Belgium's neutrality and the way the German armies razed Belgium alienated many Americans.

Even more important than propaganda in influencing the United States was the growth of American economic ties with the Allies. With its control of the sea, Britain drew upon American resources—food, fiber, arms and munitions. Total U.S. trade with the Allies more than tripled, from $800 million to $3 billion, between 1914 and 1916. At the same time, the British blockade of Germany helped reduce American commerce with the Central Powers from $170 million to practically nothing. Mounting Allied war trade helped pull the United States out of a recession and into a boom.

Expanding trade led to one of the key decisions of the war. In the early days of the fighting, the French government sought to float a $100 million loan in the United States, but Secretary of State Bryan refused to endorse the proposal. He told American bankers that such loans would violate "the true spirit of neutrality." "Money is the worst of all contrabands," Bryan declared, "because it commands everything else." A few months later, in October 1914, Bryan and Wilson approved "short-term credits" from the bankers to the Allies. These proved inadequate, however, and by August 1915 Allied war trade had grown so large that the bankers asked permission for Britain and France to float a $500 million bond issue among American investors. This time several cabinet officers joined them. They argued that the bond issue was necessary to continue the commerce and avert a depression in the United States. In a strongly worded note Robert Lansing, who had succeeded Bryan as secretary of state, warned the president what the denial of the loans and the resulting contraction of Allied purchases in the United States would mean:

> restriction of output, industrial depression, idle capital, idle labor, numerous failures, financial demoralization, and general unrest and suffering among the laboring classes. . . . Can we afford to let a declaration as to our conception of "the true spirit of neutrality," made in the early days of the war, stand in the way of our national interest, which seems to be seriously threatened?

Wilson agreed not to prohibit the loans, thereby in effect repealing the old ban. Led by J. P. Morgan & Co., a nationwide banking syndicate floated this and other Allied loans totaling more than $2.3 billion. Although these loans did not violate international law, they and the commerce they financed made real neutrality virtually meaningless. Almost from the beginning of the conflict, the United States became the major supplier to the Allied war effort.

Within the context of widespread sympathy for the Allies and the growing war trade, Wilson's strict definition of American neutral rights led to confrontation and eventually to war with Germany. In effect, the administration insisted on America's right to supply the Allies. The U.S. government's attempt to define and obtain British and German acceptance of American neutral rights followed a long and arduous route in the first three years of the war. Pursuing his policy in the face of substantial criticism at home and abroad, Wilson nevertheless succeeded in maintaining control of the nation's foreign policy. As a result, U.S. policy was characteristically Wilsonian—it appealed to principles of international law and American idealism.

When the European armies bogged down on the western front in a bloody war of attrition, the belligerents sought to throttle each other through naval blockades which quickly affected the United States as the world's leading neutral. In November 1914 the British threw a ring of mines and ships around the sea approaches to Germany and neutrals like Holland, Denmark, and the Scandinavian countries, which might transship goods to the Germans. Gradually Britain broadened the definition of contraband to include not only arms and munitions but also foodstuffs and "strategic" raw materials like cotton, which was used to make uniforms. The British Navy seized neutral ships and confiscated contraband materials. Since international law gave neutrals the right to trade with all belligerents, such highhanded action provoked much criticism in the United States. Nevertheless, in 1916 London announced that American firms found trading with Germany would be "blacklisted" and British subjects would be forbidden to deal with them.

Although he protested British violations of neutral rights, Wilson agreed to postpone the settlement of American claims until after the war. The president's decision to wait for postwar arbitration was deliberate. He realized that any action he took with regard to the British blockade would be unfair to one side or the other. It was unfair to Germany to allow Britain unilaterally to define the rules of international trade and to maintain its blockade. But insisting on free trade would take away Britain's main weapon, its navy, and thus would be unfair to the British. The problem was that Britain was a maritime power and Germany a land power. If pushed to extremes by Washington, Britain would perhaps have loosened the blockade, since the supply of American goods and money was essential to it. In 1916, angered by British infringements, Wilson *considered* asking Congress for authorization to prohibit loans and exports to the Allies. However, he never took the drastic step of using America's economic leverage through a limited or total embargo or severance of diplomatic relations.

Wilson established a much stronger position against the blockade which Berlin declared around Britain and France in February 1915. The Germans relied on two dozen submarines to interdict enemy merchant ships. But the *Unterseeboot,* or U-boat, did not operate according to the rules of cruiser warfare. These rules required raiders to stop their target, examine the manifest and cargo, and allow the crew to escape in lifeboats before sinking the vessel. U-boats, however, proved too vulnerable to observe such protocol. British officials encouraged merchant skippers to install and use deck guns and to ram surfaced submarines. Consequently, Berlin announced that within the war zone its submarines would torpedo enemy ships without warning.

In response, Wilson held the Germans to "strict accountability" for the loss of American ships that might be sunk and the lives of Americans traveling on Allied vessels. Viewing submarine warfare as barbaric, he distinguished between the loss of lives caused by the U-boat raiders and the loss of property stemming from the actions of the surface cruisers in the British blockade. The tragic potential of submarine warfare was made clear by the sinking of one of the world's largest and most prestigious passenger liners.

On the morning of May 7, 1915, the British Cunard liner *Lusitania,* on her way from New York to Southampton, steamed out of a fog bank off the southern coast of Ireland directly in front of a submerged U-boat. The commander of the *U-20* could scarcely believe the sight. Completely filling the viewfinder of his periscope was an enormous ship displacing 30,000 tons, her four giant smokestacks glistening bright red above her white superstructure and black hull. The U-boat fired a torpedo, which slammed into the ship's hull. There was a tremendous explosion. The *Lusitania* stopped dead in the water, shuddered, and within eighteen minutes had slid bow first beneath the waves. Nearly 1,200 men, women, and children, 128 of them Americans, went down with her. The ship's death plunge, a survivor recalled, "sounded like a terrible moan."

The *Lusitania* disaster brought home to many Americans the brutality of modern war. Although ex-president Roosevelt and a few others urged America to enter the war immediately, the public reacted with more shock than anger. Refusing to listen to jingoes like Roosevelt, Wilson kept his head. He decided to respond to the German action with diplomatic protests rather than with threats of force. He demanded that Germany disavow the sinking, indemnify the victims, and agree to stop attacking passenger liners. When the Germans debated his points, Wilson continued to negotiate. This was a wise decision, because the matter was not as clear-cut as it seemed. Before the *Lusitania* sailed, the German consul had published warnings in New York newspapers indicating that the German government considered her subject to attack because she had carried munitions on past voyages. The rapidity with which the *Lusitania* sank suggested that she was indeed carrying large quantities of munitions on her last voyage. The manifest, released fifty years later, confirmed this: The ship's cargo holds contained shrapnel, fuses, and 4.2 million rounds of ammunition.

Secretary of State Bryan resigned in May 1915 to protest what he considered the president's unneutral position on the *Lusitania* incident. He told Wilson that ships carrying munitions should not be allowed to carry passengers. "Germany has a right to prevent contraband going to the Allies," Bryan argued, "and a ship carrying contraband should not rely upon passengers to protect her from attack—it would be like putting women and children in front of an army." The secretary recommended that the U.S. government protest both the German and the British blockades, and he wanted to prohibit Americans from sailing on ships carrying munitions. Furthermore, he suggested that a commission be appointed to investigate and arbitrate the *Lusitania* affair. Wilson, however, refused to consider the two blockades together. He insisted that Germany repudiate its submarine tactics. Accepting Bryan's resignation, Wilson replaced him with the State Department's legal counselor, Robert Lansing, an international lawyer and a supporter of Great Britain.

Presidential persistence forced the Germans to comply for a time. In August 1915 Wilson resumed his protests when two Americans died in the torpedoing of the British steamer *Arabic*. In the so-called *Arabic* pledge Berlin agreed not to sink passenger liners without warning. For the next six months the Germans maintained this limitation on their U-boat campaign. The German government also eventually apologized for the deaths of Americans on the *Lusitania* and paid an indemnity.

The Peace Movement

As the European war continued, the American peace movement splintered into conservative and radical wings, pursuing different strategies. Many conservative peace advocates worked for a postwar league of nations which could use force if necessary to maintain peace and order. The Association for a League to Enforce Peace, headed by former president Taft and A. Lawrence Lowell, president of Harvard University, shunned discussion of proposals to end the present war through compromise and emphasized the postwar nature of its program.

In contrast, new (post-1914) peace organizations sought to conclude the bloody conflict as quickly and as fairly as possible. This spectrum of groups virtually reconstituted the peace movement. Some, like the League to Limit Armaments and the Emergency Peace Federation, were short-lived associations. But others were more enduring, notably the Women's Peace Party founded by Jane Addams, Charlotte Perkins Gilman, and others, which became the Women's International League for Peace and Freedom, and the American Union Against Militarism headed by Lillian Wald, Crystal Eastman, and Oswald Garrison Villard, which became the American Civil Liberties Union. The new shifting coalition was composed of action-oriented peace advocates, many of whom were social justice progressives. Among them were feminists, social workers, journalists, labor lawyers, and Social Gospel clergymen. They saw the war as caused by militarists, munitions makers, and imperialists, and they warned that it sacrificed social progress to archaic means of settling disputes.

Drawing upon liberal thought in Europe and America, the pacifist progressives urged that the United States play an active, but peaceful, role in ending the war and preventing future international conflagrations. They called upon the Wilson administration to summon a conference of neutral nations which might mediate among the belligerents. They also advocated terms which they believed would ensure a just and lasting peace. The liberal peace proposals provided for no annexations or indemnities, an end to secret treaties and entangling alliances, elimination of trade barriers and colonial empires, and the reduction of large armies and navies. In their place the liberal pacifists urged disarmament, neutralization of major waterways, self-determination for all peoples, democratic governments, open diplomacy, and international machinery for the judicial settlement of disputes between nations.

Wilson had been influenced for some time by the growth of the peace movement and by ideas of international organization and world law. In the White House he continued to listen to the proposals of the peace advocates, but he pursued his own policies. Initially he hoped for an early compromise peace, one which would maintain the balance of power and protect American security. Anxious to avoid U.S. intervention in the war, he attempted several times in 1915 and 1916 to mediate a conclusion to the hostilities, but without a convention of neutral nations. However, during the first two years of the war neither side was interested in mediation. Still hoping for victory, each rejected Wilson's proposals.

Many Americans feared that the president's policy of strict accountability would draw the United States into the war. In February and March of 1916 congressional Democrats from the South and West rebelled and tried to modify Wilson's position. The Gore-McLemore resolutions attempted to prohibit Americans from traveling on armed belligerent ships. But the president crushed this challenge to his leadership. Condemning the move as a pro-German ploy, he denied patronage to supporters of the resolutions. At the same time, he took the high ground of principle. In a public letter to the head of the Senate Foreign Relations Committee, Wilson refused to consent to "any abridgement of the rights of American citizens in any respect" on the ground that Americans should not allow "expediency to take the place of principle." Presidential power was persuasive; Congress tabled the resolutions. But the vote of 276 to 142 in the House indicated that there was considerable opposition to Wilson's policy.

The Sussex Pledge

Wilson also won a major victory in diplomacy as well as in executive leadership of Congress in the spring of 1916. His achievement came in the wake of a crisis which developed in March. A German submarine commander, carelessly mistaking the unarmed British steamer *Sussex* for a mine layer, torpedoed the vessel as it carried passengers and freight across the English Channel. The stricken craft limped to port, but several European passengers were killed and a number of Americans injured. Secretary of State Lansing urged Wilson to break diplomatic relations, but instead the president presented Germany with an ultimatum. If Germany did not stop sinking nonmilitary vessels—freighters or passenger liners—without warning, the United States would sever formal relations. To avoid American entry into the war, the German government agreed to Wilson's demand in May 1916 and issued the *Sussex* pledge, thereby essentially abandoning its submarine blockade.

Momentarily, Wilson had weathered the crisis. At home, he had beaten down domestic opposition to his claim that Americans had the right to travel into the naval war zone, even on the armed ships of belligerent nations. Abroad, he had forced the Germans to suspend submarine warfare. But in his dealings with the kaiser's government he had put the determination of relations between the two countries into the Germans' hands. If Berlin resumed unrestricted submarine warfare, the United States, under Wilson's policy, would be forced to break relations and would probably enter the conflict. It seemed an ominous possibility. As Wilson told his cabinet, "any little German [U-boat] lieutenant can put us into the war at any time by some calculated outrage."

THE ROAD TO BELLIGERENCY, 1916–1917

Despite the temporary easing of tensions that followed the *Sussex* pledge, the United States went to war against Germany within a year. The interval between the spring of 1916 and the spring of 1917 was a time of shaky peace.

The "Preparedness" Controversy

The state of the nation's armed forces became a major political issue for the first time since the Spanish-American War. Led by former president Roosevelt, many corporate leaders, most of them Republicans, founded organizations advocating what they called preparedness. The United States, they claimed, was woefully unprepared for war with a major power. The Regular Army contained only 80,000 men, and the Navy, with thirty-seven battleships and only a few of the new dreadnaughts or superbattleships, might not be able to protect both coasts simultaneously. Preparedness advocates did not suggest that the

United States should get ready to enter World War I; isolationist sentiment precluded that. Rather, most of those urging increased armament warned that, as the world's richest nation, the United States would be a tempting target after the war and therefore must be ready to defend its interests. Emphasizing international uncertainty and potential danger, they attempted to discredit the Wilson administration and to modernize and expand the armed forces.

Preparedness advocates urged the United States to build a navy larger than Britain's. They also recommended that the land forces be completely reorganized. The militia should be eliminated and the dual military system abolished. The Regular Army would be maintained, but it would be slashed in both size and cost. It would act primarily as a constabulary and a cadre to train millions of reservists, who would be conscripted for six to eighteen months of military training before being passed into the reserves. Such a system would provide the United States with a large, trained, mass conscript army much like those of the European nations and Japan. Universal military training among young American men, Roosevelt and the others asserted, would enhance the country's defense. It would also improve the health, self-discipline, and national spirit of American men. With characteristic exuberance, the former Rough Rider predicted that "the military tent, where all sleep side by side, will rank next to the public school among the great agents of democratization."

Opponents of conscription and expansion of the armed forces fought against what they called a radical and dangerous departure from American tradition. The National Guard, a powerful political force in the states and in Congress, lobbied to block attempts to merge it into the Regular Army. Led by groups like the American Union Against Militarism (AUAM), pacifists and other antimilitarists argued that a large and expensive army and navy were unnecessary. The United States was not threatened by any major power, they claimed, and no matter which side won, the nations of Europe would be exhausted after the war. Even if a threat should materialize, the country could continue its traditional reliance on citizen volunteers in locally raised regiments to meet future needs. "The President knows," William Jennings Bryan declared, "that if this country needed a million men and needed them in a day, the call could go out at sunrise and the sun would go down on a million men in arms." Furthermore, many of the antimilitarists—social progressives, farmers, workers, and socialists—were suspicious of big business's support of preparedness. They warned that a large navy and conscript army could be used to help corporations control labor and dissident groups at home and expand abroad. Instead of enlarging the armed forces, the AUAM asserted that the United States should call a conference of neutral nations to mediate among the belligerents.

Declaring that he did not intend to "turn America into a military camp," Wilson initially resisted the movement for increased preparedness. But he soon came to believe that some Republicans were building national defense into a major issue for the 1916 election; in addition, he realized that he might need expanded military power to enforce his strict policy toward Germany. In late summer of 1915 the president came out for expanded national defense, and after several months of debate Congress enacted a compromise measure. The lawmakers rejected proposals which would eliminate the state militia or establish national conscription. Nevertheless, the National Defense Act of 1916 expanded the land forces. It authorized increases in the size of both the Regular Army (to 223,000 men—double the previous number) and the National Guard (to 450,000 men) within five years. It empowered the president to federalize the militia in emergencies, making it part of the national armed forces and eliminating dual control. It also created the Reserve Officers Training Corps (ROTC). The Naval Appropriations Act of 1916 provided for the construction of a navy larger than Britain's within three years.

Viewing these changes in the armed forces as having been arranged by wealthy conservatives, the progressives and agrarians in Congress decided to make rich individuals and corporations pay the costs of expanding the army and building the enormous fleet. The Revenue Act of 1916, which sharply increased income, estate, and corporation taxes, represented the first major victory for advocates of a progressive tax, that is, one which taxed larger incomes at higher rates.

Re-election and a Call for Peace

Foreign policy—not defense—was a primary issue in the 1916 presidential campaign. Emphasizing the themes of peace, progressivism, and prosperity, the Democrats campaigned for Wilson on the slogan, "He kept us out of war." Although the GOP candidate, Charles Evans Hughes, ran much better than Taft had in 1912, he lost the votes of many progressives and other Americans who opposed the bellicose, interventionist speeches of ex-president Roosevelt. Wilson won the presidency by a narrow margin, and the Democrats retained control of Congress. The confused international situation helped the Democrats temporarily overcome their minority status and upset the reunited Republican party.

After his reelection Wilson made a major effort to mediate an end to the war. He asked both sides to state their terms for a cease-fire. Since each side still thought it could win, the response was disappointing. The Germans secretly wanted Lithuania and Poland, Belgium, and the Belgian Congo. Publicly, they refused to comment. The terms put forward by the Allies were clearly unfavorable to the Central Powers. The British and French demanded German withdrawal from Belgium, the return of Alsace-Lorraine, indefinite payment of indemnities, relinquishment of Germany's colonies, and dismemberment of the Austro-Hungarian Empire.

Frustrated, Wilson announced a program of his own based on proposals by the liberal peace movement. In a speech to Congress in January 1917, he called for a "peace without victory." A just rather than a vengeful peace, he said, needed to be based on principles of equality and self-determination of nations, freedom of the seas, universal disarmament, and an international organization to preserve world peace. Critics belittled Wilson's proposal. Roosevelt, for example, urged a complete Allied victory over Germany and an Anglo-American military alliance to maintain the postwar order. But liberals and war-weary people throughout the world applauded Wilson and increased his standing as an international peacemaker.

A Fateful Meeting at Pless Castle

Meanwhile, the imperial German government was making a fateful decision. Failure to achieve victory and the growing frustration and privation caused by food shortages eroded support for moderates like Chancellor Theobald von Bethmann-Hollweg, who had made the *Sussex* pledge to end unrestricted submarine warfare. By the end of

1916 the right wing and the military had gained strength in the Reichstag, the German parliament. Kaiser Wilhelm II equivocated, but he had by that time lost a good deal of his power and prestige. General Paul von Hindenburg, the popular hero of the eastern front, joined the admirals who claimed that the enlarged submarine fleet— now more than one hundred strong—could starve Britain into submission and win the war within six months.

At a meeting with the kaiser at Pless Castle on January 9, the German leaders voted to resume unrestricted submarine warfare. This time the U-boats would attack not only belligerents' ships in the war zone but also those of neutral nations like the United States. The military realized that this would bring the Americans into the war, but as the naval chief of staff had said, "The United States can scarcely engage in more hostile activities than she has already done up to this time." The Germans counted on defeating the Allies before the Americans could alter the situation by raising and training an army and sending it to Europe. On January 31 the German government announced it would resume unrestricted submarine warfare the following day, February 1, 1917. It was a risky gamble. "Despite all promises of the navy," Bethmann-Hollweg noted in his diary, "it remains a leap into the dark."

Events of the next two months led almost inexorably to war. Despite the German announcement, Wilson tried to resist the Germans' violations of America's neutral rights. He also sought to avoid mobilization and other actions which he considered precipitious. He wanted the imperial government to reconsider its decision. He also wished to assure both himself and noninterventionists in the United States that he had sincerely tried to avert armed conflict. Secretary of State Lansing recalled that in those fateful days Wilson became "more and more impressed with the idea that 'white civilization' and its domination over the world rested largely on our ability to keep this country intact, as we would have to build up the nations ravaged by the war." Thus, although interventionists like Lansing and Roosevelt urged an immediate declaration of war, Wilson proceeded cautiously toward American intervention.

On February 3 the president severed diplomatic relations with Germany. With the German blockade reinstituted, submarines soon frightened most neutral shipping from the seas, and goods piled up on the docks and warehouses of the East Coast. On February 26 Wilson asked Congress for authority to place weapons and naval gun crews on American merchant ships. He also solicited an open-ended endorsement to conduct limited naval warfare if necessary while Congress was adjourned for its summer recess. When the legislators resisted, Wilson applied pressure on them by releasing the *Zimmermann* telegram to the press. Intercepted by British intelligence, this message from the German foreign secretary to the kaiser's ambassador in Mexico City proposed that, in the event of war, the German diplomat should offer money and weapons to encourage Mexico to attack the United States in order to obtain its "lost territory in Texas, New Mexico, and Arizona." The American response was one of great indignation toward Germany. Yet many Americans still did not want war. When a dozen noninterventionists in the Senate filibustered against Wilson's proposals, the president excoriated them as "a little group of willful men." After Congress had adjourned, he armed the merchant ships by executive order.

Events of mid-March 1917 led Wilson to decide to take the United States into the war. On March 18, U-boats sank three American merchant ships, killing more than two dozen crewmen. In the same week, the outbreak of the Russian Revolution led to the overthrow of the czarist government and the abdication of Nicholas II. The establishment of a constitutional monarchy under the liberal Prince Lvov reduced the autocratic image of the Russian government and enhanced the Allies' argument that they were fighting for democracy. Still, Wilson found himself in a dilemma. American ships had been sunk and some Americans killed, and interventionists clamored for war. But many Americans remained unconvinced that the situation had changed sufficiently to threaten vital U.S. interests or justify American entry into the European conflict.

The Decision for War

Some noninterventionists suggested alternatives to full-scale belligerency. Bryan urged the president to prohibit American ships from sailing into the war zone and to submit the submarine dispute to a joint high commission for investigation and adjudication after the war. Others argued that the United States should form a league of armed neutrals and keep the sea lanes open to trade by means of a naval neutrality patrol.

Although Wilson knew of these proposals, he chose to ask Congress for a full declaration of war. The chief executive did not think a policy of armed neutrality would give the government adequate authority to mobilize public opinion, the economy, and the armed forces. He decided on full belligerency partly because he considered it the only proper course given the German assault on American shipping and neutral rights. He also believed it was essential for him to have a seat at the peace table. Only as a participating power could the United States work actively to reform international relations and create a progressive world order based on liberal, democratic, capitalist institutions and a league of nations.

Accompanied by armed cavalry, the president rode down Pennsylvania Avenue on April 2, strode up the steps of the Capitol, and delivered an inspiring war message. The kaiser's government, he said, had thrust war upon the United States: "The present German submarine warfare against commerce is a warfare against mankind." "The world," Wilson declared in what would become a historic phrase, "must be made safe for democracy."

Congress adopted the declaration of war, but only after a vigorous debate. Anti-interventionists from the rural South and Midwest warned that the country was entering the conflict to protect the investments of American bankers and munitions makers in the Allied cause. "We are going to war upon the command of gold," declared George Norris, a progressive Republican congressman from Nebraska. Nevertheless, an overwhelming majority supported the president, and the war resolution passed by a vote of 82 to 6 in the Senate and 373 to 50 in the House. On April 6, 1917, the United States officially entered World War I.

Wilson justified American entry into the war in terms of idealism and mission, rather than mundane self-interest. He did not speak of the need to protect Britain and France and prevent Germany from dominating the continent and possibly the Atlantic sea lanes. He avoided such *Realpolitik* partly because he did not realize how desperate the Allies' military situation had become and partly because neither he nor the American people thought primarily in those terms. Instead, Wilson established war objectives which were so idealistic and so difficult that virtually no peace conference could attain them. His grand vision led the American people to war, but it also doomed them to postwar disillusionment.

THE DEBATE OVER AMERICAN ENTRY

As with other great historical events, the causes of the United States' entry into World War I were complex. Historians have little difficulty identifying the precipitating cause as Germany's resumption of unrestricted submarine warfare. But there is much less unanimity on the role of Wilson's policies or the influence of underlying strategic and economic forces.

Although the president emphasized German violation of neutral rights, neither American tradition nor law nor economic necessity required him to guarantee the right of Americans to travel on armed belligerent ships. While he couched his policies in terms of international law and principle, Wilson was responsible for defining the growth of trade with Britain as a legitimate and profitable expression of neutral rights. He rejected definitions by other neutrals—Spain, the Netherlands, and the Scandinavian countries—which banned such passenger travel and embargoed guns and ammunition. In addition, he refused to consider the German and British blockades similarly or to hold Germany to a postwar accounting, as he did in the case of Britain. Thus, by 1917 Wilson found himself constrained by the framework created by his earlier decisions about American rights. Within his strict definition of neutrality the German decision to attack all shipping in the combat zone made war with the United States inevitable. However, there were larger forces at work that must be considered.

Some scholars, such as George Kennan, have argued the importance of strategic realism in explaining the American entry into the war. The United States went to war, they suggest, to preserve a favorable balance of power in Europe and maintain Anglo-American control of the sea lanes. This argument proved particularly popular during the cold war as the United States linked its defense to that of Western Europe against the Soviet Union. Although a few of Wilson's private comments support the assertion that he understood American security to be involved in the European war, this was not his primary concern and he did not try to educate the public to it.

During the 1930s revisionist critics like Walter Millis and Charles Tansill asserted that the United States became a belligerent to protect its loans to the Allies and its trade in arms and munitions. Little evidence exists that the bankers or munitions makers had much immediate influence on Wilson's decision for war. The Nye Committee of Congress, which subpoenaed corporate records, proved only that these corporations had made enormous profits throughout the war. Rather, the bankers influenced the administration most directly in 1915, when they persuaded Wilson to agree to the provision of loans to the Allies to avert a depression in the United States. That decision facilitated the growth of the American economy by rejecting governmental interference with the expanding war trade.

More recently, New Left critics of American foreign policy like William A. Williams have offered a broader economic argument. With considerable justification, they claim that the United States went to war partly to establish an international Open Door for expanding American capitalism. Although Wilson thought primarily in terms of universal principles of law and morality, his world view included the need to open markets to American business. He sought to generate American prosperity and opportunity as well as to reform international relations. Wilson's economic policy, as the historian N. Gordon Levin has shown, was part of his foreign policy, whose goal was to encourage the development of a liberal, democratic, capitalist world order which, he believed, would benefit all nations.

Wilson's policy toward Germany and his decision to take the United States into World War I were part of the development of international activism and interventionism by policy makers in the Progessive Era. His immediate predecessors—McKinley, Roosevelt, and Taft—had emphasized the United States' growing role in world affairs and its responsibility to shape and improve its environment. As the world's richest and most powerful neutral, the United States could not be unaffected by a war for dominance in Europe and, consequently, in other areas as well. Given the prevailing legal, strategic, economic, and idealistic forces, it is likely that any president would eventually have taken the country into World War I.

Within the limits set by national interests at the time, by public opinion and pressure groups, and by tradition and recent developments in foreign policy, Wilson gave U.S. policy his own particular stamp. Another president might have entered the war earlier and justified it on different grounds. A different president might have joined it later or chosen armed neutrality. Wilson's neutrality policy achieved its basic goal of avoiding American belligerency and preserving trade with honor until early 1917, when the Germans decided to end their policy of restraint. By that time the United States had missed the bloodiest years of the war. Not until the closing six months of the conflict, in 1918, did large numbers of American soldiers arrive in France. The war took the lives of 100,000 Americans compared to an estimated ten million Europeans.

Although progressives were divided over American entry in 1917, Wilson employed the rhetoric of reform—idealistic fervor, national purpose, and governmental activism—to justify his policy. Thus, he tried to link the progressive crusades at home and abroad into a war for progressive aims, even though both the war and U.S. entry meant the failure of the progressive attempt to reform international relations so as to eliminate war. The war and the defective peace which followed marked the temporary collapse of the progressive ideal that through active interventionism a great power could help shape its environment and improve its security and international relations.

THE MODERNIZATION OF FOREIGN POLICY

Twenty years of experience under presidents from both major parties during the Progressive Era testified to the weakening of continental isolationism and the beginning of the United States' emergence as an activist, interventionist world power. Despite considerable support for isolationism on the part of traditionalists, practitioners of the new diplomacy abandoned the policy of merely setting an example to the world or reacting to foreign events. Instead, by extending the domestic search for order and improvement overseas, interventionists sought to use America's power to shape its international environment and promote international progress.

Activism and Expansion

Although American activism varied from one region to another, the new interventionists focused primarily on the Western Hemisphere. Defense of the Panama Canal and its approaches became a strategic priority. The Caribbean and Central American countries became "important to us," Secretary of State Root explained, because the Panama Canal put them "in the front yard of the United States."

Powerful nations often dominate small neighbors, but Americans tended to obfuscate their relationship with "client states" by emphasizing such liberal aims as teaching local inhabitants democratic self-government and improving their living conditions. Despite this rhetoric, the primary U.S. goals included security for American trade and naval routes and the development of an area of economic profit. Heavy-handed as it was, Washington's policy achieved its main aim— American hegemony in the Caribbean—though at the cost of numerous military interventions and much local ill will.

In other areas U.S. activity also increased, but Americans proved much less able to dominate events. In the Far East, the United States built naval bases at Pearl Harbor in Hawaii and Subic Bay in the Philippines to protect its string of island territories. But on the mainland of Asia it was relatively ineffective in resisting the determined challenges of Russia and Japan to Manchuria and the integrity of China. In Europe, expanded economic connections and a changing balance of power were accompanied by additional diplomatic initiatives. Active participation in the conferences at The Hague and Algeciras represented a major departure from the American tradition of noninterference in European affairs. Closer ties with Europe and increased interventionism led to participation in World War I and contributed to the Allied victory.

Activism abroad had important effects at home. American exports doubled, increasing from $1.5 million in 1900 to $3 million in 1915. U.S. investments overseas more than tripled during the same years, increasing from less than $1 billion to more than $3 billion. Growing sales abroad, especially during World War I, encouraged continued prosperity at home. Wartime dislocation of international trade patterns also helped American business capture Latin American markets from the British and Germans. In international finance, American war loans to the Allies meant that the United States would emerge from the conflict as the world's creditor nation. All of these trends encouraged the expansion of American multinational corporations as well as numerous other business ventures in the 1920s.

The United States modernized its diplomatic service to meet the demands of growing foreign trade and expanded American commitments. Isolationists had not seen the need for an extensive diplomatic corps. As late as 1897 Champ Clark, a congressional leader from Missouri, had recommended that the diplomatic corps be abolished as an unnecessary expense. But in the two decades after the Spanish-American War Congress reorganized and enlarged the diplomatic and consular services to put them on a more permanent, full-time, professional basis. The State Department established a more efficient information system and created its first specialized geographic branch, the Far Eastern Division. It also encouraged professionalization by inaugurating a training period for new officers and advocating selection and promotion on the basis of merit.

The combined diplomatic and defense budgets climbed by more than one-third—from $200 million to $300 million annually—in the first fourteen years of the twentieth century. The armed services accounted for the major part of this expansion. During the Progressive Era the Navy obtained a modern high-seas fleet which ranked third in the world. It also built substantial new bases at home, in the Caribbean, and in the Pacific. A more centralized command structure was created to increase its efficiency. As a result of inefficient mobilization during the Spanish-American War, the government also reorganized the military forces. Congress established a general staff to coordinate the work of the previously autonomous bureau chiefs and set up a series of specialized postgraduate command schools for officers. The lawmakers also made provisions for drafting the National Guard into federal service in an emergency. President Wilson used this provision during the mobilization on the Mexican border in 1916 and when the United States entered World War I the following year.

Although Congress rejected universal military training, pressure for such training emboldened Wilson and the legislature to adopt conscription—the Selective Service System—once the country had gone to war. This was the first time in the history of the United States that compulsory military service was used as the primary means of raising the army. The draft and the enormous supply of manpower it provided on a predictable basis helped Wilson obtain an army of more than 3 million men and send and maintain an expeditionary force of 2 million in France. It served as a precedent for future wars.

In the Progressive Era, for the first time in generations, foreign relations became a major concern. Americans debated the effect of the new U.S. interventionism on traditions like isolationism, neutrality, and the Monroe Doctrine, on institutions and ideals, and on the security and prosperity of the nation as a whole. Each of the three chief executives of the period encouraged expansion and in doing so helped strengthen the powers of the presidency. Roosevelt became the first president to leave the country while in office (he went to the Caribbean), and Wilson was the second, traveling to Europe for the peace negotiations.

As international affairs grew in importance, Congress expanded its watchdog role in foreign policy. For the first time, the legislature held hearings dealing extensively with foreign affairs. In 1910 a Democratic House committee inquired into Roosevelt's part in the Panamanian Revolution of 1903, and in 1919 the Senate Foreign Relations Committee held substantial hearings on the Versailles Peace Treaty. The lawmakers began to expose presidential actions and important treaties to the new foreign policy interest groups in a congressional forum.

Despite this new interest and involvement in world affairs, Americans maintained much of their former isolationism. Many believed that the United States could retain its traditional policies despite changes in international relations.

An Ambivalent Legacy

American views on foreign affairs lagged behind the altered international situation. Policy and institutions were transformed more rapidly than attitudes. Most Americans assumed that the country could enter the modern world while maintaining its nineteenth-century traditions of relatively free security and freedom of action. The modernizers—militant expansionists and reform internationalists—influenced many people but failed to convince the majority of Americans of the need for sustained drastic change. Even Wilson's combination of evangelistic mission with interventionism could not sustain a continuous commitment to active engagement and responsibility in international affairs. The new outward thrust was counterbalanced by traditional American parochialism.

The growth of the United States' world role in the first two decades of the twentieth century did not result in a complete transformation of U.S. foreign policy. A new activist interventionism, pursued by corporations, private reform groups, and the president and his advisers in the diplomatic service and the armed forces, emerged. It was aimed at shaping the country's external environment and promoting international progress. But this did not end the influence of American isolationism. Rather, diplomacy in the Progressive Era was a transitional stage in the erratic evolution of the United States to the global commitments and involvement that would characterize American foreign policy in the cold war era.

CHAPTER 8

The New Interventionism

"Those who are young today," Walter Lippmann wrote in 1914, "are born into a world in which the foundations of the old order survive only as habits or by default. Scientific invention and blind social currents have made the old authority impossible. . . . Our time believes in change." Lippmann was right. The Progressive Era proved to be a time of extraordinary change. In many ways it marked the birth of modern America.

A generation earlier, people had debated national political issues which now seem generally archaic: reconstruction policies toward the South, pensions for Union veterans, tariff levels, and whether the currency should be backed by gold alone or by silver as well. But industrialization, immigration, and urbanization transformed America and the nature of the political debate. In the Progressive Era national parties clashed over big business, antitrust policy, federal regulation, women's rights, the government's role in determining working conditions, the conservation of natural resources, and the extent of U.S. intervention overseas. These were issues which would dominate politics for much of the twentieth century.

The change in issues reflected basic alterations in the way Americans lived and worked. Industrialization was accompanied by the spread of factories and congested, unhealthy cities. It contributed to widespread poverty and labor violence, while concentrating great power in the hands of new industrial and financial elites. Yet industrialization also brought many benefits—jobs, goods, wealth, and power—and the anxiety with which many people viewed it was mixed with admiration and awe.

At the turn of the century the United States entered a new era of economic growth, becoming the first industrial nation to commit itself to mass production and consumption of consumer goods. The consumer society meant a dramatically increasing material standard of living and seemed to offer a new frontier for economic expansion when seemingly limitless western land was no longer available. These developments encouraged Americans to continue to believe that they were a chosen people with a unique mandate to lead the way to a more perfect world.

THE INTERVENTIONIST IMPULSE

Despite their confidence, large numbers of Americans concluded that the problems accompanying industrialization meant that they could no longer rely solely on providence or evolution for automatic progress in keeping with the country's heritage. They lost their faith in the long-held utilitarian concept of a natural harmony of self-interests and in the functioning of a self-regulating society. Given the dangers which were evident by the turn of the century, many Americans questioned whether the economy and society benefited from allowing decisions which affected everyone to be determined entirely by individuals and by market forces. With the optimism and new sense of power which came from developments in science, technology, and organization theory, the new interventionists decided that it was necessary to modify the concept of unrestricted individualism and the marketplace ideal. They thought that intervention and intelligent direction could ensure continued growth and progress that would be consistent with the ideal of an efficient and liberal democratic society.

The new interventionists did not eliminate individualism, laissez faire, or the market system, or even make them secondary. These beliefs remained powerful and primary long after the Progressive Era.

Rather, what happened in the first years of the new century was that Americans made the first successful national attempt since the mercantilist system of the eighteenth century to place significant limitations on the market system. This shift to a mood which supported intervention and purposeful direction was probably the most important change of the Progressive Era.

The number of collective decisions to limit the self-regulating marketplace increased substantially. Officials in a somewhat expanded government made a few of these decisions. But many more were made by people in organizations in the private sector—supercorporations (themselves often conglomerations of formerly independent companies), trade associations, labor unions, professional bodies, or other voluntary associations. Interventionists created new mechanisms for dealing with the problems caused by blind social forces accompanying industrialization. Using the example of the supercorporations, which could greatly influence their environment, interventionists employed organization and intervention as tools for imposing conscious direction on society. Writing in 1914, Lippmann noted the dramatic change:

> We can no longer treat life as something that has trickled down to us. We have to deal with it deliberately, devise its social organization, alter its tools, formulate its method, educate and control it. . . . The scientific spirit is the discipline of democracy, the escape from drift. . . . Men have to substitute purpose for tradition; and that is, I believe, the profoundest change that has ever taken place in human history.

By focusing on the progressives and on the expansion of governmental power, historians have frequently neglected the broader basis of change in the era. They have concentrated on the transient nature of the shifting coalitions which formed around specific issues. In doing so, they have often misunderstood the widespread dissatisfaction with many of the results of unrestricted individualism, an unregulated marketplace, and a self-regulating society. The dominant development of the era was the emergence of an interventionist mood on a national scale. The need for some kind of purposeful, collective intervention, for what Lippmann called mastery over drift, became apparent not only to radicals and moderate reformers like the progressives but to many conservatives as well.

Many conservatives, for example, supported some degree of intervention in the marketplace because of new industrial conditions. As Thomas A. Edison wrote to his friend Henry Ford in 1912,

> This is a pretty raw, crude civilization of ours—pretty wasteful, pretty cruel. . . . Our production, our factory laws, our charities, our relations between capital and labor, our distribution—all wrong, out of gear. We've stumbled along for a while, trying to run a new civilization in old ways, but we've got to start to make this world over.

Conservatives created instruments for collective decision making in the private sector such as the giant corporations, trade associations, philanthropic foundations, and coordinating bodies like the National Civic Federation. Many of them also helped other interventionists achieve new governmental mechanisms for order, including regulatory agencies, social control devices like prohibition and immigration restriction, and a modern army, navy, and diplomatic service for a more active foreign policy.

Yet, despite the breadth of the forces for change, the Progressive Era cannot be understood without progressivism. Although it was neither a unified social movement nor a single coalition of voters, progressivism cannot be dismissed for its diversity. Nor can it be disregarded because of conservative aspects of its nature and legacy. Rather, contemporaries correctly saw it as the dominant motif of the period.

The core of progressivism was the progressive ethos—a combination of moral idealism and pragmatic, piecemeal reform with a sweeping vision of democracy and rejuvenated national community. Evangelistic modernizers, progressives had a sense of morality and mission which led them to try to impose their standards on an increasingly diverse society and, in fact, through cultural imperialism, on the world as well. The reformer Frederic C. Howe, writing his memoirs in 1925, put it candidly:

> Evangelical religion [and] . . . early assumptions as to virtue and vice, goodness and evil . . . explain the nature of our reforms, the regulatory legislation in morals and economics, our belief in men rather than in institutions and our messages to other peoples. Missionaries and battleships, anti-saloon leagues and Ku Klux Klans, Wilson and Santo Domingo are all part of that evangelistic psychology that makes America what she is.

The progressives' spirit, like that of the nation's founders, the Jacksonians, and later the New Dealers, set the style, the rhetoric, and much of the substance of the agenda and leadership of their time.

Progressivism also provided a significant number of leaders, both in private and public organizations and in government, who translated that spirit into an ideal which helped mobilize millions of Americans into myriad campaigns for progress. "It is this union of the idealistic and the efficient," a young intellectual named Randolph Bourne wrote in 1913, "that gives the movement its hold on the disinterested and serious youth of today." A generation earlier, in the spoilsman days of the Gilded Age, young men from elite families had avoided politics as disreputable. But progressives resurrected public service and political leadership as honorable callings. Unselfish service came to be seen as an ideal, partly because resurgent Protestant evangelism coalesced with such secular developments as professionalization and bureaucratization. The altruist, the expert, and the civil servant were seen as people who put the good of society above their own interests. Leaders like Jane Addams, Gifford Pinchot, Theodore Roosevelt, and Woodrow Wilson inspired a generation of young men and women to enter community and public service. They also influenced the course of public debate for several decades.

The rhetoric of reform, the common language which progressivism gave to an era, proved more effective in mobilizing action than in analyzing developments. It masked the differences among people who used the same political phrases. The conflicting aims of many progressives and others were muted by the interventionists' emphasis on process—purposeful, intelligent, collaborative decision making—rather than on specific goals such as reducing prices, providing socially acceptable wages, or limiting the size of corporations. Progressives sought to establish a general public interest among different and often competing groups. But defining that concept might have destroyed the coalition which made possible much of the interventionist legislation. To the extent that progressives and other interventionists stressed larger abstract goals of a higher morality, a general public interest, and a unique mission for ensuring progress at home and abroad, they served as missionaries of a particularly American form of modernization.

MODERNIZATION, AMERICAN STYLE

Because of a different environment, culture, and tradition, the United States placed much less emphasis on governmental intervention and acted much more slowly than the industrializing countries of western Europe in establishing a regulatory welfare state. Beginning in the 1880s, for example, the German government under Bismarck insured industrial workers for loss of income because of sickness or accident and guaranteed them old-age pensions. The Germans established the principle that such risks should be carried by society and not solely by individuals. Under pressure from rapidly expanding trade and craft unions and from socialist labor parties and middle-class reformers, other western European nations adopted similar programs. Britain added a system of national unemployment insurance and, under the Liberal governments of Campbell-Bannerman and Lloyd George, sought to increase economic and political democracy by restricting the power of the House of Lords and raising taxes on the wealthy to pay for the emerging welfare state.

The United States experienced industrialization and the drive toward political and social democracy somewhat differently because of its relative abundance and the absence of an entrenched aristocracy and a restless proletariat, and because of the country's emphasis on individualism, laissez faire, and a relatively free marketplace. America's social democracy was much less oriented toward labor and socialist ideology than that of Europe. The lack of widespread class consciousness among industrial workers and notoriously weak labor unions contributed to a reform program which was moderate, pragmatic, and centered on specific problems. More influential than labor were the agrarians of the South and West and the broad middle class. Within these groups religious and missionary traditions gave American social democracy a particularly moralistic air and an evangelical tone. Furthermore, there was no counterpart on the European continent to the United States' antimonopoly tradition. European political and legal systems proved much more permissive to allowing independent manufacturers to join together in cartels to avoid destructive price competition at home or abroad. Ironically, the American antitrust tradition, which outlawed such cartels, resulted in the largest integrated supercorporations in the world.

Structural obstacles and suspicion of strong central government helped limit the growth of governmental power in the United States. Taxes, for example, took only 3 percent of average income compared to 9 percent in Britain and 12 percent in France. Traditionalists and many fiscal conservatives in Congress, the judiciary, and the media restricted governmental expansion. In the political system, power was fragmented among various branches of government and in the division of the federal-state system itself. The new supercorporations and other powerful interest groups contested many reforms, thereby forcing significant compromises. In this accommodation the poor and the unorganized had virtually no influence. Most people had little knowledge of the details of contemporary issues or legislation. Even the reformers who understood the issues were often divided. Furthermore, progressives overestimated the length of time that reform activism could be sustained before sufficient opposition gathered to blunt it and it lost its momentum.

THE CYCLE OF REFORM

The life cycle of progressivism as a nationwide political movement illustrates the dynamic quality of the American political system. Dramatic events and shifts in public mood can, under favorable circumstances and effective leadership, reduce the power of previous constraints, at least temporarily. At such a time a broad national consensus for collective action can lead to the achievement of significant change. Such a departure generally requires a special combination of occurrences to unsettle the political situation. During the Progressive Era, the interventionist mood stemmed from the traumatic disruptions of the depression of the 1890s, which helped convince many Americans that industrialization would not automatically cure its own ills and that purposeful action was required. Following the depression, the prosperity and economic growth in the first decade of the twentieth century encouraged optimism, hope, and generosity. Investigative journalists—the muckrakers—helped to sustain and direct reform. New political leaders came to power promising significant changes.

Progressivism emerged in the cities in the late 1890s and reached its peak nationally in the decade between 1907 and 1916. Then the movement began to divide as more conservative reformers became convinced that the tempo of reform had become too rapid and the scope too broad and that a period of stability was required to absorb the changes already made. American participation in World War I aroused and then dissipated the militant optimism of progressivism. "We were not used to smelling blood from vast human slaughterhouses," William Allen White recalled. The strains of the war and the debate over the peace shattered progressivism as a national movement. "We poor panting crusaders for a just and righteous order were left on a deserted battlefield," White mourned, "our drums punctured, our bugles muted, our cause forgotten."

In the 1920s progressivism as a broad, national political force faded from American life. The coalition which had supported its reforms splintered further over ethnocultural issues—prohibition, compulsory "Americanization," and immigration restriction—raised by the continuing search for a homogeneous national culture. Further blows were dealt to the movement by the death of its political leaders like Roosevelt and Wilson and the aging of others, such as La Follette. Many wealthy patrons of reform movements died, while others turned their attention to the arts or to other causes. The nation focused on the growth of business, the flood of new consumer goods, mass entertainment, changing life styles, and the divisive ethnocultural issues which dominated the decade. Although a number of the reforms and reformers continued, the national mood of the Progressive Era evaporated in the boosterism, consumerism, individual self-concern, and aid to business which characterized the 1920s.

THE LEGACY OF THE PROGRESSIVE ERA

Despite the demise of progressivism, the era significantly influenced American society. Interventionists began to acclimate Americans to new mechanisms for social change and order in a complex and interrelated urban, industrial society. Most progressives and other interventionists sought to provide new means of coordination and direction without creating the kind of powerful state apparatus which emerged in Europe. Although they called for modification of laissez faire and the marketplace ideal, they wanted new private and governmental mechanisms which would ensure progress while maintaining the nation's aims.

Despite the democratic rhetoric of the time, the politics and institutions developed in the Progressive Era provided an ambiguous legacy. In retrospect, the progressives were rather naive reformers. They proved better at obtaining power than at using it. In ousting incumbents, they had few equals, but once in office they could not agree on the specific aims of government. They sought a general public interest, but they did not define it. Given the conflicting aims of the interventionist groups which helped create the new mechanisms of management, it was perhaps impossible to define a commonly accepted goal. But without such a definition, or adequate guidelines for the exercise of power, the new institutions could be used by interests with other philosophies when the national mood and political power shifted. The regulatory commissions, for example, often became dominated by some of the powerful interest groups they were designed to control.

The fact that the most liberal progressives later claimed that the institutions had betrayed their original purpose was less a reflection of the actual aims of these bodies than of the democratic rhetoric of the Progressive Era. That rhetoric often masked not only the conflicting aims of competing groups but wide differences in philosophy as well. It was evoked by those who emphasized rights and those who stressed duties; it was employed both to encourage freedom and to increase repression. In the long run interventionists created mechanisms which could be used for different purposes. In retrospect, the ambiguity had been present from the beginning.

In their search for new people and new systems to direct social change, progressives and other interventionists promoted patterns of rationalization, predictability, and efficiency; most important, they created new organizations. To replace what they regarded as reliance on chance and ad hoc local responses, interventionists turned to the methods of scientific investigation—data gathering, analysis, and prognosis—and to the establishment of permanent associations or agencies.

Despite their ambiguity, the organizations of the Progressive Era proved one of the period's most important legacies.

Interventionists gave a major boost to the creation of nationally organized voluntary associations which could mediate between increasing social demands and the need for some kind of collective action, on the one hand, and, on the other, older American traditions of individual autonomy, private property, and limited government. Although they recognized the need for some expanded governmental power to balance the growth of private power centers, progressives and most other interventionists did not want to end primary reliance on voluntary action and initiative in the community itself. The corporations demonstrated the benefit of organization and intervention in the marketplace. As a result, many workers, professionals, producers, shippers, and others formed associations for self-protection and promotion.

The Progressive Era also showed that nationally organized voluntary associations could intervene to improve society. The tuberculosis society, the settlement house association, and youth organizations like the Boy Scouts, Camp Fire Girls, YMCA, and YWCA tried to alleviate problems by altering environmental conditions, attitudes, and behavior. So, in fact, did more coercive organizations like the Anti-Saloon League and the Immigration Restriction League. The irony of the Progressive Era included not only the ambiguity of its mechanisms of organization and intervention but also the fact that progressives, although desiring a common public interest, often created interest groups which ultimately changed the way the national government functioned and contributed to the rise of the broker state.

The New Politics

For all their talk of restoring government to "the people" and curbing "the interests," the progressives obtained mixed results. Many of the insurgents' innovations were designed to help them gain office by expanding the power of their particular constituency, primarily the middle class. Thus, they circumvented party bosses by emphasizing popular government. They enlarged the nominating process by creating direct primaries in several states, and they achieved direct election of U.S. senators through a constitutional amendment. They developed a new kind of personal and issue-oriented politics which party machines often found difficult to handle.

In practice, however, much of their emphasis on democracy proved illusory. Measures like the initiative and referendum have been employed most successfully by the best-financed and -organized special-interest groups, especially conservative organizations. The recall has rarely been effective in removing public officials. And while progressive reforms helped insurgents gain power, they also diminished the political involvement of many lower-income people—blacks as well as Asian, Hispanic, and European immigrants—whom the progressives deliberately disfranchised. Furthermore, the progessives' emphasis on personalities and issues was no substitute for party loyalty and discipline as a means of mobilizing masses of voters. Voter turnout (as a percentage of eligible voters), which had begun to decline after the election of 1896, shrank rapidly in the Progressive Era, evidence of increasing voter apathy despite extensive political activity.

The experience of Europe, where socialist labor and liberal reform parties emerged in these years, was not matched in the United States, where attempts to create substantial socialist and progressive parties failed. The structure of the two-party system remained basically unaltered. The Progressive party died when Roosevelt deserted it, and the Socialist party was drained by Wilsonian reforms and crippled by repression and internal schism during and immediately after World War I. The dominant Republican party repudiated much of Roosevelt's reform activism and statism, and the Democractic party spent much of the 1920s paralyzed by bitter divisions between its urban and rural wings. It took the Great Depression and Franklin D. Roosevelt to unite those elements, enlist millions of new voters, and forge the Democractic party into the new majority coalition which would dominate national politics for more than two decades.

Progressives did, however, create the modern presidency. Theodore Roosevelt and Woodrow Wilson took advantage of the centralizing forces of the period, the mass media, and the growth of foreign affairs to attract popular loyalty and enlarge the public's expectations of presidential leadership. In departing from the limited view of executive power of the post–Civil War period, Roosevelt and Wilson showed that the modern president could sometimes bridge the separation of powers and overcome other obstacles to strong positive governmental action. Herbert Hoover and Franklin Roosevelt continued the expansion of the presidency in meeting the exigencies of the Great Depression. Thus, progressives created an institution which could help the nation take effective action against national problems but could also become an "imperial presidency" which went beyond both consensus and constitutional limitations on executive power in both domestic and foreign affairs. Like the other progressive mechanisms, the modern presidency could be used for good or ill.

Responding to Big Business

By the end of the Progressive Era, national administrators in both major parties had responded to the problem of industrial concentration. Interventionists evolved four different approaches to managing the organizational revolution and the new economic order. These alternatives came to be lumped under general rubrics: socialism, the New Freedom, the New Individualism, and the New Nationalism. The Progressive Era did not resolve the debate among these alternatives, but it left an institutional legacy based on each of them.

The concept of public ownership, a central part of socialism, was applied primarily to local utilities. Governmental ownership of gas and water facilities, and sometimes of electrical production and transit lines, removed these utilities as sources of corruption and often meant lower prices for consumers. Public control of water and power and the principle of conservation contributed to the development in the 1930s of the Tennessee Valley Authority, the largest federal experiment in regional conservation and development through public ownership and planning.

But public ownership was too radical for most Americans, who supported more traditional concepts like Wilson's "New Freedom" idea, in which the government would intervene in the economy only to the extent necessary to break up monopolies and help restore the discipline of the marketplace. Attempts to limit concentration included tariff reduction, regionalization and public supervision of banking through the Federal Reserve System, restrictions on business practices through the Clayton Antitrust Act, and the growing antitrust bureaucracy in the Department of Justice. Although virtually abandoned in World War I and the 1920s, the New Freedom idea was restored temporarily during the New Deal through federal regulation of the stock market, limitation of utilities' holding company empires, and a temporary revival of the investigation and prosecution of concentration in industry.

The new "Cooperative Individualism" espoused by some progressives, such as Herbert Hoover, envisioned both government and private institutions playing a more positive role to encourage socially beneficial economic growth. In a marketplace in which "destructive" price competition was reduced, social duties could be assigned not to government but to responsible private associations. Functional groups in business, labor, and other sectors could receive advice from government agenices on how to achieve social harmony and community action without stultifying bureaucracy. The National Civic Federation and many trade associations favored this alternative to a powerful administrative state. In the 1920s Hoover, first as secretary of commerce and then as president, became the leading spokesman for this kind of partnership among responsible, interdependent social groups. But the Great Depression undermined his plans as those groups turned to the federal government for assistance and sustenance.

The Progressive Era's most substantial legacy in the area of governmental policy was the New Nationalism of Theodore Roosevelt, with its emphasis on national planning and regulation and its contribution to the origin of the managerial and social-service state. In the public interest, federal agencies supervised activities in the private sector which affected the nation as a whole: the consolidation and trade practices of big business, railroad acquisitions and rate making, the manufacture and sale of drugs, food preparation and meatpacking practices, the development of natural resources, and the currency reserves of the banking system. The size of the federal government, which had grown from 95,000 civilian employees in 1880 to 230,000 in 1900, nearly doubled again by 1917, when the employee total reached 430,000. New or expanded agencies like the Interstate Commerce Commission, the Federal Trade Commission, the Federal

Reserve Board, the Forestry Service, the Bureau of Mines, and the Food and Drug Administration greatly increased the federal government's role in the economy. They also served as models for mobilization agencies in World War I, for new regulatory bodies like the Federal Radio Commission (later the Federal Communications Commission) and the Civil Aeronautics Board in the 1920s, and for a host of New Deal agencies, such as the National Recovery Administration, the Agricultural Adjustment Administration, the Securities Exchange Commission, and the National Labor Relations Board, in the 1930s.

The independent regulatory commission, the key mechanism of most progressives and many other interventionists for maintaining the public interest in certain sectors of the economy, proved a complex and ambiguous device. Given the contradictory goals of restricting combination and protecting consumers while promoting economic growth and a healthy industry, progressives were never able adequately to define an enduring public interest. Rather, the regulatory agencies tended to become independent bureaucracies concerned primarily with their own status and well-being. Although their original proponents often claimed—with much justification—that the commissions had become too responsive to the industries they were designed to regulate, the charge oversimplified the origins, obstacles, and subsequent development of most regulatory commissions. These agencies responded most directly to changes in the power of various groups caused by fluctuations in political circumstances. Commissioners saw themselves as operating within a much narrower range of policy options than most progressives recognized. Even when they sought to act boldly, commissioners found themselves restricted by the courts, the legislatures, business interests, and changing public opinion. Finally, they were limited by the inherent nature of each industry, which in the long run proved to be the single most important context of governmental regulation.

The early history of the Federal Trade Commission (FTC) illustrates the complexity of the problem. Originally, radical progressives hoped it would control big business and promote fair competition. But many corporation managers expected it to encourage cooperation between business and government to stimulate further economic growth. During its early years the FTC began some investigations of business practices, but during World War I it turned its attention to encouraging cooperation among businesses in order to expand production of war matériel.

After the end of the war the commission returned briefly to investigating business. But when it recommended radical restructuring of the meatpacking industry, including some public ownership, a conservative Congress called for an investigation of the FTC and transferred jurisdiction over the meatpackers to the more friendly Department of Agriculture. During the Republican administrations of the 1920s, a chastised and restaffed FTC supported efforts by competing businesses to cooperate through trade associations, and provided governmental advice on business opportunities and economic growth. Not until the New Deal did the FTC, with new powers and personnel, again seek to regulate business practices in the public interest. Like the FTC, other regulatory commissions shifted their roles repeatedly in response to changing appointments, new circumstances, and different public and governmental attitudes toward business.

Regardless of occasional gestures toward antitrust action and some federal regulation, big business and big finance remained relatively unimpaired. Although a few giants like Standard Oil and American Tobacco suffered temporary setbacks from governmental action, the supercorporations lost little of their power or prerogatives, despite widespread public hostility toward the trusts. The most effective challenge to monopoly came from new competitors as the economy evolved toward oligopoly; it was the concentration of power in a few giant firms in each major industry. In their relationship with government, corporation managers and financiers were not able to obtain everything they wanted or block everything they opposed, but they wielded substantial influence in shaping legislation or modifying its implementation. Although the power of big business fluctuated— greater in the 1890s and the 1920s than in the Progressive or New Deal eras—it was always able to block the most radical efforts against it.

Many Americans feared the complete breakup of big business would create such chaos that it would jeopardize economic growth. Many rejected governmental ownership because they believed in private property and individual initiative and were skeptical of the efficiency of governmental operation. As a result the governmental response to industrial and financial concentration in the Progressive Era did more to help Americans adjust to the new corporate economy than it did to curb the new centers of power. Not until the New Deal, with its dramatic expansion of the power of government and of other groups such as organized labor, did big business begin to feel significant public influence and constraints.

Reducing the Harshness of Industrialism

Protective intervention began to ameliorate some of the harshness of the factory and wage systems. Many states passed laws for a basic standard of protection for industrial workers—mine and factory safety, workmen's compensation, outlawing of child labor, and minimum-wage and maximum-hour standards for women workers—but enforcement was often inadequate. Not until the New Deal did the federal government obtain the power to establish wage and hour standards for male and female workers and set up nationwide systems of unemployment insurance and pension and other social security benefits.

Industrial workers benefited from protective legislation and the general economic growth of the period, but they made their most substantial gains through direct collective intervention in the marketplace. Although most progressives showed little support, trade unionism and the collective bargaining agreement emerged as the predominant mechanisms for protecting and improving labor's position. Unlike European unions, with their mass membership and socialism, the American Federation of Labor remained limited primarily to skilled workers, moderate in its goals, and only reluctantly political. It was not until the Great Depression that the mass production workers were organized by an offshoot of the AFL, the Congress of Industrial Organizations (CIO), and labor became one of the enduring substantial components of a major political party—the New Deal coalition of the Democratic party.

Henry George and others had long pointed to the growing gap between the rich and poor, the expansion of poverty, and the hardship caused by the wage system, which threw workers back on their own resources during downturns in the business cycle. Progressive Era interventionists provided some protection for the urban poor. They obtained laws aimed at ameliorating conditions in tenements and ensuring safe water, milk, and meat. They helped make cities somewhat cleaner and healthier places to live. Reformers also supplemented church and ad hoc private charities with new, permanent, professional secular organizations of social workers, youth workers, and public health nurses and physicians. Nevertheless, poverty remained widespread, and it was not until the Great Depression demonstrated the inadequacy of local efforts that the federal government established programs of relief for the unemployed which went far beyond any previous private or municipal assistance.

The monetary and fiscal innovations of the Progressive Era also served more as precedents for future intervention than as mechanisms of great immediate influence. In one of their most important victories, reformers obtained a federal income tax as a means of tapping the new sources of wealth in the corporate economy. Keeping the tax rates low, however, they chose to use it to pay for expanding governmental functions rather than as a device to redistribute wealth. Yet despite the income tax, the gap between rich and poor grew wider during the Progressive Era. The wealthiest 10 percent of the population increased its share of total personal income from 34 to 38 percent between 1910 and 1920, while the poorest 60 percent watched its share drop from 35 to 30 percent.

In an attempt to provide a system of currency and bank reserves which would be more responsive to business conditions, Congress created the Federal Reserve System, but its managers failed to ease the painful economic contractions which began in 1920 and 1929. Although the interventionists of the Progressive Era took the first steps toward creating a federal budget, they did not establish mechanisms for countercyclical spending. Not until the New Deal did the government adopt deficit spending to stimulate economic growth or provide federal insurance for bank deposits and greater monetary controls for the Federal Reserve Board to manipulate the money supply and shore up the banking system.

The Challenges of Pluralism and Modernism

Some of the most repressive interventionist measures of the Progressive Era came from attempts to maintain a relatively homogeneous society and culture. In an increasingly heterogeneous society the failure of progressives and conservatives to achieve a consensus on values and behavior set the stage for violent clashes between nativists and ethnic minorities and between modernizers and those who were committed to the traditional culture. Cultural interventionism left a bitter legacy.

For blacks, the Progressive Era meant primarily the solidification of racial segregation in the South and the rise of urban ghettos and *de facto* segregation in the North. Yet despite the attempt to keep blacks subordinate, there were hopeful signs. New institutions like the NAACP and the National Urban League began to work for blacks' rights. The concentration of blacks in northern cities contributed to cultural developments like the Harlem Renaissance and the black nationalist movement of Marcus Garvey in the 1920s and the growth of black voting blocs, which became significant in local and ultimately national elections.

To deal with what they considered the "problem" of the new immigrants, interventionists used a combination of education and coercion. When voluntary "Americanization" measures worked too slowly, nativists turned to government to restrict or prevent disapproved behavior through efforts to prohibit the use of alcohol, enforce sabbatarian and antivice laws, and suppress foreign-language newspapers and parochial schools. The Americanization movement gained momentum from the nationalist mood of World War I and grew during the hysteria over radicals and foreign influence which pervaded the postwar era. Immigration restriction, begun in 1917, was expanded and made permanent in the 1920s through legislation which directly excluded most southern and eastern Europeans and nearly all Asians and which remained in effect until 1965. Such suppression, combined with the intense debates over U.S. entry into World War I and the Treaty of Versailles, produced a counterreaction. New immigrant voters began to mobilize politically in defense of some cultural pluralism and to support urban presidential candidates such as Alfred E. Smith and Franklin D. Roosevelt.

The issue of what kind of belief and value system should be dominant in America also continued to divide modernizers and traditionalists as they struggled over the direction of change. For example, prohibition, which became widespread during the Progressive Era, grew into a major symbolic issue in the 1920s. Some progressive and conservative interventionists had supported it as a means of improving society. But to many of those who were committed to the traditional culture, affirmation of abstinence as a national ideal became intertwined with the desire to uphold the values of small-town and rural Protestant America as opposed to secular and permissive trends or Catholic culture, which they identified with modern metropolitan America. National prohibition, first adopted as a wartime measure, was seemingly made permanent in 1919 by the passage of the Eighteenth Amendment, one of the most extensive examples of national cultural intervention.

Traditionalists and fundamentalists also struggled against many of the changes being made by modernizers in what was being preached in churches, taught in schools, and shown in movie theaters. Their reaction against modernization became extreme in legislation like the Tennessee law which prohibited the teaching of the theory of evolution in public schools (and led to the conviction of biology teacher John Scopes in the famous "monkey trial") and in the vigilantism of the revived Ku Klux Klan. Despite such resistance, the complex transformation of moral values, religious beliefs, and social and sexual customs which accelerated during the Progressive Era became even more widespread in the following decades.

The International Legacy

Interventionists of the Progressive Era found a new frontier of activism and economic growth abroad, but they did not achieve agreement among Americans over the nation's proper role in the world. Much of the old isolationism remained, despite the internationalists' efforts not to drift in reaction to events but actively to shape and improve the environment abroad. Yet the internationalists created a number of new organizations—ranging from trade groups to the ideological associations which made up the modern peace movement—and devised a variety of mechanisms for implementing their policies. Among these were arbitration and conciliation treaties, a world court, a league of nations, and a modernized army, navy, foreign service, and presidency. The United States intervened in the Caribbean and the Far East. After obtaining a few formal colonies, it developed a string of protectorate client states in the Caribbean. But it also attempted to go beyond imperialism to a new, Americanized world order created through cooperative economic development, scientific knowledge, and moral commitment. This was the liberal, capitalistic international order Wilson envisioned in his Fourteen Points and in his concept of the League of Nations.

The United States' entry into World War I represented both a logical culmination of growing interventionism and the failure of the progressives' hope that Americans could be active abroad and improve international relations at little cost. The era left a dual legacy. Reaction against the war and the Treaty of Versailles led to a resurgence of isolationism which precluded many formal U.S. commitments and interventions. The Great Depression and the rise of aggressive military regimes in Italy, Japan, and Germany increased American isolationism, which reached its peak in the neutrality legislation of the 1930s. But there was also continued internationalism in the form of economic expansion and diplomatic attempts to build postwar cooperation without military intervention. The fragile structure of international realtions crumbled in the 1930s, but as the United States moved toward global commitments in World War II and during the cold war, active interventionism and the Wilsonian ideal of collective security were resurrected from the Progressive Era.

PROGRESSIVISM AND OPTIMISM

Despite its ambiguous legacy, the Progressive Era was instrumental in shaping modern America. In those years interventionists made the first successful national effort to curtail some of the more destructive features of unrestricted individualism, an unregulated marketplace, and blind social forces. They provided new private and governmental mechanisms for consciously directing and improving society. The interventionists thought these means were consistent with America's traditions and ideals. Progressives, the most optimistic of the interventionists, believed that with the proper mechanisms they could eliminate virtually any social problem: corruption, drunkenness, disease, and even war itself. Despite the practical, modern nature of their devices, their exuberance made them more like nineteenth-century moral reformers than like later generations, who were chastened by depression and two world wars. The progressives were not faced with such disillusionment. Nor did they confront the brittle tension between the desire to ensure the rights of all citizens and expand benefits to them and the realization of limits to economic growth—a paramount issue today. For all its naive, shortsighted, and sometimes repressive aspects, the activism of the Progressive Era interventionists toward the challenges of their time enabled them to provide ideas and institutions which would continue to shape the direction of American society for more than half a century.

The disillusionment with progressivism which has characterized much historical writing in recent years has provided many new insights into the movement. Critics of progressivism as diverse as Richard Hofstadter and Gabriel Kolko have pointed out its confusion, conservatism, racism, and repression. Prohibition, immigration restriction, racial segregation, and imperialism are, of course, part of its legacy. But while there is considerable truth in these critical appraisals, undue attention to such features militates against an accurate understanding of progressivism.

Taking a broader view, I conclude that the evidence supports a more positive emphasis. Repression and other distasteful aspects of the era—the "sour side" of interventionism—were not the aims of most progressives and were not the overarching concerns of the era. Rather, the emphasis was on positive achievements. While recognizing the role of class and regional conflict in generating progressive protest, it is important to realize that progressivism also represented a continuation of a basic American optimism and faith in Americans as a chosen people with a unique destiny to improve the lot of humankind. In addition, progressives combined an evangelical mentality with a new scientism. Together with nonprogressives, they intervened purposefully in the functioning of society through new mechanisms—national associations, regulatory commissions, agencies for investigation and arbitration, and even a league of nations—to achieve Americans' traditional aim of social betterment in a new urban-industrial society and changing world. Interventionism was a tool which could be used by different groups for various purposes, but despite the differences the end result was that the nation as a whole moved ahead.

This interpretation of the Progressive Era may be considered idealistic and perhaps naive, but I think it is supported by a fair and balanced examination of the evidence. It is true that elements of narrow-mindedness and even reaction accompanied both the origins and the outcomes of progressivism. But when one looks at the main purpose of progressivism—to improve society—and measures its positive accomplishments realistically against the obstacles, alternatives, and relatively narrow opportunities for change, the progressives achieved a substantial amount. Within a span of only a few years, progressives helped make the United States a better country. One of the most important messages of the Progressive Era is that in the right circumstances, with faith in themselves and their destiny, the American people can dramatically improve the quality of their lives and their society. It is a message of hope, not cynicism and despair; and in fact that may be the greatest legacy of the Progressive Era.

Bibliography

A period as important as the Progressive Era was bound to generate substantial interest as subsequent generations attempted to understand the origins and meaning of modern America. What follows represents only a sample of the studies of the period which have been published to date. For further references consult such bibliographies as Arthur S. Link and William M. Leary, Jr., comp., *The Progressive Era and the Great War, 1896–1920* (1969); George E. Mowry, *The Progressive Era, 1900–1920: The Reform Persuasion* (1972), in the pamphlet series of the American Historical Association; and Robert Wiebe, "The Progressive Years, 1900–1917," in William H. Cartwright and Richard L. Watson, Jr., eds., *The Reinterpretation of American History and Culture* (1973).

The nature of progressivism has remained the single most controversial aspect of the era. In a provocative article, "An Obituary for 'The Progressive Movement,'" *American Quarterly* (Spring 1970), Peter Filene has suggested that the concept itself should be abandoned. A good sense of the current debate may be found in two excellent collections of original essays: Lewis L. Gould, ed., *The Progressive Era* (1974), and John D. Buenker, John C. Burnham, and Robert M. Crunden, *Progressivism* (1977).

Progressive historiography has followed a twisting course. The positive achievements of the movement were first chronicled by Benjamin

251

DeWitt, *The Progressive Movement* (1915), and Harold U. Faulkner, *The Quest for Social Justice, 1898–1914* (1931). Disillusionment set in with the Great Depression. John Chamberlain, *Farewell to Reform* (1932), called progressivism only pseudoreformist. In the post-World War II period, historians became more concerned with the causes of reform. Russell B. Nye, *Midwestern Progressive Politics* (1959), traced its origins to regional reform and populism. But Richard Hofstadter, *The Age of Reform: From Bryan to F.D.R.* (1955), and George E. Mowry, *The Era of Theodore Roosevelt, 1900–1912* (1958), stressed the discontinuities between populism and progressivism, describing the latter as led by small businesspeople and urban professionals. In his path-breaking but now widely challenged theory of a "status revolution" to explain the origin of the progressive movement, Hofstadter argued that the reformers belonged to an older class of community leaders and resented being displaced by a new industrial and financial elite. According to this theory, progressives were fundamentally motivated by status anxiety and other psychological characteristics rather than by political or economic goals. However, critics have shown that the progressive leaders and their opponents shared the same general socioeconomic characteristics and that status anxiety is not, on the whole, a primary determinant of political behavior.

In the 1960s New Left historians, often disillusioned with reform in general, asserted that the new corporate and financial elite, not a declining gentry, had dominated progressivism. Gabriel Kolko, in *The Triumph of Conservatism* (1963), argued that big business used progressivism to forestall more radical reform and ensure profits by curtailing competition. Kolko stated that big business sought, obtained, and benefited from governmental regulation. While providing much information about competition within oligopolistic industries and about the interest of business in economic legislation, Kolko often misused evidence and provided a distorted, one-dimensional view which neglected governmental actions which were opposed by business. The book also neglected important divisions within American business, omitted ways in which compromise legislation was derived from interaction between big business and other groups, and avoided dealing with the changing nature of regulatory agencies. It is true that members of the new corporate and financial leadership had significant influence on many aspects of the progressive movement, but they did not completely dominate it and they did not always achieve what they desired. A more accurate view is supported in more complex and sophisticated studies by Sidney Fine, *Laissez-Faire and the General Welfare State* (1956); Samuel P. Hays, *Conservation and the Gospel of Efficiency* (1959); Robert Wiebe, *Businessmen and Reform* (1962); Gerald D. Nash, *State Government and Economic Development: A History of Administrative Policies in California, 1859–1933* (1964); and Ellis W. Hawley, *The New Deal and the Problem of Monopoly* (1966). Of particular interest in this regard is the controversy over the key progressive issue of railroad regulation. The conflicting interpretations of Kolko, Robert W. Harbeson, and Albro Martin are examined, along with pertinent documents, in David M. Chalmers, ed., *Neither Socialism nor Monopoly: Theodore Roosevelt and the Decision to Regulate the Railroads* (1976). For a case study see Stanley P. Caine, *The Myth of a Progressive Reform: Railroad Regulation in Wisconsin, 1903–1910* (1970).

Currently, the most influential interpretation of the Progressive Era is the organizational or bureaucratic school, which emphasizes modernization theory. Avoiding the old dichotomy of "the people" against "the interests," this new interpretation sees the reformers of the period as representatives of a confident new middle class of managers, experts, bureaucrats, and professionals who sought to achieve order and efficiency through techniques of rationalization and administrative control which many of them had helped to develop in business, science, and the professions. Among the first historians to apply this approach to the period were Samuel P. Hays, *The Response to Industrialism, 1885–1914* (1957), and Robert H. Weibe, *The Search for Order, 1877–1920* (1967). A useful collection of essays employing the new interpretation is Jerry Israel, ed., *Building the Organizational Society* (1972).

The diversity of progressivism has led to much exciting new work. David P. Thelen, *The New Citizenship: Origins of Progressivism in Wisconsin, 1885–1900* (1972), emphasizes the role of the depression of the 1890s in bringing disparate groups together into a potentially radical, consumer-oriented political coalition. The new political history, which stresses ethnocultural issues and loyalties, has led to the discovery of significant urban, ethnic, working-class support for many reforms which previously were attributed solely to middle-class progressives. John D. Buenker, *Urban Liberalism and Progressive Reform* (1973), is a wide-ranging example. Focusing more closely on political parties is Lewis L. Gould, *Reform and Regulation: American Politics, 1900–1916* (1978).

The leading figures of the era continue to intrigue biographers. Among the most recent biographies are David P. Thelen, *Robert M. La Follette and the Insurgent Spirit* (1976); Allen Davis, *American Heroine* (Jane Addams) (1973); Robert C. Twombly, *Frank Lloyd Wright* (1973); and Justin Kaplan, *Lincoln Steffens* (1974). The political leaders of the period come alive in some fine biographies, including Arthur S. Link's multivolume study *Woodrow Wilson* (1947–1965) and a briefer treatment by John A. Garraty (1956); and biographies of Theodore Roosevelt by Edmund Morris, *The Rise of Theodore Roosevelt* (1979); William H. Harbaugh, *Power and Responsibility* (1961); and the more interpretive John M. Blum, *The Republican Roosevelt* (1954, rev. ed. 1977). On others see Paolo E. Coletta, *The Presidency of William Howard Taft* (1973); David Burner, *Herbert Hoover: The Public Life* (1978); Joan Hoff Wilson, *Herbert Hoover: The Forgotten Progressive* (1975); Louis W. Koenig, *Bryan* (1971); and biographies of conservatives like Nathaniel W. Stephenson, *Nelson W. Aldrich* (1930); Richard Leopold, *Elihu Root and the Conservative Tradition* (1954), and William Harbaugh, *Lawyer's Lawyer: The Life of John W. Davis* (1973).

The social and political thought in the era is examined in Clyde Griffin, "The Progressive Ethos," in Stanley Coben and Norman Ratner, eds., *The Development of an American Culture* (1970); David M. Noble, *The Progressive Mind, 1890–1917* (1970); Arthur A. Ekirch, Jr., *Progressivism in America* (1974); Morton White, *Social Thought in America: The Revolt Against Formalism* (1957); the stimulating work of Henry Steele Commager, *The American Mind* (1950); and Henry F. May, *The End of American Innocence* (1959). Henry M. Littlefield provides a delightfully provocative interpretation in "The Wizard of Oz: Parable on Populism" in *The American*

Quarterly (Spring 1964). A comparison with European developments is included in C. Vann Woodward, ed., *The Comparative Approach to American History* (1968), and Robert Kelley, *The Trans-Atlantic Persuasion* (1969).

The continuation of progressivism as part of a larger search for order in the 1920s is brilliantly examined in Ellis W. Hawley's volume in this series, *The Great War and the Search for a New Order, 1919-1933* (1979). Specific aspects are studied in Clark A. Chambers, *Seedtime for Reform: American Social Service and Social Action, 1918-1933* (1968); and Otis L. Graham, Jr., *An Encore for Reform: The Old Progressives and the New Deal* (1967). William E. Leuchtenburg, *The Perils of Prosperity, 1914-1932* (1958), is a highly readable classic.

Social change was so broad and pervasive during the first two decades of the twentieth century that many social movements of the time have been subjects of historical study. A good general background is provided in John A. Garraty, *The New Commonwealth, 1877-1890* (1968). Organized labor is the topic of Marc Karson, *American Labor Unions and Politics, 1900-1918* (1958); Milton Derber, *The American Idea of Industrial Democracy, 1865-1965* (1970); Irwin Yellowitz, *Labor and the Progressive Movement in New York State, 1897-1916* (1965); Melvyn Dubofsky, *When Workers Organize: New York City in the Progressive Era* (1968); and *We Shall Be All: A History of the Industrial Workers of the World* (1969). Socialism has been portrayed by the contrasting interpretations of David A. Shannon, *The Socialist Party of America* (1955), and James Weinstein, *The Decline of Socialism in America, 1912-1925* (1967). William Preston, Jr., *Aliens and Dissenters: Federal Suppression of Radicals, 1903-1933* (1963), is especially thorough.

Literature on women in the Progressive Era is growing rapidly. Lois W. Banner, *Women in Modern America* (1974), offers a good overview. Aileen Kraditor, ed., *Up from the Pedestal* (1969), provides selections from works by major feminist writers. Robert Smuts, *Women and Work in America* (1959), focuses on working-class women. William L. O'Neill, *Everyone Was Brave* (1969), attempts to provide an overall synthesis. Aileen Kraditor, *The Ideas of the Woman Suffrage Movement* (1965), and Eleanor Flexner, *A Century of Struggle* (1959), deal with the suffrage movement. William O'Neill, *Divorce in the Progressive Era* (1967), and David M. Kennedy, *Birth Control in America: The Career of Margaret Sanger* (1970), focus on specific aspects of the changing status of women. Annette Kar Baxter with Constance Jacobs, *To Be a Woman in America, 1850–1930* (1978), makes insightful use of visual documents.

Race and ethnicity have received increasing attention. Immigrants are dealt with in Philip Taylor, *The Distant Magnet* (1971); Thomas Kessner, *The Golden Door: Italian and Jewish Immigrant Mobility in New York City, 1880–1915* (1977), which documents substantial social mobility; James Olson, *The Ethnic Dimension in American History* (1979); and John M. Allswang's statistical analysis of political behavior, *A House for All Peoples: Ethnic Politics in Chicago, 1890–1936* (1971). John Higham, *Strangers in the Land* (1955), examines nativist reaction. The leadership and conditions of black Americans in the Progressive Era are examined in Jack T. Kirby, *Darkness at the Dawning: Race and Reform in the Progressive South* (1972); August Meier, *Negro Thought in America, 1880–1915* (1963); Elliott M. Rudwick, *W. E. B. Du Bois* (1960); Louis R. Harlan, *Booker T. Washington* (1972); and Allan H. Spear, *Black Chicago: The Making of a Negro Ghetto, 1890–1920* (1967).

Progressivism has also been studied by locale and by issue. Bruce M. Stave, ed., *Urban Bosses, Machines, and Progressive Reformers* (1972), is an excellent collection of essays on the urban milieu. The diversity of progressivism in different states can be seen in several works, including Robert S. LaForte, *Leaders of Reform: Progressive Republicans in Kansas, 1900–1916* (1974); Sheldon Hackney, *Populism to Progressivism in Alabama* (1969), which emphasizes discontinuity; and Richard Abrams, *Conservatism in a Progressive Era: Massachusetts Politics, 1900–1912* (1964). Prohibition and its relationship to progressive reform has fascinated many scholars. Joseph R. Gusfeld, *Symbolic Crusade: Status Politics and the American Temperance Movement* (1963), relates it to the declining status of certain groups; James Timberlake, *Prohibition and the Progressive Movement, 1900–1920* (1970), sees it as reflecting white Anglo-Saxon Protestant progressivism. Lewis Gould, *Progressives and Prohibitionists: Texas Democrats and the Wilson Era* (1973), emphasizes its role as an issue of the reform wing of the Democratic party. David Musto, *The American Disease: Origins of Narcotic Control* (1973), examines the roots of American attitudes toward narcotics and federal controls. Allen F. Davis, *Spearheads for Reform: The Social Settlements and the Progressive Movement, 1890–1914* (1967), and Paul T. Ringenbach, *Tramps and Reformers, 1873–1916* (1973), deal with the amelioration and control of poverty. Gerald W. McFarland, *Mugwumps, Morals & Politics, 1884–1920* (1975), traces one set of reformers and finds them split over progressive reforms. Broader than its title is William Graebner's *Coal-Mining Safety in the Progressive Period: The Political Economy of Reform* (1976), which examines an effort to achieve the benefits of centralized politics without centralizing the political system.

The emergence of the corporate economy has been the subject of much new research. An overview is provided in Glenn Porter, *The Rise of Big Business, 1860–1910* (1973); Stuart Bruchey, *The Growth of the Modern American Economy* (1975); Thomas Cochran, *Business in American Life* (1972); and Harold U. Faulkner, *The Decline of Laissez-Faire, 1897–1917* (1951). Dudley Dillard, *Economic Development of the North Atlantic Community* (1967), compares aspects of development on both sides of the Atlantic. John Tipple, *The Capitalist Revolution: A History of American Social Thought, 1890–1919* (1970), is an excellent collection of documents with a valuable commentary. Specific aspects are covered in Alfred D. Chandler, Jr., *Strategy and Structure: Chapters in the History of Industrial Enterprise* (1962); Stephen E. Ambrose, ed., *Institutions in Modern America* (1967); Vincent Carosso, *Investment Banking in America* (1970); and Daniel Boorstin, *The Americans: The National Experience* (1974). The impact of industrialization on workers is examined in Herbert Gutman, *Work, Culture and Society in Industrializing America* (1976); Melvyn Dubofsky, *Industrialism and the American Worker, 1865–1920* (1975); David Brody, *Steelworkers in America* (1960); and Graham Adams, Jr., *Age of Industrial Violence, 1910–1915* (1966).

The modernization of society is not dealt with comprehensively in any single work. However, various studies shed light on the process by which social institutions were transformed. Among these are Caroline

F. Ware et al., *The Twentieth Century* (1966); The President's Research Committee on Social Trends, *Recent Social Trends in the United States* (1933); Robert and Helen Lynd, *Middletown: A Study in Modern American Culture* (1929); and Gilman M. Ostrander, *American Civilization in the First Machine Age, 1890–1940* (1970). More specific areas are treated in Blake McKelvey, *The Urbanization of America, 1860–1915* (1963); Bert N. Adams, *The American Family* (1971); Robert I. Rotberg and Theodore K. Robb, eds., *The Family in History* (1971); Joseph F. Kett, *Rites of Passage: Adolescence in America, 1790 to the Present* (1977); Lawrence Cremin, *The Transformation of the School: Progressivism in American Education, 1876–1956* (1961); and Raymond Callahan, *Education and the Cult of Efficiency* (1962). The early development of the American motion picture industry and its influence on society is examined in Robert Sklar, *Movie-Made America: A Social History of the American Movies* (1975). See also Anthony Slide, *Early American Cinema* (1970); George C. Pratt, *Spellbound in Darkness* (rev. ed., 1973); and Richard Griffith and Arthur Mayer, *The Movies* (1978).

Science, law, and medicine have received increasing attention. A. Hunter Dupree, ed., *Science and the Emergence of Modern America, 1865–1916* (1963), is a standard work. On developments in the legal profession see the contrasting views of James Willard Hurst, *The Growth of American Law: The Law Makers* (1950), and the more critical study by Jerold S. Auerbach, *Unequal Justice: Lawyers and Social Change in Modern America* (1976). Changes in health care are investigated in George Rosen, *From Medical Police to Social Medicine* (1974); John D. Thompson, *The Hospital* (1975); Lloyd C. Taylor, Jr., *The Medical Profession and Social Reform, 1885–1945* (1974); John C. Burnham, *Psychoanalysis and American Medicine, 1894–1918* (1967); and Nathan G. Hale, Jr., *Freud and the Americans: The Beginnings of Psychoanalysis in the United States, 1876–1917* (1971). Donald K. Pickens, *Eugenics and the Progressives* (1968), studies an area of concern to many progressives and conservatives.

Since the United States emerged as a world power in the Progressive Era, the foreign policy of the period has triggered much debate. Examples of the "realist" school, which criticized policy makers for failing to educate the American public to the responsibilities of world power, are George Kennan, *American Diplomacy, 1900–1950* (1950), and Robert Osgood, *Ideals and Self-Interest in American Foreign Relations* (1953). New Left revisionists, who emphasized the influence of economic forces in the determination of an expansionist foreign policy, include William A. Williams, *The Tragedy of American Diplomacy* (2nd ed., 1972); Lloyd C. Gardner, *Imperial America: American Foreign Policy Since 1898* (1976). Less interpretive accounts are contained in the relevant chapters in Richard W. Leopold, *The Growth of American Foreign Policy: A History* (1962), and Thomas G. Paterson et al., *American Foreign Policy: A History* (1977). See also Ernest R. May, *Imperialism: A Speculative Essay* (1968), and John A. S. Grenville and George B. Young, *Politics, Strategy, and American Diplomacy: Studies in Foreign Policy, 1873–1917* (1966).

The institutions which affected America's relationship with other countries underwent significant transformation in the Progressive Era. State Department modernization is examined in Robert P. Schulzinger, *The Making of the Diplomatic Mind: The Training, Outlook, and Style of U.S. Foreign Service Officers, 1908–1939* (1975). Changes in the armed forces are studied in Peter Karsten, *The Naval Aristocracy* (1972); Russell F. Weigley, *History of the United States Army* (1967); Richard D. Challener, *Admirals, Generals, and American Foreign Policy, 1898–1914* (1973); Arthur Ekirch, Jr., *The Civilian and the Military* (1956); John Garry Clifford, *The Citizen Soldiers: The Plattsburg Training Camp Movement, 1913–1920* (1972); and John W. Chambers, *Draftees or Volunteers* (1975), and the forthcoming *The Politics of Progressivism: The World War I Draft and Modernization in the United States*. American industrial investments abroad has been explored in Mira Wilkins, *The Emergence of Multi-national Enterprise: American Business Abroad from the Colonial Era to 1914* (1970).

Various aspects of the peace movement in this period are portrayed in John W. Chambers, ed., *The Eagle and the Dove: The American Peace Movement and United States Foreign Policy, 1900–1921* (1976); C. Roland Marchand, *The American Peace Movement and Social Reform, 1898–1918* (1972); Charles Chatfield, *For Peace and*

Justice: Pacifism in America, 1914–1941 (1971); Warren F. Kuehl, *Seeking World Order: The United States and International Organization to 1920* (1969), and Sondra R. Herman, *Eleven Against War: Studies in American Internationalist Thought, 1898–1921* (1969).

American foreign policy varied toward particular areas of the world. Primary attention went to the Caribbean and has been examined by Dana G. Munro, a former State Department official, in *Intervention and Dollar Diplomacy in the Caribbean, 1900–1921* (1964), and the revisionist Daniel F. Smith, *The U.S. and Revolutionary Nationalism in Mexico, 1916–1932* (1972). See also P. Edward Haley, *Revolution and Intervention: The Diplomacy of Taft and Wilson in Mexico, 1910–1917* (1970); Lester D. Langley, *Struggle for the American Mediterranean: United States–European Rivalry in the Gulf-Caribbean, 1776–1904* (1976); and Walter La Feber, *The Panama Canal: The Crisis in Historical Perspective* (1978). For a discussion of U.S. occupation of its Caribbean protectorates, a number of books are pertinent: Allan R. Millett, *The Politics of Intervention: The Military Occupation of Cuba, 1906–1909* (1968); James H. Hitchman, *Leonard Wood and Cuban Independence, 1898–1902* (1971); and Hans Schmidt, *The United States Occupation of Haiti, 1915–1934* (1971). The U.S. role in the Far East is treated in contrasting manner by Paul A. Varg, *The Making of a Myth: The United States and China, 1897–1912* (1968), and a revisionist work by Jerry Israel, *Progressivism and the Open Door: America and China, 1905–1921* (1971). Also valuable are Akira Iriye, *Across the Pacific: An Inner History of American–East Asian Relations* (1969) and *Pacific Estrangement: Japanese and American Expansion, 1897–1911* (1972). The American occupation of the Philippines is examined in William J. Pomeroy, *American Neo-colonialism: Its Emergence in the Philippines and Asia* (1970), and Peter Stanley, *A Nation in the Making: The Philippines and the United States, 1899–1921* (1974). The single most important peacetime change in American diplomatic relations in Europe is described in Bradford Perkins, *The Great Rapprochement: England and the United States, 1895–1914* (1968).

American involvement in World War I remains controversial. Favorable scholarly accounts, stressing the threat to American interests posed by a German victory and emphasizing the complexity of the forces leading to American entry, include Arthur S. Link, *Woodrow Wilson,* Vols. III–V (1960–1965), a collection of essays, *Wilson, the Diplomatist* (1963), and Link's briefer history of the period, *Woodrow Wilson and the Progressive Era, 1910–1917* (1954); Ernest R. May, *The World War and American Isolation, 1914–1917* (1959); Ross Gregory, *The Origins of American Intervention in the First World War* (1971); and Patrick Devlin, *Too Proud to Fight: Woodrow Wilson's Neutrality* (1975). Otis L. Graham, Jr., *The Great Campaigns: Reform and War in America, 1900–1928* (1971), criticized Wilson for not following a more conciliatory policy toward Germany. The most detailed critique of Wilson's policy from the perspective of revisionists who emphasize economic forces is still Charles C. Tansill, *America Goes to War* (1938). For an account of the widespread opposition to American interventionism, see John M. Cooper, Jr., *The Vanity of Power: American Isolationism and the First World War, 1914–1917* (1969).

The presidents remained the chief architects of American foreign policy during the Progressive Era. For understanding Roosevelt, Howard Beale's *Theodore Roosevelt and the Rise of America to World Power* (1956) is still valuable, but it should be supplemented with Raymond Esthus, *Theodore Roosevelt and the International Rivalries* (1970), and the biographies by Blum and Harbaugh. Walter and Marie Scholes treat Roosevelt's successor in *The Foreign Policies of the Taft Administration* (1970). Wilson's diplomacy is examined in the greatest detail by Arthur Link in the works cited earlier. Additional aspects of Wilson's foreign policy are dealt with in Alexander L. and Juliette L. George, *Woodrow Wilson and Colonel House: A Personality Study* (1956), a provocative psychological analysis, and N. Gordon Levin, Jr., *Woodrow Wilson and World Politics: America's Response to War and Revolution* (1968), which stresses Wilson's desire for a liberal, democratic, capitalist world order. For an insightful conceptual analysis of the institution, see Richard M. Pious, *The American Presidency* (1979).

The real flavor of the Progressive Era—of what it was like to live in those exciting days—can be recaptured only by consulting primary sources, material written at the time or recalled later by participants. References to many published primary sources may be found in the works cited earlier. A good place to begin is *The Literary Digest,* which summarized debate in the nation's newspapers and included photographs and political cartoons. A number of valuable documents, accompanied by insightful commentary, are included in Howard H. Quint et al., eds., *Main Problems in American History* (4th ed., 1978). John Spargo, *The Bitter Cry of the Children* (1906), is a vivid example of Progressive Era indignation. Walter Lippmann's *Drift and Mastery* (1914) and Herbert Croly's *The Promise of American Life* (1909) illustrate a major thread of progressive thought. Additional insight can be gained from letters and autobiographies. Among the best are *The Letters of Theodore Roosevelt,* edited by Elting E. Morison and John M. Blum (1951–1954); *The Papers of Woodrow Wilson,* being edited by Arthur S. Link, (1966–   ); and *The Letters of Lincoln Steffens,* edited by Ella Winter and Granville Hicks (1938). Valuable memoirs include Jane Addams, *Twenty Years at Hull House* (1910); Emma Goldman, *Living My Life* (1931); Henry Adams, *The Education of Henry Adams* (1918); Mary Antin, *The Promised Land* (1912); and William Allen White, *Autobiography* (1946). Finally, many Americans are using oral history and genealogical techniques as they seek to relate the experiences of their own ancestors to historical developments in the American past. A good guide with which to begin such an investigation is Jim Watts and Allen Davis, *Generations: Your Family in Modern American History* (2nd ed., 1978).

Index